House Prices and the Macroeconomy

House Prices and the Macroeconomy: Implications for Banking and Price Stability

Charles Goodhart and Boris Hofmann

OXFORD
UNIVERSITY PRESS

OXFORD
UNIVERSITY PRESS

Great Clarendon Street, Oxford OX2 6DP

Oxford University Press is a department of the University of Oxford.
It furthers the University's objective of excellence in research, scholarship,
and education by publishing worldwide in

Oxford New York

Auckland Cape Town Dar es Salaam Hong Kong Karachi
Kuala Lumpur Madrid Melbourne Mexico City Nairobi
New Delhi Shanghai Taipei Toronto

With offices in

Argentina Austria Brazil Chile Czech Republic France Greece
Guatemala Hungary Italy Japan Poland Portugal Singapore
South Korea Switzerland Thailand Turkey Ukraine Vietnam

Oxford is a registered trade mark of Oxford University Press
in the UK and in certain other countries

Published in the United States
by Oxford University Press Inc., New York

© Charles Goodhart and Boris Hofmann, 2007

British Library Cataloguing in Publication Data
Data available

Library of Congress Cataloging in Publication Data
Data available

Typeset by Newgen Imaging Systems (P) Ltd., Chennai, India
Printed in Great Britain
on acid-free paper by
Biddles Ltd., King's Lynn, Norfolk

ISBN 0-19-920459-4   978-0-19-920459-5

10 9 8 7 6 5 4 3 2 1

Acknowledgements

We would like to thank Chris Allsopp, Ben Bernanke, Efrem Castelnuovo, Andrew Filardo, Jürgen von Hagen, Bernd Hayo, Gerhard Illing, Colin Mayer and various anonymous referees for helpful comments on the different chapters of this book and Andrew Farlow for extensive comments on the first draft of the book manuscript. We also thank Marina Emond for very helpful editorial assistance. The views expressed in this book do not necessarily represent the views of the institutions the authors are or have been affiliated with.

Contents

List of Figures

List of Tables

Introduction

The macroeconomic implications of asset price fluctuations have received increasing attention in academic and policy circles recently, in large part due to the recent boom–bust bubbles in the equity and now in the housing markets. Most studies in this area have focused on financial asset prices, while the role of house prices has not been explored to the same extent. Over recent years we have tried to fill this gap by investigating the role of asset prices, especially house prices, for various aspects of the macroeconomy. In this book we bring together the outcome of this research.

In the first chapter, which serves as a general introduction to the topic of this book, we provide an overview of the various channels through which house prices may affect economic activity. We also present some stylized facts and discuss how institutional features of the housing and mortgage market can determine the strength of the effect of house prices on the economy.

The remainder of the book is structured into three parts. The first part, consisting of Chapters 2 to 5, investigates the role and usefulness of house prices as determinants or indicators for goods price inflation and economic activity. In Chapter 2, we assess the predictive power of asset prices—i.e. exchange rates, equity prices, house prices, and other standard indicators such as the output gap, interest rates and money growth—for future consumer price inflation in industrialized countries. The results suggest that house prices are in general useful predictors of future inflation.[1] In Chapter 3, we derive, on the basis of reduced-form coefficient estimates and VAR impulse responses, Financial Conditions Indices (FCIs), weighted averages of the short-term real interest rate, the effective real exchange rate, real house and real share prices, for the G7 countries. We find that house and share prices get a substantial weight in such an index and that the derived Financial Conditions Indices contain useful information about future inflationary pressures.[2] Chapter 4 assesses the role of house prices in simple empirical versions of the New Keynesian model for the US and the euro area. We find that the real interest rate does not have a significantly negative effect on the output gap in standard specifications of the model. On the basis of an extended specification of the IS curve, also including house prices,

---

[1] Chapter 2 is a reprint of Goodhart and Hofmann (2000a).
[2] Chapter 3 is based on Goodhart and Hofmann (2001).

we are able to restore a significantly negative interest rate effect on aggregate demand in all countries.[3] In Chapter 5 we assess the historical and more recent experiences with goods and asset price deflations. The main finding of this chapter is that there is no innate disadvantage in goods and services price deflation as such. Episodes of goods price deflation have often been consistent with continuing strong growth. On the other hand, we show that a fall in asset prices, especially in house prices, has commonly had a severe contractionary effect on output.[4]

The second part of the book, consisting of Chapters 6 to 8, analyses the effect of house prices on the financial system. In Chapter 6, we show that house prices significantly affect credit creation in the industrialized countries. Impulse response analysis suggests that innovations to house prices, possibly reflecting changing beliefs about future economic conditions or speculative activity in house markets, may give rise to significant and persistent cycles in bank lending, and are thus a potential explanation for the persistent cycles in bank lending observed in the past.[5] In Chapter 7 we argue and show that the financial liberalizations of the 1970s have increased the sensitivity of the banking sector to house price fluctuations and have therefore also increased the procyclicality of the financial system. We further argue that the policy response to this increased procyclicality, the regulation of bank capital in the form of capital adequacy requirements, is itself inherently procyclical and may therefore further amplify business cycle fluctuations. Finally, we show that the new Basel II Accord may considerably accentuate the procyclicality of the regulatory system.[6] In Chapter 8, we assess the two-way dynamic interaction between credit and house prices and the usefulness of real-time indicators of bubbles in the housing and credit market as indicators of future fragility in the banking sector. We find that there is a significant two-way interaction between bank credit and house prices: house prices significantly affect credit and vice versa. The other main finding of this chapter is that deviations of both house prices and credit from their long-run trends are useful indicators of future banking sector distress. These results suggest that mutually reinforcing boom–bust cycles in house and credit markets may occur and enhance the likelihood of future financial fragility.[7]

The third and final part of the book, Chapters 9 to 11, discusses policy implications of the nexus between house prices, economic activity and financial stability. Chapter 9 discusses the role of asset prices in the measurement of inflation. Assets represent claims on future consumption. A change in a nominal asset price may reflect a change in the expected real future services to be derived from the

---

[3] Chapter 4 is based on Goodhart and Hofmann (2005b).
[4] Chapter 5 is based on Goodhart and Hofmann (2003).
[5] Chapter 6 is a reprint of Hofmann (2004).
[6] Chapter 7 is a reprint of Goodhart, Hofmann, and Segoviano (2004).
[7] Chapter 8 is based on Goodhart, Hofmann, and Segoviano (2005).

asset, or a change in the relative price of an unchanged flow of future services. For such reasons, Alchian and Klein (1973) argued that a correct measure of inflation should include asset prices, since such an index would also account for the expected cost of future consumption. In this chapter we assess the theoretical and empirical case for including asset prices, again notably housing, in a broader index of the cost of living.[8] In Chapter 10 we argue that the central bank may need a second instrument in order to be able to address the procyclicality of the financial system, as the first instrument, the interest rate, is predicated on the stabilization of inflation and economic activity. Such a second instrument could take the form of a time-varying loan-to-value ratio (LTV), which is lowered during the boom and raised during the bust.[9] The concluding Chapter 11 takes stock and summarizes the implications of house price fluctuations for monetary and regulatory policies.

[8] Chapter 9 is a reprint of Goodhart (2001).
[9] Chapter 10 is a reprint of Goodhart and Hofmann (2004b).

1

House Prices and the Macroeconomy: Overview

Like other asset prices, house prices should equal the discounted stream of future housing returns, i.e rents, in the long run. To the extent that rents and discount factors are affected by macroeconomic shocks, these shocks should also be reflected in house prices. However, housing has many features which make it distinct from other assets, like equity. Real estate is not only an asset but also a durable consumption good for households, providing shelter and other housing services. As a result, a house is often the largest and most important asset of households and therefore accounts for a major share of household wealth. Because of that, and also because it is immobile and can therefore not easily be put out of a creditor's reach, it is also commonly used as collateral for loans, so that a large share of financial sector assets is tied to housing values. House price fluctuations may therefore have a major effect on economic activity and the soundness of the financial system. As a result, house price fluctuations may significantly amplify the effects of macroeconomic shocks, like supply, demand, or monetary policy shocks, and non-fundamental movements or bubbles in house prices may give rise to imbalances in the economy and in the financial system.

The housing market also differs from other asset markets in various respects. Due to the length of the approval and construction process the supply response in housing markets to changes in market conditions is very sluggish. Furthermore, residential property markets often lack transparency, as housing is a local good and the availability of price information is often very limited. As a result, house prices may respond more strongly to macroeconomic shocks than other goods and asset prices, and persistent deviations of house prices from their long-term fundamental value may occur.[1]

A particular issue for the analysis of the effects of house prices on the macroeconomy is data availability and data quality. Sufficiently representative and regularly collected data for residential property prices are now available for a large number of industrialized countries, although the available data are in most

---

[1] For a more detailed discussion of these issues see Zhu (2003).

cases not directly comparable across countries, partly due to differences in the definition of the representative property, but also due to differences in data collection (Arthur 2003). Also, whereas residential property accounts for the largest part of the overall property stock, house price movements are not necessarily fully representative of the price developments in other property markets. As we document in Chapter 7, in some countries commercial property prices appear to be substantially more volatile than residential property prices. This may indicate that commercial property price dynamics fundamentally differ from residential property price developments, but it may also simply reflect the fact that for many industrialized countries, the available commercial property price series are for prime commercial property in the capital city's centre and may therefore not be representative of country-wide developments. Data for price developments in the market for industrial property are, with a few exceptions, not available at all. For this reason, most studies, including this book, focus on the macroeconomic implications of house price fluctuations.

1.1   House prices and economic activity

Figure 1.1 shows the four-quarter rate of change in real house prices[2] (solid line) and the output gap (dotted line), measured as the percentage gap between real GDP and trend real GDP,[3] over the period 1980 to 2004 for a sample of 16 industrialized countries. The graph suggests that there is a close correlation between house prices and the economic cycle. Turning points in the *change* in real house prices generally lead business cycle turning points. Figure 1.1 also suggests that turning points in the *level* of real house prices in many countries lag business cycle turning points, as the change in real house prices often turns negative (positive) only after business cycle peaks (troughs). Over the last couple of years, the positive correlation between house prices and the output gap appears to have weakened, as in many countries house prices have kept growing despite a slowdown in economic activity. This does not necessarily imply, however, that the relationship between house prices and economic activity has broken down. The recent slowdown in economic activity was to a large extent caused by the bursting of the stock market bubble in 2001 and further reinforced by the terrorist attacks of 11 September. The result was a shift of funds from the stock market to other asset markets, including housing, and a monetary easing which drove interest rates to record lows, which has led to a booming housing market and thus a decoupling of housing prices and the economic cycle.

---

[2] The nominal house price data originate from the BIS and were converted to real terms by deflation with the GDP deflator.

[3] Trend real GDP was calculated using a standard Hodrick–Prescott filter with a smoothing parameter of 1,600.

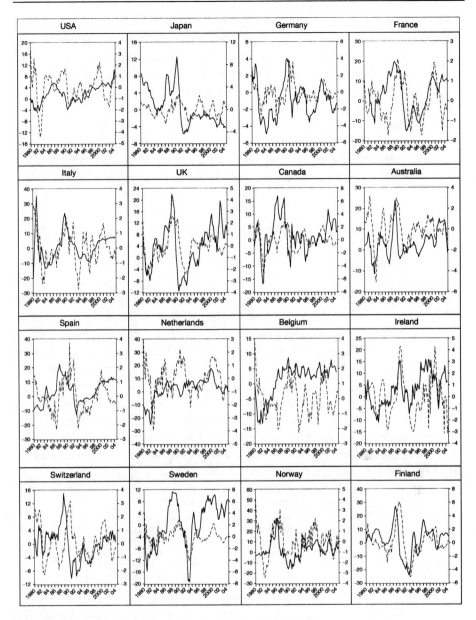

Figure 1.1. House prices and economic activity, 1980–2004

Note: Each graph shows the four-quarter rate of change in real house prices (solid line, left-hand scale) and the output gap (dotted line, right-hand scale), measured as the percentage gap between real GDP and trend real GDP, calculated using a standard Hodrick–Prescott filter with a smoothing parameter of 1,600.

The documented stylized facts, therefore, suggest that there is a rather close correlation between house prices and economic activity, with house prices generally leading developments in the real economy. From an asset-pricing point of view, house prices may be leading macroeconomic developments because they are forward-looking. Fluctuations in house prices may reflect expected future movements in economic activity, which also affect the returns on housing and their discount rate. In this case, house prices would merely be a sideshow of macroeconomic developments. However, given the peculiarities of the housing market briefly discussed above, especially the general lack of transparency and liquidity, this is unlikely to be the main explanation of the documented close correlation between house price growth and the output gap. A more convincing interpretation is that house prices have a direct, causal effect on economic activity and on the financial sector and thus amplify macroeconomic shocks or are autonomous sources of macroeconomic and financial fluctuations.

1.2   House prices and private consumption

House prices may affect economic activity via various, often interrelated channels. The bulk of the empirical literature focuses on the wealth effect of house price movements on private consumption. A (permanent) change in house prices affects households' perceived lifetime wealth. Changes in perceived lifetime wealth in turn determine the spending and borrowing plans of households as they wish to smooth consumption over the life cycle.[4] Table 1.1 shows the ratio of housing and financial wealth to GDP in some major OECD countries in 1995 and in 2000. The figures reveal that housing wealth accounts for a large share of household wealth and in some countries is even a more important component of wealth than are total financial assets. More recent data are unfortunately not available, but given the bust in stock markets and the boom in housing markets since 2000, the importance of housing wealth in total household wealth is likely to have further increased in recent years.

Table 1.1. Household assets as a percentage of GDP, 1995–2000

	Housing assets		Financial assets	
	1995	2000	1995	2000
USA	120	130	292	341
Japan	222	192	252	278
Germany	191	191	149	180
France	170	206	165	234
Italy	234	220	189	227
UK	146	191	261	299
Spain	298	334	150	187
Netherlands	112	182	254	297

Sources: Altissimo *et al.* (2005); OECD; various national statistical offices.

[4] The life-cycle model of household consumption was originally developed by Ando and Modigliani (1963). A formal exposition of the life-cycle model can be found in Deaton (1992) and Muellbauer (1994).

However, what matters for the effect of house prices on consumption is not only the size of the housing wealth of a country, but also its distribution. If an increase in house prices is related to an increase in current or future (expected) rents, it will have not only a positive wealth effect on landlords and owner-occupiers, but also a negative income effect on tenants, who have to pay higher rents.[5] So the overall effect on aggregate non-housing consumption is not clear a priori, since higher house prices simply cause a redistribution of resources between tenants and prospective new buyers on one side and homeowners on the other. In principle, the higher the share of owner-occupiers, the more likely it is that the wealth effect of a change in house prices dominates the income effect. Table 1.2 reports the development of owner-occupancy rates in industrialized countries since 1980. The figures show that owner-occupancy rates vary widely across countries and that many countries, especially those in southern Europe, have experienced a substantial increase in owner-occupancy rates over the last two decades. In 2002, Spain and Italy had the highest share of home ownership. Home ownership is also high in the Anglo-Saxon countries, while Germany has the lowest owner-occupancy rate.

There are various potential causes of the cross-country differences in owner-occupation rates. The regulation of the rental market, for example with respect to the level and adjustment of rents as well as contract termination, is likely to play a key role, as rent regulation hindering the upward adjustment of rents potentially increases the attractiveness of renting. We are not aware of a cross-country assessment of the strictness of rent regulation. The available information suggests that in many industrialized countries there remain significant impediments to the adjustment of rents to market conditions, though there have been revisions allowing for more flexibility, at least in new rental contracts.[6] Another important determinant of the differences in home-ownership patterns across countries are cross-country differences in housing-related tax incentives and subsidies and in transaction costs in the housing market. Due to the large number of different tax incentives, subsidies and housing policy measures and also data limitations, it is hard to make an overall assessment.[7] Finally, whether households are able to acquire real estate property also depends to a significant extent on the borrowing constraints they face in the mortgage market, as these constraints determine the general availability of mortgage finance.[8]

[5] See ECB (2003) for a more detailed discussion.

[6] ECB (2003) provides a chronology of main changes in rent regulation for the EU countries.

[7] ECB (2003) provides some key information on housing taxes, transaction costs and the general evolution of housing policy in the EU over the 1990s.

[8] On the basis of microeconomic data for 14 OECD countries, Chiuri and Japelli (2003) show that typical LTVs and owner-occupancy rates are negatively correlated, especially for young households.

Table 1.2. Characteristics of housing and mortgage markets in industrialized countries

	Owner-occupancy rates (% of all households)		Maximum loan-to-value ratio (LTV)	Valuation for lending based on market prices	Housing equity withdrawal available
	1980	2002			
Australia	71	70	80	Yes	Yes
Belgium	59	71	80–85	Yes	No
Canada	62	66	75	Yes	Not used
Denmark	52	51	80	No	Yes
Finland	61	58	75	Yes	Yes
France	47	55	80	Yes	No
Germany	41	42	60	No	No
Ireland	76	77	90	Yes	Yes
Italy	59	80	50	Yes	No
Japan	60	60	80	Yes	Yes
Netherlands	42	53	75	Yes	Yes
Norway	74	77	80	Yes	Yes
Spain	73	85	80	Yes	Not used
Sweden	58	61	80	Yes	Yes
UK	58	69	90–100	Yes	Yes
USA	65	68	75–80	Yes	Yes

Sources: OECD (2004); Tsatsaronis and Zhu (2004).

There is a large theoretical literature showing that, due to informational asymmetries in credit markets which give rise to adverse selection and moral hazard problems, the borrowing capacity and borrowing costs of households are largely determined by the collateral they can offer. [9] As we have already noted above, due to their large weight in household wealth portfolios and their immobile character, houses represent the most important collateralizable asset against which households can borrow in order to finance consumption or housing investment. Figure 1.2 shows the co-movement of the level of real house prices and household indebtedness, measured as the ratio of total household liabilities to household disposable income for eight countries for which sufficiently long time-series data from the national accounts were available. The graphs suggest that there is a very close correlation between real house prices and household debt, lending support to the view that household borrowing capacity is closely linked to the value of housing collateral. A noteworthy exception is Germany, where the correlation

---

[9] Bernanke and Gertler (1989), Kiyotaki and Moore (1997) and Bernanke *et al.* (1999) have developed modified real business cycle models where firms' borrowing capacity depends on their collateralizable net worth and show that fluctuations in firms' net worth amplify macroeconomic shocks and can give rise to a powerful financial accelerator effect. Aoki *et al.* (2004) show, on the basis of the model of Bernanke *et al.* (1999), that a financial accelerator effect also arises in the household sector via house prices when households' ability to borrow depends on the value of housing collateral. For a survey of the literature on credit market frictions and their macroeconomic implications see Walsh (2003: ch. 7).

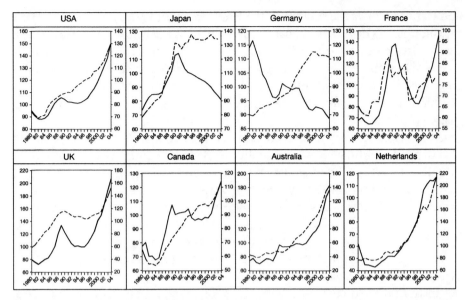

Figure 1.2. House prices and the household debt, 1980–2004

Note: The figure shows the level of real house prices (solid line, left-hand scale, 1995 = 100) and the ratio of total household liabilities to household disposable income (dotted line, right-hand scale, %).

Sources: BIS; OECD; Debelle (2004).

between house prices and household indebtedness appears to be rather negative. A possible explanation for this rather implausible finding is the construction boom following German unification, which led to an increase in housing supply and thus downward pressures on house prices and, at the same time, an increase in household debt as most of the new buildings were debt-financed.

A couple of more recent studies have argued that the ability of households to borrow against rising house prices and, as a result, the strength of the nexus between house prices and the macroeconomy depends on the structural characteristics of the mortgage market.[10] Household borrowing against real estate collateral is usually restricted by a wealth constraint, a loan-to-value ratio (LTV) restricting the loan from exceeding a certain proportion of the value of the house, and/or an income constraint restricting mortgage interest payments from exceeding a certain proportion of the borrower's income. While cross-country data on the latter are generally not available, data on maximum or typical LTVs are available for a large number of industrialized countries. The available data for maximum LTVs are shown in Table 1.2. The figures suggest that in most countries the maximum LTV is about 75 to 80%. Only in Ireland and the UK are LTVs significantly higher at 90%, or even up to 100%. On the other hand, in Italy

---

[10] See Maclennan *et al.* (2000); ECB (2003); OECD (2004); Tsatsaronis and Zhu (2004).

and Germany LTVs are substantially lower at 50% and 60% respectively. These maximum LTVs have to be seen in connection with the valuation method that is used to determine the value of the property to which the LTV is applied. Here the available information, which is also reported in Table 1.2, suggests that in most countries mortgage lending is based on current market values. Exceptions are Germany and Denmark, where valuations are to a significant extent based on historical prices.

The possibilities for home-owners to borrow against their housing wealth also depend on the general availability of housing equity withdrawal (HEW) products. HEW is defined as the difference between net mortgage lending to households and residential investment by households. In principle, the aggregate household sector can withdraw housing equity by (1) increasing or refinancing the mortgage loan—which would not require a transaction in the housing market—or (2) through a transaction in the secondary property market whereby the buyer can obtain a larger loan due to the higher house value.[11] Whether these alternatives are possible and how intensively they are used depends on the structure of the mortgage markets and on the respective legal regulations. If the only possibility for a house owner to utilize a rise in the house value for higher consumption is (2), that is first to sell the house, then the overall effect of increasing house prices on consumption should be smaller than in the case where opportunity (1) is also available. Table 1.2 indicates the availability of HEW products in industrialized countries. HEW products are now available and used in most industrialized countries. Notable exceptions are the four large continental European countries: Germany, France, Italy and Spain.

Several studies have in the meanwhile investigated the effect of house price movements on private consumption. House prices are generally found to have a stronger effect on consumption than equity prices (Case *et al.* 2001; Ludwig and Sløk 2004). Regarding cross-country differences, the evidence is, however, inconclusive. The results in Ludwig and Sløk (2004), which are also discussed in Altissimo *et al.* (2005), suggest that house price movements have a stronger effect on consumption in the euro area countries than in the USA and the UK, while the evidence reported in OECD (2004) suggests exactly the opposite.[12]

· [11] For the individual household, Davey (2001) identifies five different ways to withdraw housing equity: (1) Last-time sales: the seller of a house does not buy a new house; (2) Trading down: the seller moves to a cheaper property and reduces the mortgage by less than the price difference; (3) Over-mortgaging: the seller moves and increases the mortgage by more than the price difference; (4) Re-mortgaging: the home-owner takes a new, higher mortgage without moving or investing in the property; (5) Further advances and second mortgages: the home-owner increases an existing mortgage (further advance) or takes a second mortgage without moving or investing in the property.

[12] For further references see Altissimo *et al.* (2005) and HM Treasury (2003).

1.3 House prices and investment

The most direct effect of house price fluctuations on economic activity is via residential investment. An increase in house prices raises the value of housing relative to construction costs, i.e. the Tobin q for residential investment. New housing construction becomes profitable when house prices rise above construction costs. Residential investment is therefore a positive function of house prices. Construction costs are composed of building costs and the cost of land, neither of which is directly observable.[13] As a consequence, the Tobin q for housing investment is, like the Tobin q for business investment, also not observable. Partly because of this, only a few studies have attempted to assess the effect of property price movements on construction activity.[14] In any case, the share of residential investment in the GDP of OECD countries is generally rather small, so that the effect via this channel is likely to be of limited importance.

Fluctuations in house prices may also affect the ability of firms to borrow and finance business investment. As we pointed out above, the financial accelerator models of Bernanke and Gertler (1989), Kiyotaki and Moore (1997) and Bernanke *et al.* (1999) suggest that asset prices determining firms' net worth is an important propagator of business and financial cycles. However, as we have also discussed above, residential property price movements are not necessarily representative of price developments in commercial and industrial property markets, so that a change in house prices does not necessarily indicate a change in the value of firms' collateralizable real estate. Also, little is known about the structural features of the market for business loans, such as the role of real estate collaterization, LTVs, etc. As a result, the implications of house price movements for business investment are not as clear as for private consumption and residential investment and, probably for this reason, have also not yet been empirically explored.

1.4 House prices and the financial system

Figure 1.3 shows the four-quarter rate of change in real house prices and the four-quarter rate of change in real bank credit to the private non-banking sector[15] since

---

[13] Some studies use the deflator for private residential investment as a proxy (e.g. Girouard and Blöndahl 2001).

[14] See Girouard and Blöndahl (2001) for evidence for some OECD countries.

[15] The bank credit data originate from the BIS and were converted into real terms by deflation with the GDP deflator. The growth rates were calculated on the basis of data for outstanding stocks. The credit series are not fully comparable due to differences in definition of banking institutions, but also due to differences in data compilation, such as the treatment of non-performing loans. The series also do not fully reflect total credit creation in the economy, as lending by other financial institutions (OFIs) is generally not covered.

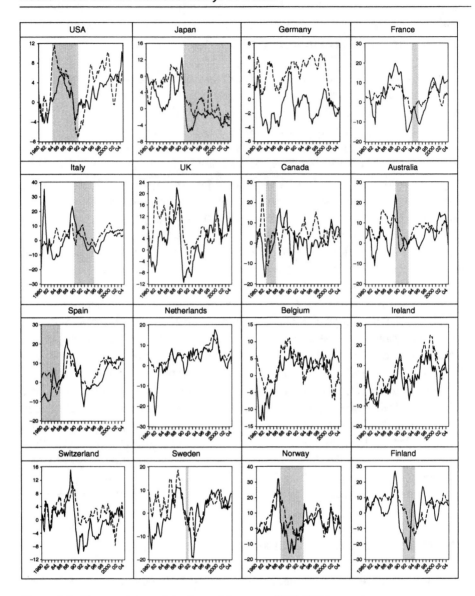

Figure 1.3. House prices and the financial system, 1980–2004

Note: The figure shows the four-quarter rate of change in real house prices (*solid line*), the four-quarter rate of change in real bank credit to the private non-banking sector (*dotted line*), and episodes of systemic and borderline financial crises (*shaded area*) from Caprio and Klingebiel (2003).

1980 for our sample of 16 countries. The figures reveal a very close correlation between real house price inflation and real credit creation. Over the last 25 years, most countries have experienced at least one joint boom–bust cycle in housing and credit markets, with house price generally leading credit growth. The graphs also show that, in contrast to the correlation between the output gap and house prices, the correlation between bank lending and house prices does not appear to have weakened in recent years.

The coincidence of cycles in credit and housing markets has various potential causes. As we discussed above, house prices may affect consumption and investment via wealth effects and Tobin's q, which also affects bank lending via credit demand. On the other hand, house prices affect the value of collateral which borrowers can offer and thus the availability of credit for borrowing-constrained households and firms. Thus, via their effect on private sector balance sheets, house prices may also affect credit supply. Additional credit supply effects may arise via the effect of house prices on the balance sheets of banks. Such an effect may arise directly to the extent that banks own property, and indirectly by affecting the value of loans secured by real estate. Chen (2001) has developed a general equilibrium model based on the models of Bernanke and Gertler (1989) and Kiyotaki and Moore (1997) in which both borrowers' and banks' net worth influences the supply of credit. Just as borrowers' net worth acts as an incentive mechanism and collateral for the banks, bank capital acts in these models as an incentive mechanism and as collateral for the bank's providers of loanable funds, such as the depositors. As a result, the availability of loanable funds to banks depends on their capitalization. Via their effect on the value of banks' housing wealth and, more importantly, on the value of loans secured by housing collateral, fluctuations in house prices therefore also affect the capitalization of the banking system and, hence, credit supply.

Thus, house prices may affect both credit demand and credit supply. Moreover, bank lending may also affect property prices via liquidity effects. This potential two-way causality between bank lending and house prices may give rise to mutually reinforcing cycles in credit and real estate markets.[16] A rise in house prices, caused by more optimistic expectations about future economic prospects, raises the borrowing capacity of firms and households by increasing the value of collateral. Part of the additional available credit may also be used to purchase property, pushing up property prices even further, so that a self-reinforcing process may evolve.

Such boom–bust cycles in house prices and bank lending may leave banks' and households' balance sheets heavily exposed to housing values, so that a collapse of house prices and bank lending may trigger banking sector distress. The shaded areas in Figure 1.2 indicate episodes of systemic and borderline financial crises according to Caprio and Klingebiel (2003). The graphs reveal that boom–bust cycles in house prices and bank lending were in several countries followed by banking sector distress. Except perhaps for the case of the rather long-lasting savings-and-loan crisis in the US, over the chosen sample period all banking crisis episodes in our sample of countries were preceded by boom–bust cycles in housing and credit markets.

---

[16] The possibility of mutually reinforcing cycles in credit and asset markets has already been stressed by Kindleberger (1978) and Minsky (1982).

Part I

House Prices and Economic Activity

2

House Prices as Predictors of Consumer Price Inflation?

2.1 Introduction

There is a consensus among 'mainstream' economists about how asset price fluctuations should be treated for purposes of monetary policy in principle, but no consensus in practice. The mainstream would have the monetary authorities, usually an independent central bank, give primacy to achieving price stability, preferably defined as an inflation target, where inflation is itself measured by some variant of the Retail or Consumer Price Index (RPI or CPI). Such an index consists of prices of current goods and services, but not assets directly.[1] The consensus in principle is that the monetary authorities, whom we will henceforth term the Central Bank, or CB, should adjust their current policy in so far as asset price fluctuations have predictive content for future RPI or CPI inflation. This was the message of Gertler *et al.* (1998), Vickers (1999), and Bernanke and Gertler (1999).

Bernanke and Gertler write:

The inflation-targeting approach dictates that central banks should adjust monetary policy actively and pre-emptively to offset incipient inflationary or deflationary pressure. Importantly for present purposes, it also implies that policy should not respond to changes in asset prices, except insofar as they signal changes in expected inflation. Trying to stabilize asset prices per se is problematic for a variety of reasons, not the least of which is that it is nearly impossible to know for sure whether a given change in asset values results from fundamental factors, non-fundamental factors, or both. By focusing on the inflationary or deflationary pressures generated by asset price movements, a central bank effectively responds to the toxic side effects of asset booms and busts without getting into the business of deciding what is a fundamental and what is not. It also avoids the historically relevant risk that a bubble, once "pricked", can easily degenerate into a panic. Finally, because inflation targeting both helps to

[1] The conceptual validity of this position was strongly challenged by Alchian and Klein (1973). While we find their logic compelling, practical attempts to incorporate asset prices systematically into an index, or measure, of inflation have proved intractable (see Shibuya 1992 and Shiratsuka 1999).

provide stable macroeconomic conditions and also implies that interest rates will tend to rise during (inflationary) asset price booms and fall during (deflationary) asset price busts, this approach may reduce the potential for financial panics to arise in the first place.

Where the difficulties lie *in practice* have been in trying to assess exactly what might be the quantitative implications of current asset price changes for future inflation. There is uncertainty on this both in theory and empirically.

2.2 Some theoretical considerations

Nominal monetary shocks have real effects on activity primarily because certain prices and wages are 'sticky' and do not adjust pro rata. With prices/wages being sticky, the initial effect of monetary shocks is likely to be on (much more) flexible asset prices. Indeed, in theory, this combination of flexible asset prices and sticky goods/labour prices could lead to 'overshooting' in asset prices, though strong empirical support for such phenomena is in practice hard to uncover.

Be that as it may, the initial effects of monetary shocks are likely to be via asset prices, and much of the subsequent transmission mechanism will occur as a result of higher asset prices stimulating expenditures and activity, e.g. Tobin's q effects on investment, wealth effects on consumption, or the effect of exchange rate changes on net trade. Such a transmission mechanism, however, is uncertain, variable and hard to measure at all accurately. Structural innovations have made the velocity of money (in all its definitions) somewhat unpredictable, so the rate of growth of the money stock is an unreliable gauge of the thrust of monetary policy, and/or of the near-term future development of inflation. Whereas policy changes are mainly brought about via changes in nominal wholesale interest rates, the interest rate level/change is also a dubious guide to the measure of policy. For example, was the change previously anticipated, or not, and what is the associated level/change in real interest rates? Indeed, what exactly is meant by the term 'real interest rate' when borrowers may be, indeed usually are, more concerned about future asset price inflation than about goods price inflation? Moreover, as Allan Meltzer (1999a) emphasizes, there are times and occasions, e.g. in a quasi-liquidity trap, as appeared to exist in Japan during 1998/9, when the rate of monetary expansion can have positive effects on activity but the nominal rate of interest on short-term riskless assets is held at a quasi-fixed low nominal level.

Consequently neither monetary growth nor the level (or change) of nominal interest rates gives an unambiguous or straightforward measure of policy. Moreover, the effect of policy will depend for example on the state of confidence, on prior balance sheet positions, on expectations of the future course of inflation and of policy itself. These time-varying and often largely unobservable factors will cause the link from monetary policy to asset prices, and then on to subsequent activity and inflationary pressures, to be variable and uncertain.

This line of analysis still assumes that the causal path runs from monetary shocks to asset prices to output; the point here is that the path is time-varying, so that asset prices may be useful information variables to help assess the strength of the transmission mechanism. But there is equally a causal mechanism running from asset price shocks to monetary and real variables. Stronger asset prices will raise collateral, and encourage more borrowing (see Bernanke and Gertler 1999). If stronger asset prices lead to expectations of higher future activity and higher profits, they will again stimulate bank lending and monetary expansion, at a constant level of interest rates. In so far as higher asset prices stimulate expectations of future asset price increases and capital gains, the relevant real interest rates to borrowers intending to purchase such assets fall. While in theory, except in cases of a bubble, asset prices should always jump to a level that equates expected returns, adjusted for risk, on all assets, in practice there often do seem cases, both in housing and equity markets, where expectations of abnormal future capital gains appear, at least superficially, to be driving bank lending, monetary growth and large segments of real expenditures.

Asset prices may, therefore, provide useful additional information (additional to monetary growth and interest rates) in assessing likely future movements in real activity and inflation. But which asset prices might be most useful in this respect? The asset market heretofore predominantly used for this purpose has been the foreign exchange market. In a small open economy so many activities, transactions and relative profitability depend on the exchange rate that it is surely the most important asset market for such an economy. It is in that spirit that the exchange rate has often been combined with the interest rate to form a Monetary Conditions Index, or MCI. There is a large literature on the estimation and use of MCIs (for recent examples (and bibliographies) see Eika *et al.* 1996 and Peeters 1999).

Although in small open economies the exchange rate most probably represents the most important asset market, it is not necessarily the most informative indicator of either the thrust of domestic monetary policy or of future trends in activity and inflation. Like every other asset market in an economy, the foreign exchange rate can be affected by shifts in tastes, supply shocks, expectations of future returns and profits, and risk premia of various kinds, in addition to concerns about current and future interest rates, monetary growth and inflation. As is the case with all other asset markets, e.g. land, commercial property, housing and equities, only a subset of these factors reflect variables relating to monetary growth, real output and current (goods and services) price inflation. However, what distinguishes the foreign exchange market from other domestic asset markets is that the former is (much more) sensitive to such developments in the foreign economy. Thus, to take only one example, a depreciation in the exchange rate may come about because of a collapse in output and prices abroad, and not because of a domestic expansion. So, although the importance of the exchange rate to economic developments is undeniable, the information content of exchange rate changes, taken on their own without further analysis, may be quite low.

The theoretical literature provides sufficient arguments for considering asset prices other than just the exchange rate. There are several channels through which property and equity prices may affect inflation, and the bond yield can, in theory, provide a measure of the private sector's expectations of future inflation.

An increase in property or equity prices which increases private sector wealth will lead to higher consumption demand, and may finally feed through to higher consumer prices. For the OECD countries the share of residential property in private sector wealth is between 60% and 80%, the share of commercial property between 5% and 20%, and the share of equities between 5% and 35% (see Borio, Kennedy and Prowse 1994: table AI.2, p. 80). This implies that a change in residential property prices will affect private sector wealth much more strongly than the same change in commercial property or equity prices, and is thus also more likely to affect consumer prices.

A relationship between investment demand and equity prices is implied by Tobin's q-theory of investment (Tobin 1969). Tobin's q is defined as the market value of capital relative to the replacement cost of capital. If q rises because of an increase in equity prices, firms can buy more capital for the equity they issue. This makes it more attractive for firms to acquire new capital and so increases investment demand, which may again feed through into higher goods and services prices.

Residential property prices may also affect consumer prices via wages. Higher house prices raise the cost of living for workers, causing them to demand higher wages.[2] Firms may react to higher wage demands by raising their prices, so that eventually goods and services prices increase.

Another connection between asset prices and economic activity arises from imperfections in the credit market. According to the credit view, firms and households may be constrained in their borrowing because of asymmetric information in credit markets, giving rise to adverse selection and moral hazard problems. The lower the net worth of firms and households, the more severe these problems and thus the borrowing constraints will be, since there will be less collateral available to secure loans. A rise in asset prices raises the borrowing capacity of firms and households by increasing the value of collateral. The additionally available credit can be used to purchase goods and services and may thus lead to higher consumer price inflation. Part of the additionally available credit may also be used to purchase assets, pushing up asset prices even further, so that a self-reinforcing process can evolve. The role of credit-market conditions has already been considered by Fisher (1933) amongst others to explain the Great Depression. The interaction of credit and asset prices was reassessed by

[2] Bover, Muellbauer and Murphy (1989) find a long-run coefficient of about 0.2 on log UK house prices in a log-wage equation.

Minsky (1986),[3] and has regained some popularity recently (see e.g. Bernanke and Gertler 1989; Kiyotaki and Moore 1997; Bernanke, Gertler and Gilchrist 1999). These recent theoretical studies show how the interaction between credit limits and asset prices transmits shocks to the economy and may cause large and persistent business cycle fluctuations. This phenomenon is also referred to as the 'financial accelerator'. From the credit perspective, property prices are more likely than equity prices to have an effect on consumer prices, as property is more likely to serve as collateral than is equity.

Long-term nominal interest rates reflect, according to the expectations theory of the term structure, expected future short-term nominal interest rates. In so far as real interest rates and risk premia can be expected to remain constant, the yield spread, i.e. long-term nominal interest rates less short-term nominal interest rates, would provide a measure of expected future inflation. Thus the yield spread may be a useful indicator of future inflationary pressures (see e.g. Mishkin 1990).

If, then, we are concerned to assess whether asset price movements contain useful information (in addition to interest rates and monetary growth) on future activity and inflationary pressures, there seems no necessary presumption that attention should be concentrated on just the exchange rate. The question would seem to be empirical, rather than determined by a priori theory.

2.3   Some empirical considerations

The variables that one might consider using to assess future inflation depend on the horizon of that assessment. For a one-month-ahead assessment one might consider such variables as recent inflationary trends, the exchange rate, oil and other commodity prices, seasonal factors, announced tax changes, etc. For a decade-ahead assessment, one might consider the strength of the political regime and the possibility of conflict, the fiscal and monetary regimes, and worldwide inflation trends.

For an operationally independent central bank with a mandate to maintain price stability by achieving a low and stable rate of inflation, the appropriate horizon for an inflation assessment would seem to focus on a horizon of about four to eight quarters ahead. The main instrument that such a central bank can use is its ability to control short-term interest rates. The consensus is that policy changes in such rates have their main impact on inflation about two years on. Moreover, the ability to assess what else might be happening to the economy, which monetary policy might need to counteract, increasingly deteriorates the

---

[3] Minsky saw the interaction between asset prices and money/bank expansion as an engine of instability in a capitalist economy, which required mitigation and intervention both by fiscal policy, 'big government', and by the monetary authorities acting as lender of last resort.

further ahead one tries to peer. Very few forecasts (as contrasted with simulations) are pushed beyond a two-year horizon.

The question that we want to address here, therefore, is whether various measures of asset price inflation now (and in the recent past) help to assess future goods and services price inflation, e.g. as measured by some version of the RPI or CPI or GDP deflator, between four and eight quarters into the future. This is, after all, the exercise which most monetary policy committees have to undertake.

Our prior beliefs, based on experience and historical study, were that fluctuations in the equity market are less closely associated with the economy, the banking system and subsequent inflation than are fluctuations in property prices. With our preliminary results seeming to support this view, we made special efforts to obtain price indices for housing and property, though the latter in particular are generally harder to obtain from standard publicly available data sources than are other key asset prices, e.g. equity indices and the exchange rate. We were able to obtain quarterly data on residential property prices for 11 countries (Australia, Canada, Finland, France, Ireland, the Netherlands, New Zealand, Norway, Sweden, the UK and the USA) and semi-annual data for residential land prices for Japan.[4] We were even less fortunate in our search for commercial property prices; we could only get a quarterly time series for Australian commercial property prices and a semi-annual data set for Japanese commercial land prices. Details on the house prices series used in the empirical analysis and their sources are given in Table 2.1. All other series used in the empirical analysis were taken from the IMF International Financial Statistics or the OECD Main Economic Indicators database.

A variable may have an important, and close, causal relationship with some second variable, while at the same time *not* have a stable statistical lead relationship with that second variable. The causal relationship, though strong, may vary depending on circumstances. We have already hinted that this may be so for the relationship between exchange rates and domestic inflation. Again the statistical lead relationship may be disturbed because of structural and behavioural changes; this may have been the case for the relationship between (broad) money and inflation over short- and medium-term horizons. Nor do statistically strong, and often apparently robust, lead relationships necessarily require strong and direct causal links. Whatever the analytical interpretation may be, our question is whether we can find evidence that current asset price inflation helps (in a statistically significant sense) to assess future goods and services price inflation. For this purpose we examined a 'reduced form' equation, where we regressed the

---

[4] We were also able to obtain annual residential property price series for Germany and Spain. As the exercise we undertook involved the estimation of many parameters, the degrees of freedom were close to zero in our regressions with annual data. Therefore we decided not to present the results for these regressions here, but they are available on request from the authors.

Table 2.1. Description and sources of house price series

Country	Series used	Source
Australia	RBA Dwelling Price Index	Central bank
Canada	Average resale housing price index	Canadian Real Estate Association
Finland	National house price index	Central bank
France	Price of old apartments in Paris	Chambre des Notaires
Ireland	Average prices of new houses for which loans have been approved by all lending agencies	Department of the Environment
Japan	Nationwide land price index	Japan Real Estate Institute
Netherlands	Average housing prices	Central bank
New Zealand	Average house prices	Central bank
Norway	National house price index	Central bank
Sweden	Single-family house price index	Central bank
United Kingdom	Index of house prices	Department of the Environment
United States	Median sales prices of new one-family houses	Bureau of the Census

rate of consumer price inflation (Δcpi) in $t + 4$ or $t + 8$ on its own current and lagged values and the current and lagged values of other explanatory variables. As we were especially interested in the predictive power of property prices, share prices and the yield spread, we estimated a baseline equation including real GDP growth (Δgdp),[5] broad money growth (Δm), the nominal short-term interest rate (ir) and the rate of change in the nominal exchange rate (Δexr) as explanatory variables,[6] and an extended asset price equation, where we added the rate of change in residential property (house) prices (Δhp), the rate of change in share prices (Δsp) and the yield spread (ys)[7] to the list of regressors.[8]

Thus we get the baseline equation:

$$\Delta cpi_{t+i} = \alpha + \beta_0 \Delta cpi_{t-j} + \beta_1 \Delta gdp_{t-j} + \beta_2 \Delta m_{t-j} + \beta_3 ir_{t-j} + \beta_4 \Delta exr_{t-j}$$

[5] For Ireland we could not obtain a long enough series for real GDP, so we used industrial production instead. The use of the output 'gap' as an alternative measure of the pressure of demand is discussed further in §2.4 below.

[6] In preliminary regressions we also included the rate of change in wages (hourly earnings) and the rate of change in the US oil price in the baseline equation. As the coefficients of these variables came out either insignificant or wrongly signed, we decided subsequently to omit these variables from the regression. The reason for the bad performance of these variables is most likely their quick effect on inflation, which renders them useless in an attempt to predict inflation four or eight quarters ahead.

[7] The yield spread could not be included in the regressions for Finland and Sweden, as there was no long-term bond yield for a long enough period available for these countries.

[8] As we were aiming at a standardized specification we did not make use of our commercial property/land price data for Australia and Japan, but the regression results obtained when we included these series are available on request from the authors.

and the extended asset price equation:

$$\Delta cpi_{t+i} = \alpha + \beta_0 \Delta cpi_{t-j} + \beta_1 \Delta gdp_{t-j} + \beta_2 \Delta m_{t-j} + \beta_3 ir_{t-j} + \beta_4 \Delta exr_{t-j} + \beta_5 \Delta hp_{t-j}$$
$$+ \beta_6 \Delta sp_{t-j} + \beta_7 ys_{t-j}$$

with $i = 4, 8$ for the one- and two-year horizon respectively, $j = 0, 1, \ldots$ The expected sign of the coefficients is positive for the lagged dependent variable, Δgdp, Δm, Δhp, Δsp and ys, and negative for ir and Δexr.[9]

With so many regressors the question of how to determine lag lengths becomes crucial. As a first measure, to save degrees of freedom we assumed that when assessing future inflation, only information of the current and the previous year should be taken into account. But this measure alone would still have left 65 coefficients to be estimated in the extended asset price regression equation. One way to economize on the number of freely estimated parameters in such a situation is to use an information criterion to determine the optimal lag length. As we did not want to impose the restriction that the optimal lag length is the same for all regressors, we would have had to run regressions for all possible combinations of lag lengths. The high number of possible combinations in such an exercise made us reject this option. Instead we decided to use successive four-quarter moving averages of the variables.[10] Thus, we created information windows, the first window representing the information on the variable from the current year, and the second window representing the information on the variable from the previous year. Therefore we included for each variable the average of the lags 0–3 and 4–7 in the regression. For the lagged dependent variable we only included the average of the lags 0–3.

We estimated the equations and eliminated successively wrongly signed and insignificant variables in order to see which variables survive in the end. Significance was assessed based on Newey–West autocorrelation and heteroscedasticity-consistent standard errors. The results of this elimination strategy for the one- and two-year horizon regressions are summarized in Table 2.2. The full results are presented in Tables 2.3 and 2.4. Table 2.2 shows for each specification the percent of regressions (countries) where the coefficient of at least one lag-window of a variable appeared correctly signed and significant, i.e. significant at least at the 10% level. The last row shows the average adjusted coefficient of determination ($\bar{R}^2$).

It becomes clear that, when predicting future inflation, current inflation plays a crucial role, with the current-year lag-window coming out significantly in all the regressions at the one-year horizon and in nearly all the regressions at the

---

[9] The nominal effective exchange rate is measured as the amount of foreign currency per unit of home currency.

[10] For another application of this approach see Gordon (1998).

Table 2.2. Summary of the regression results for Δcpi

	One-year horizon		Two-year horizon	
	Excluding asset prices	Including Asset prices	Excluding asset prices	Including asset prices
Δcpi	100	100	91.7	83.3
Δgdp	50	33.3	41.7	33.3
Δm	83.3	58.3	66.7	58.3
ir	50	50	66.7	58.3
Δexr	25	25	41.7	50
Δhp	—	50	—	58.3
Δsp	—	25	—	33.3
ys	—	10	—	33.3
Average $\bar{R}^2$	73.3	76.3	64.3	70

Note: The table shows for each specification the percent of regressions where the coefficient of at least one lag-window of a variable appeared correctly signed and significant, i.e. significant at least at the 10% level, in the regression; the last row shows the average adjusted coefficient of determination.

two-year horizon. But that is not a surprising result. We were more interested in the performance of the other variables, especially of asset prices.

Real GDP growth does not perform very well at either horizon. When asset prices are included in the regressions, it appears to be significant in only one-third of the countries at both horizons. Broad money growth performs very well at the one-year horizon and still pretty well at the two-year horizon in the baseline regressions. When asset prices are included, the significant outturns for broad money growth drop by 25 percentage points at the one-year horizon and by 8 percentage points at the two-year horizon. The short-term interest rate comes out significant in between a half and two-thirds of the countries, performing better at the two-year horizon. The change in the exchange rate performs relatively poorly at the one-year horizon, but nearly doubles its significant outturns at the two-year horizon. Perhaps surprisingly, the exchange rate seems to be a better indicator for inflation at the longer horizon.

Asset prices in general seem to be more useful indicators for inflation at the two-year horizon than at the one-year horizon. Among them, residential property price inflation performs the best, coming out significantly in 50% and 58% of the countries respectively. Share price inflation and the yield spread[11] do not perform so well, with both achieving their best result at the two-year horizon with at least one significant lag-window in one-third of the countries. The average adjusted coefficient of determination improves when asset prices are included, though not overwhelmingly. The improvement is more marked at the two-year horizon.

---

[11] It should be remembered that the performance of the yield spread is assessed on the basis of 10 regressions instead of 12, as we could not include the yield spread in the regressions for Finland and Sweden.

Table 2.3. Full regression results for the one-year horizon

	Δcpi 1	Δcpi 2	Δgdp 1	Δgdp 2	Δm 1	Δm 2	ir 1	ir 2	Δexr 1	Δexr 2	Δhp 1	Δhp 2	Δsp 1	Δsp 2	ys 1	ys 2	R^2
Australia 1972:2–1998:3	0.74***		0.29**		0.23*			−0.34**									0.66
	0.73***		0.32**		0.15			−0.26**			0.1*						0.68
Canada 1982:1–1998:3	0.66***		0.37***	0.29***		0.13**											0.82
	0.61***		0.23***	0.2***		0.15***					0.05**		0.03***				0.87
Finland 1981:1–1998:2	0.65***				0.22***	0.11**	−0.17*	−0.35**	−0.1***	−0.1**							0.86
	0.65***				0.22***	0.11**	−0.17*	−0.35**	−0.1***	−0.1**							0.86
France 1983:2–1998:3	0.63***			0.27***	0.3***	0.27***			−0.07								0.9
	0.63***			0.27***					−0.07								0.9
Ireland 1979:1–1998:2	0.74***				0.3***	0.27***			−0.3***								0.79
	0.52***										0.22***	0.23***		0.03**			0.87
Japan 1969:2–1998:2	0.63***				0.5***		−0.54*										0.67
	0.74***				0.25		−0.71**				0.22						0.69
Netherlands 1973:1–1998:3	0.69***					0.17*		−0.19	−0.12								0.75
	0.69***					0.17*		−0.19	−0.12								0.75
New Zealand 1980:2–1998:2	0.76***		1.03***						−0.1								0.6
	0.76***		1.03***						−0.1								0.6
Norway 1974:4–1998:3	0.52***		0.13		0.12**	0.3***		−0.39***		−0.22***							0.69
	0.65***		0.11		0.1	0.28***		−0.44***		−0.19*			0.03*	0.03**			0.74
Sweden 1979:2–1998:3	0.45***				0.16*	0.32***		−0.24									0.65
	0.3***		0.19		0.13**	0.31***			−0.07			0.16**					0.7
UK 1971:2–1998:3	0.84***					0.1**		−0.77***	−0.06								0.65
	0.68***		0.43**			0.06**		−0.78***	−0.05			0.19***					0.7
USA 1966:1–1998:3	0.89***		0.24**			0.28***		−0.37***	−0.07**	−0.07**							0.76
	0.86***					0.24***		−0.33***	−0.04	−0.05	0.12**					0.3*	0.79

Note: For each country the first row displays the results for the regression excluding asset prices, the second row displays the results for the regression including asset prices; the table displays the coefficients and significance levels for the first (1) and second (2) lag-window for each variable; *, **, *** denotes significance at the 10%, 5% and 1% level respectively; all variables with *t*-statistics≥1 were retained.

Table 2.4. Full regression results for the two-year horizon

	Δcpi 1	Δcpi 2	Δgdp 1	Δgdp 2	Δm 1	Δm 2	ir 1	ir 2	Δexr 1	Δexr 2	Δhp 1	Δhp 2	Δsp 1	Δsp 2	ys 1	ys 2	R̄²
Australia	0.76***		0.57***				-0.45**										0.47
1973:2–1998:3	0.7***		0.51***				-0.41**				0.09*						0.5
Canada	0.48***	0.21***	0.43***		0.06												0.74
1983:1–1998:3	0.45***	0.22***	0.28***								0.06***	0.03	0.02**				0.84
Finland	0.43***				0.17**	0.18**	-0.46***		-0.1***								0.73
1982:1–1998:2	0.5***	0.1			0.12**	0.12	-0.34***		-0.1***				0.02**				0.78
France	0.37***	0.11	0.22**						-0.1***								0.77
1984:2–1998:3	0.37***	0.11	0.22**						-0.1***								0.77
Ireland	0.65***				0.4***	0.42***	-0.51**										0.71
1980:1–1998:2	0.29***				0.08	0.33***					0.2***	0.17***	0.05***	0.04***		0.43**	0.88
Japan	0.51***				0.65***		-0.92***			-0.08							0.66
1970:2–1998:2	0.5***				0.56***		-1.2***			-0.08		0.18**					0.69
Netherlands	0.23				0.14	0.28**		-0.25									0.64
1974:1–1998:3	0.23				0.14	0.28**		-0.25									0.64
New Zealand	0.49**								-0.16**	-0.08							0.41
1981:1–1998:2	0.49**								-0.16**	-0.08							0.41
Norway	0.22*		0.14*		0.26***	0.37***		-0.5***	-0.16	-0.25*							0.68
1975:4–1998:3	0.28**				0.29***	0.34***		-0.66***	-0.23**	-0.2			0.03**				0.7
Sweden	0.32**				0.35***	0.14**		-0.5***	-0.09								0.62
1980:2–1998:3	0.28**				0.32***	0.12**		-0.37***	-0.13**		0.13*						0.68
UK	0.86***	0.64**	0.54		0.08	0.09*	-0.93***										0.58
1972:2–1998:3	0.27				0.08	0.03	-0.42*		-0.08	-0.11**	0.19***	0.25***			0.74*		0.78
USA	0.67***				0.29***	0.39***	-0.43***		-0.08**								0.71
1967:1–1998:3	0.82***	0.16**			0.22***	0.32***	-0.65***		-0.06		0.07**					0.34*	0.73

Note: For each country the first row displays the results for the regression excluding asset prices, the second row displays the results for the regression including asset prices; the table displays the coefficients and significance levels for the first (1) and second (2) lag-window for each variable; *, **, *** denotes significance at the 10%, 5% and 1% level respectively; all variables with coefficients with *t*-statistics ≥ 1 were retained.

So how do we assess the result of this exercise? For the one-year-ahead prediction we see broad money growth coming first and the short-term nominal interest rate and the rate of change in house prices sharing second place. Real GDP growth comes fourth, the rate of change in the exchange rate fifth and the yield spread last.

For the two-year-ahead prediction the interest rate and house price inflation catch up with money growth and all three share first position. The rate of change in the exchange rate improves to fourth place and the other three variables come jointly fifth. Thus, altogether, broad money growth, the short-term nominal interest rate and house price inflation are the winners of this race.

Most studies of the determinants of inflation use the rate of inflation as the dependent variable, and there are certainly good reasons to believe that in most developed countries both the inflation rate and the short-term nominal interest rate will be stationary in the long run. We tested all variables for stationarity using a standard augmented Dickey–Fuller Test and, as is commonly the case, the results suggested that consumer price inflation and the short-term nominal interest rate appeared to be non-stationary, while all other variables generally appeared to be stationary. Our conjecture is that regime shifts make inflation and interest rates appear I(1) in short samples, but that they will be stationary in the long run. However, in order to take the possibility of non-stationary inflation and interest rates into account, we decided to estimate a second specification with the change in consumer price inflation ($\Delta^2 cpi$) instead of with the level as the dependent variable, and with the change in short-term nominal interest rates (Δir) instead of with the level as a regressor.

For this specification we exactly repeated the exercise we did before. The summary of the results can be found in Table 2.5. Real GDP growth appears to be a much more useful predictor of the change in the inflation rate instead of the

Table 2.5. Summary of the regression results for $\Delta^2 cpi$

	One-year horizon		Two-year horizon	
	Excluding asset prices	Including asset prices	Excluding asset prices	Including asset prices
Δgdp	83.3	66.7	75	66.7
Δm	25	25	25	25
Δir	33.3	58.3	25	25
Δexr	8.3	25	16.7	16.7
Δhp	—	41.7	—	50
Δsp	—	16.7	—	25
ys	—	33.3	—	41.7
Average $\bar{R}^2$	26.3	32	28.9	38.1

Note: The table shows for each specification the percent of regressions where the coefficient of at least one lag-window of a variable appeared correctly signed and significant, i.e. significant at least at the 10% level, in the regression; the last row shows the average adjusted coefficient of determination.

level, coming out significantly in at least two-thirds of the regressions for all specifications. The change in the interest rates does not appear to be a good indicator for future changes in inflation except for the one-year horizon, where the significant outturns jump to 58% when asset prices are included. Broad money growth and the exchange rate perform quite badly, never appearing significant in more than 25% of the regressions.

Again the usefulness of asset prices seems to increase with the forecast horizon, and again the rate of change in house prices is the best performer. The yield spread seems to be quite a useful predictor of the change in the inflation rate at the two-year horizon, being significant in more than 40% of the regressions. Share price inflation does not appear to be a very useful predictor of the change in inflation either. The average improvement in fit from including asset prices is more marked than in the other specification, but the low levels of the $\bar{R}^2$ show that all variables together cannot explain future changes in the inflation rate very well. Surprisingly, the average fit is better at the two-year horizon.

The outcome of this horse race is significantly different from the one we ran before. At both horizons real GDP growth is the clear and undisputed winner. At the one-year horizon the change in interest rates comes second, house price inflation third and the yield spread fourth. At the two-year horizon house price inflation and the yield spread move up to second and third place respectively. Therefore real GDP growth and house price inflation are the winners and broad money growth, the change in the exchange rate and share price inflation are the losers of this race.

2.4 Conclusions

What do we make of these results? First, inflation is highly autocorrelated, so one needs to examine the explanatory value of other variables *after* taking account of such autocorrelation. The results we obtained show that it is also crucial *how* this autocorrelation is taken into account, i.e. whether the inflation rate is assumed to be a non-stationary process or not. Augmented Dickey–Fuller Test results suggest that inflation is I(1). Our conjecture, however, is that regime shifts make inflation and interest rates appear I(1) in short samples, but that they will be stationary in the long run. Therefore our conclusions will focus on the implications of our results for the prediction of the level of the inflation rate and not its change. The results obtained for the change in the inflation rate, which sometimes contradict the former results, must be seen as qualifications of these conclusions.

In many current standard models, for nearly closed economies, inflation is taken as determined by a measure of real activity, past (or expected) inflation and interest rates; in more open economies the exchange rate is added (sometimes in a composite MCI form). What is surprising about the results we obtained from estimating these reduced-form equations is how comparatively poorly (relative to our prior expectations) real GDP growth did in explaining the non-autocorrelated movement in inflation.

One may argue that our measure of real activity, real GDP growth, is a poor proxy of the actual output gap and therefore of future inflationary pressures. Usually the output gap is calculated by using some kind of trend filter, e.g. the Hodrick–Prescott filter, to get a measure of potential output. These trend filters use information of past and future GDP to filter out the trend. As we do not know future GDP today, such a measure of trend GDP is based on data not available when assessing future inflation and would therefore not properly reflect the information available for the assessment. Nonetheless we ventured to rerun all regressions using a measure of the output gap based on the Hodrick–Prescott filter instead of real GDP growth and it appeared that this measure of the output gap did not perform better.

Perhaps these results mainly reflect structural shifts in the output gap over our data period, which were not picked up in the simple measures of the 'gap' adopted. No doubt adjustments to the output gap series could result in a closer econometric relationship between a pressure-for-demand variable and the fluctuations in inflation. But one would ask then whether similar adjustments (data mining?) could be made for the other variables as well.

The other weak performer was the (percentage) change in the exchange rate. This is surprising given that the role of the exchange rate as an indicator of future inflationary pressures has already received a lot of attention in the literature and in central banking practice. But it is not surprising in the light of the qualifications pointed out below.

The three explanatory variables that appeared much stronger (than we had earlier anticipated) in these results, especially at the two-year horizon, are the change in monetary-type variables, the rate of growth of broad money itself, current and past short-term interest rates, and, especially, current and prior house price inflation. If there is a message in these results, it is that monetary variables in general, and house price movements in particular, need to be given more weight in the assessment of inflation, particularly at a two-year horizon, than is done in some current models, which primarily incorporate the monetary transmission mechanism via the effects of real interest rates on real expenditures (and of nominal interest rates on exchange rates). One of the problems may be that views about key economic interrelationships are dominated by the experience of the USA, which is the leading economy with the best data and where the best economists congregate. Like other research workers, we find that the yield spread is a useful additional predictor of inflation in the USA, but rather rarely outside the USA. House prices do have a weaker, but just significant, effect there, but, unlike many other countries, cyclical movement of housing prices has been comparatively mild in the USA (in aggregate), perhaps because the ready availability of land and cheap wooden building has increased the elasticity of supply. Be that as it may, the addition of housing prices does not provide any real help in explaining US inflation, and US experience becomes projected as a universal truth.

In contrast, many other countries around the world experienced at least two strong cycles in housing prices, in the early 1970s and late 1980s, and these preceded strong inflationary surges. Correlation does not prove causation, and it could possibly be that the cycles in housing prices and in goods and services price (CPI) inflation were largely independent, or driven by common factors. In truth, there have only been a few cycles, and hence only a small number of (real) degrees of freedom in our data set.

That suggests that we should extend this research to explore the effects of housing prices (and of other asset prices) on inflation over a much longer time horizon, using annual data. This will be our next research exercise in this field. In the meantime it would be as well to keep a weather-eye on housing price inflation as a guide to trends in future CPI inflation.

At the beginning of this chapter we noted that most economists would agree that movements in asset prices *should* be taken into account by the monetary authorities insofar as they signal changes in expected inflation. What we have done here is to run a horse race between a benchmark forecasting equation with, and without, a set of non-standard asset prices. We claim that such asset prices, especially house prices, do help in the majority of cases in the context of our data set to assess (predict) future CPI inflation.

We very much doubt whether this will cause the sceptics to revise their position. The criterion usually adopted is *not* in practice whether asset prices can help predict inflation in a 'reduced-form', simple framework as used here; but rather how, and why, changes in such asset prices may be shown to enter the structural equations of a larger, more coherent, forecasting model. That would be a different, and probably much more difficult, exercise.

3

Financial Conditions Indices

3.1 Introduction

A Monetary Conditions Index (MCI), a weighted average of the short-term interest rate and the exchange rate, has commonly been used, at least for open economies, as a composite measure of the stance of monetary policy. The MCI concept is based on empirical findings that inflationary pressures are determined by excess aggregate demand and that monetary policy mainly affects aggregate demand via its leverage over short-term interest rates and the real exchange rate. Changes in the stance of monetary policy affect short-term money market interest rates, which in turn influence the investment and saving decisions of households and firms and thus domestic demand conditions. A change in short-term interest rates changes, ceteris paribus, the interest rate differential vis-à-vis the rest of the world and may thus lead to a change in the real exchange rate, which in turn affects the competitiveness of domestic firms vis-à-vis foreign firms and thus external demand conditions.

Recent developments in theoretical and empirical research on the monetary transmission process imply that property and equity prices may also play an important role in the transmission of monetary policy via wealth and balance sheet effects. Monetary policy can affect property and equity prices via arbitrage effects and/or a change in discounted expected future dividends, which gives rise to the wealth effect and the balance sheet effect of monetary policy. Thus, from a theoretical point of view there is a strong case to consider other asset prices besides interest and exchange rates as indicators of the stance of monetary policy as well. In the following we will try to derive an extended Monetary Conditions Index or Financial Conditions Index (FCI) for the G7 countries. FCI weights are derived based on coefficient estimates of reduced form demand equations and impulse responses of an identified VAR.

3.2 Constructing Financial Conditions Indices: strategies and problems

3.2.1 The general strategy

We are aiming at the construction of an aggregate measure of monetary or financial conditions, a Financial Conditions Index (FCI), consisting of a short-term interest rate, the real effective exchange rate, real house prices and real share prices.[1] Our FCI is defined as $FCI_t = \sum_i w_i(q_{it} - \bar{q}_{it})$ where q_{it} is the price of asset i in period t, $\bar{q}_{it}$ is the long-run trend or equilibrium value of the price of asset i in period t, and w_i is the relative weight given to the price of asset i in the FCI.[2]

As with the construction of MCIs, there are three possibilities for estimating the weights of the respective asset prices in an FCI:

- simulations in large-scale macro-econometric models
- reduced-form aggregate demand equations
- VAR impulse responses

Large-scale macro-econometric models are used by national central banks and governmental organizations, some of which are available for public access. However, large macro-econometric models with an explicit role for house prices are not available, mainly due to a lack of data availability, a problem that we bypass by resorting to interpolated data in some cases. Since the role of property prices is a centrepiece of this chapter, we could not use large-scale macro-econometric models for this reason and thus had to go for the other two options.

The reduced-form model consists of a Phillips curve relating CPI inflation to the output gap and an IS equation relating the output gap to deviations of the short-term real interest rate, the effective real exchange rate, real house prices and real share prices from their long-run trend. The FCI is constructed on the basis of the estimated coefficients in the aggregate demand equation. Alternative FCI weights are derived on the basis of impulse responses in a VAR consisting of the same variables that appear in the reduced-form model.

---

[1] It would also have been desirable, of course, to include a long-term interest rate, since in many countries long-term interest rates are more relevant for aggregate demand conditions than short-term interest rates. The problem we faced was that we wanted to concentrate on real variables, and it is not clear how to construct a measure of real long-term interest rates. What one would need is a measure of expected inflation for a horizon equal to the maturity of the bond underlying the long-term yield. We tried to construct a measure of inflation expectations based on a three-year moving average of inflation, but the real long-term interest rate thus constructed always appeared with the wrong sign in the output gap equations, indicating that this measure is probably a rather poor proxy of real long-term rates. For this reason we decided to exclude long-term interest rates from the analysis.

[2] This definition does not conform to the usual definition of an MCI, where the interest rate and the exchange rate are set in relation to their level in a base period. Since house prices and share prices are trending variables, such a definition would have led to trending FCIs. To avoid that we set our asset prices in relation to some measure of long-run trend or equilibrium.

3.2.2   Modelling long-run trends in asset prices

How should one model long-run trends in asset prices? The short-term real rate of interest poses the smallest difficulty in this respect, since it is usually considered to be mean-reverting. But what about real exchange rates, real house prices and real share prices? A look at Figure 3.1, which displays the development of these asset prices over 1972–98, makes clear that the assumption of mean reversion would not appropriately characterize the process that drives these variables. There is a large literature arguing that asset prices are random walks and that it is not possible to identify equilibrium values of asset prices. On the other hand, there is also a large, and growing, literature on how to model equilibrium asset prices. Our view is that it is generally possible to identify periods of misalignment in asset prices, if only *ex post*, so that we venture to follow the second approach here by assuming that asset prices follow (possibly time-varying) determinist trends but not stochastic ones.

The most commonly used equilibrium concept for real exchange rates, Purchasing Power Parity, implies in its traditional form that real exchange rates are mean-reverting.[3] However, there are also real determinants of the real exchange rates which could give rise to long-run deterministic trends in real exchange rates. For example, the Balassa–Samuelson effect implies that if a country has higher long-run productivity growth in its tradeable goods sector than its trading partners, then its real exchange rate will appreciate in the long run. Thus, there can be a long-run trend in real exchange rates. For this reason, we model the long-run trend of real exchange rates by regressing the real exchange rate on a constant and a linear trend.

We take the same approach for real house prices, on the basis of a related argument. Given that house prices are tied to construction costs, real house prices will follow a long-run deterministic trend since productivity in the construction sector is growing at a slower pace than overall productivity. Thus, the long-run trend in house prices is also modelled by regressing real house prices on a constant and a linear trend.

For real share prices the case is more difficult. According to standard asset pricing models, today's share prices should reflect the discounted sum of future real dividends. If the discount rate and the expected growth rate of future dividends are constant, real share prices are given by $P = D/(r - g)$, where D is real dividends, r is the discount rate and g the long-run growth rate of dividends. Since dividends are related to real activity, it would seem to be possible to model long-run trends in share prices by a linear trend too. Visual inspection of real share price

---

[3] There are several competing concepts for calculating equilibrium exchange rates, most of which require large macro-econometric models. Following all of them up is therefore beyond the scope of this paper. MacDonald (2000) provides a comprehensive survey of all the concepts.

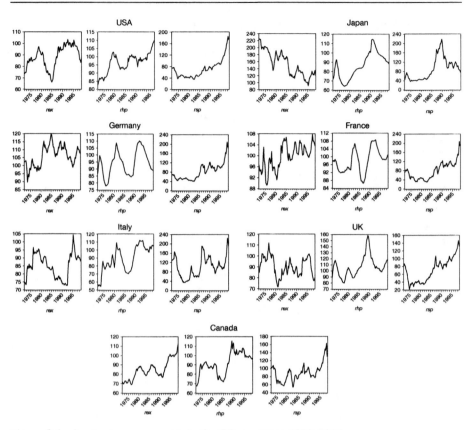

Figure 3.1. Asset price movements in the G7 countries, 1972–1998

Note: rex is the CPI-based effective real exchange rate (units of home goods per unit of foreign goods), *rhp* is the real house price index and *rsp* is the real share price index.

movements shows, however, that we are unable to keep track of share prices with a linear trend. Real share prices rather seem to have followed three different regimes over the period 1970–98: a high, constant level before the first oil price shock in 1974, a low constant level after the first oil price shock, and an upward trend since the early eighties. The problem is that the expected long-run growth rate of dividends cannot be assumed to be constant. Adverse supply-side conditions, caused by the increase in oil prices and union wage pressure in some countries, are likely to have had an adverse effect on expected future dividend growth and thus to have caused the drop in share prices in the early 1970s. Share prices remained at their low levels until the early eighties, when oil prices started to recede and conservative governments in many countries put in place policy measures to improve the supply side of their economies, thus causing an increase in expected future dividend growth. Thus, the long-run trend of real share prices has been time-variable due to the effect of expectations. For this reason we calculate the trend in real share prices using a Hodrick–Prescott

Table 3.1. Unit-root tests for asset price gaps

	Interest rate	Exchange rate	House prices	Share prices
USA	−1.88*	−2.49**	−2.09**	−4.80***
	−3.62***	−1.58	−1.75*	−3.93***
Japan	−3.01***	−2.92***	−4.23***	−3.11***
	−4.85***	−2.20**	−2.99***	−2.99***
Germany	−3.28***	−2.59***	−3.23***	−4.02***
	−5.02***	−2.29**	−1.75*	−3.09***
France	−1.91*	−3.45***	−3.78***	−4.04***
	−3.35***	−3.36***	−1.95**	−3.23***
Italy	−1.87*	−2.11**	−2.35**	−3.59***
	−3.00***	−2.08**	−2.54**	−2.37**
UK	−2.30**	−2.71***	−3.62***	−4.16***
	−4.13***	−2.32**	−2.01**	−3.97***
Canada	−2.15**	−1.68*	−2.21**	−3.78***
	−3.56***	−1.50	−1.91*	−3.45***

Note: The table displays, for each country and asset price, first the Augmented Dickey–Fuller and then the Phillips–Perron test statistic based on regressions with four lagged differences and a lag truncation of four respectively and without intercepts and trends. *, ** and *** indicate rejection of the unit-root hypothesis at the 10%, 5% and 1% level respectively. The respective critical values are −1.62, −1.94 and −2.58 (MacKinnon 1991).

Filter with a high smoothing parameter of 10,000, in order to obtain a smooth, time-variable trend.

Table 3.1 reports unit-root test statistics for the derived asset price gaps. In most cases the null of non-stationarity is clearly rejected, so that valid test statistics can be obtained from regressions with these gap measures.

When estimating FCI weights using reduced-form equations and VARs, we inherit several potential caveats from the MCI literature (see Eika, Ericsson and Nymoen 1996 and Ericsson *et al.* 1998). The main criticisms that also apply to our analysis are

- parameter non-constancy
- model dependence of the derived weights
- non-exogeneity of regressors

Parameter non-constancy is potentially a problem in our analysis. Our sample period covers the post-Bretton Woods period, which could be seen as a single regime with fixed exchange rates in continental Europe and mainly flexible exchange rates in the rest of the G7. However, our sample period can still be seen as covering more than one regime. The 1970s were characterized by the oil shocks, rather accommodative monetary policy and, in some countries, labour disputes. In the 1980s inflation receded due to a change in the paradigm of macroeconomic policy in the G7 countries, with a strong emphasis on stability and, in most G7 countries, on the improvement of supply-side conditions. The 1990s saw German reunification and the bursting of asset price bubbles in Japan, leaving the country in an ongoing depression. Thus, parameter non-constancy is a potential problem for our analysis, which we try to cover mainly by doing standard breakpoint tests.

Model dependence of estimated effects is a potential caveat that applies to any kind of empirical analysis. We were unable to construct (or use) large-scale macro-econometric models, nor could we include every variable that possibly affects aggregate demand and inflation, so that the weights we derive certainly depend on the way we specified our model. We hope, however, that the model specification we chose is adequate for the question at stake.

Non-exogeneity of regressors might be seen as a problem that applies with particular force to our analysis, since property and share prices are often characterized as forward-looking variables, so that including them as regressors might introduce a simultaneity bias in the estimating equations. However, simultaneity problems may already arise from including interest rates and exchange rates in the analysis. The Central Bank raises interest rates in anticipation of future positive output gaps, and exchange rates appreciate in anticipation of positive gaps, which could trigger rising interest rates. Thus, including property and share prices in the analysis does not introduce a problem that has not potentially been there before. In the literature on monetary policy transmission and monetary policy rules it is always assumed that the information set of the Central Bank can be characterized by lags of endogenous and exogenous variables, so that no simultaneity problem arises. But why should asset markets have information on future output and inflation that are superior to those of the Central Bank? There is no reason why this should be the case, even if stock market investors were always fully rational.

3.3 Financial Conditions Indices for the G7 countries

FCI weights are derived on the basis of reduced-form estimates of coefficients in a simple aggregate demand equation and impulse responses from an identified VAR. The sample period of the analysis is the first quarter 1973 to the fourth quarter 1998, thus covering the post-Bretton Woods and the pre-EMU era.

3.3.1 Reduced-form estimates

In order to assess the importance of financial variables in the conduct of monetary policy, we estimate an extended version of the standard inflation targeting model proposed by Rudebusch and Svensson (1998). In this framework the economy is modelled by a backward-looking supply or Phillips curve and a backward-looking demand or IS curve:

$$\pi_t = \alpha_1 + \sum_{i=1}^{n_1} \beta_{1i}\pi_{t-i} + \sum_{j=1}^{n_2} \beta_{2j}y_{t-j} + \sum_{k=0}^{n_3} \beta_{3k}dpo_{t-k} + \varepsilon_t \tag{1}$$

$$y_t = \alpha_2 + \sum_{i=1}^{m_1} \gamma_i y_{t-i} + \sum_{j=1}^{m_2} \lambda_{1j} rir_{t-j} + \sum_{k=1}^{m_3} \lambda_{3k} rex_{t-k}$$

$$+ \sum_{l=1}^{m_4} \lambda_{4l} rhp_{t-l} + \sum_{p=1}^{m_5} \lambda_{5p} rsp_{t-p} + \sum_{q=1}^{m_6} \lambda_{6q} y_t^{OECD} + \eta_t \qquad (2)$$

π is four-quarter inflation in the consumer price index,[4] measured as the four-quarter change in the log CPI, y is the percent gap between industrial production and potential industrial production, where potential industrial production is calculated using a Hodrick–Prescott Filter with a smoothing parameter of 1,600. *dpo* is the quarter-to-quarter change in the world price of oil. This variable acts as a proxy for supply shocks and helped to eliminate heteroscedasticity. *rir* is the *ex-post* real short-term interest rate, measured as the short-term money market rate less quarterly inflation. *Rex*, *rhp* and *rsp* are respectively the percent gap between the real effective exchange rate,[5] real house prices, and real share prices and their long-run trend values, measured as described above. y^{OECD} is the OECD-output gap.

The Phillips and IS curves were estimated separately by OLS over the sample period 1973:1–1998:4. The lag order has been chosen by a general-to-specific modelling strategy, keeping all lags between the first and the last significant lag. Tables 3.2 and 3.3 report the sum of the coefficients of the exogenous variables with *t*-statistics in brackets and some diagnostics: the adjusted coefficient of determination ($\bar{R}^2$), a supremum F-test (Sup-F) for unknown breakpoint (Andrews, 1993), a test for first order autocorrelation (LM1) and a test for autocorrelation up to order five (LM5), White's test for heteroscedasticity (H) and a Jarque–Berra test for normality (N). *, **, and *** indicate significance of a coefficient or a test statistic at the 10%, 5% and 1% level respectively.

Table 3.2 reports the estimates of the G7 Phillips curves. The output gap is significant at the 1% level in all countries, with an estimated effect on inflation ranging between 0.057 (Germany) and 0.14 (UK). The oil price is also significant in all countries, with a particularly strong effect on inflation in Italy and the UK. The estimates of the lagged dependent variables are not reported due to space constraints. In all cases, the sum of the lagged inflation terms was not significantly different from 1. The fit and the diagnostics of the estimated equations are satisfactory, with no indication of severe misspecification. Only for Japan and the UK is there some weak evidence of non-normality in the residuals. However, despite the inclusion of the change in the world price of oil we still had to include dummy variables for a couple of large outliers in periods around the

---

[4] We used four-quarter-inflation instead of quarterly inflation because year on year inflation is certainly the much more relevant measure of inflation when it comes to policy decisions and quarterly inflation contains a substantial amount of noise that is filtered out when taking four-quarter differences.

[5] The exchange rate is measured as units of home currency per unit of foreign currency, so that an increase in the real exchange rate is a real depreciation.

Table 3.2. OLS estimates of the Phillips curves, sample 1973:1–1998:4

Country	Coefficient estimates (sum)		Diagnostics		
(lags)	gap	dpo	$\bar{R}^2$ Sup-F	LM1 LM5	H N
USA	0.066***	0.006***	0.98	0.01	37.56
(1–9,1–3,0–2)	(2.92)	(4.46)	2.48	1.77	1.92
Japan	0.085***	0.002*	0.98	1.18	33.33*
(1–9,1,2)	(3.41)	(1.77)	10.63	7.42	4.07
Germany	0.057***	0.002***	0.95	1.77	14.71
(1–5,1–4)	(3.05)	(2.79)	2.11	5.12	0.09
France	0.064***	0.006***	0.99	2.39	14.40
(1–5,1)	(3.46)	(6.09)	7.37	5.57	0.58
Italy	0.096***	0.014***	0.99	0.92	30.27
(1–7,1,0–3)	(3.60)	(6.55)	5.07	8.66	0.73
UK	0.14***	0.014***	0.97	1.23	33.97
(1–5,1,0–4)	(3.07)	(5.44)	4.45	8.21	7.33**
Canada	0.099***	0.002**	0.98	0.19	28.07
(1–6,1–3,0–1)	(4.68)	(1.97)	2.90	2.43	2.78

Note: The dependent variable is four-quarter inflation. gap is the output gap, dpo the quarterly change in the world price of oil. The table shows the sum of the coefficient estimates with t-statistics in brackets. $\bar{R}^2$ is the adjusted coefficient of determination, Sup-F is a test for unknown breakpoint based on Andrews (1993), LM1 and LM5 are tests for autocorrelation of order one and up to order five respectively, H is White's test for heteroscedasticity (White 1980) and N is a Jarque–Berra test for normality. *, **, and *** indicate significance of a coefficient or a test statistic at the 10%, 5% and 1% level respectively.

oil price shocks in order to eliminate heteroscedasticity and non-normality in some cases.[6]

Table 3.3 reports the estimates of the IS equations. Except for the real exchange rate in the US, all asset prices enter significantly the IS equations in all countries. Again, due to space constraints, we do not report the estimates for the lagged dependent variable. The output gap shows significant persistence in all countries, with the sum of lagged output gap coefficients being equal to 0.7 on average, but significantly smaller than 1. The OECD-output gap enters significantly only in Germany and Italy and was thus eliminated in the other countries. Again, the fit and the diagnostics do not give any indication of misspecification, with only weak evidence for non-normality for Canada and the US. As for the Phillips curves, well-behaved residuals could often only be obtained by including dummy variables for large outliers in the equation, most of which are related to the oil price shocks.[7]

[6] The included impulse dummies were 74Q1 for Japan, 74Q1 and 93Q1 for Germany, 80Q1 and 82Q3 for France, 76Q1 and 76Q2 for Italy, and 75Q2 and 75Q3 for the UK.

[7] The included impulse dummies were 75Q1 and 80Q2 for the US; 74Q3, 74Q4, 75Q1 and 93Q4 for Japan; 74Q4 and 75Q2 for France; 74Q4, 75Q1, 79Q1 and 81Q3 for Italy; 74Q4, 75Q2, 75Q3, 79Q2 and 82Q2 for the UK; and 75Q1, 80Q2, 83Q1 and 85Q1 for Canada.

Table 3.3. OLS estimates of the demand equations, sample 1973:1–1998:4

Country	Coefficient estimates					Diagnostics		
(lags)	rir	rex	rhp	rsp	oecd	$\bar{R}^2$ Sup-F	LM1 LM5	H N
USA	−0.111*	−0.009	0.061**	0.032***	—	0.92	0.77	33.40
(1–4,1–4,1,1,1)	(−1.94)	(−0.57)	(2.13)	(2.98)	—	4.38	4.15	5.50*
Japan	−0.109***	0.022**	0.115***	0.016*	—	0.93	2.19	19.22
(1–4,6,1,1–3,1)	(−2.94)	(2.04)	(3.12)	(1.98)	—	2.92	8.17	2.74
Germany	−0.316***	0.065***	0.092**	0.047***	0.309***	0.84	0.23	18.04
(1–5,1–2,1,1,1)	(−4.02)	(2.82)	(5.09)	(4.92)	(3.97)	2.25	4.69	0.56
France	−0.173***	0.063*	0.058***	0.029***	—	0.80	0.15	23.17
(1,1–3,1,1,1)	(−4.13)	(1.71)	(2.97)	(3.51)	—	5.76	2.78	0.75
Italy	−0.116***	0.042*	0.036**	0.03***	0.560***	0.84	1.70	37.06
(1–4,3,1,1,1−6)	(−3.11)	(1.75)	(2.41)	(3.52)	(5.22)	4.52	5.56	2.34
UK	−0.066**	0.036***	0.020**	0.022**	—	0.88	0.68	16.35
(1–4,1,1,1,1)	(−2.39)	(2.99)	(2.13)	(2.46)	—	1.29	9.28	4.15
Canada	−0.078**	0.041**	0.034***	0.033***	—	0.94	0.04	23.75
(1–4,1,1,1–2,1)	(−2.15)	(2.17)	(2.77)	(3.22)	—	2.62	6.01	5.27*

Note: The dependent variable is the output gap. *rir* is the ex-post short-term real rate of interest, *rex* is the effective real exchange rate gap, *rhp* is the real house price gap, *rsp* is the real share price gap and *oecd* is the OECD-output gap. The table shows the sum of the coefficient estimates with *t*-statistics in brackets. R^2 is the adjusted coefficient of determination, Sup-F is a test for unknown breakpoint based on Andrews (1993), LM1 and LM5 are tests for autocorrelation of order one and up to order five respectively, H is White's test for heteroscedasticity (White 1980) and N is a Jarque–Berra test for normality. *, **, and *** indicate significance of a coefficient or a test statistic at the 10%, 5% and 1% level respectively.

3.3.2 VAR estimates

The reduced-form model estimated in the previous section is based on a particular view of the transmission mechanism. Asset prices affect the output gap, which in turn affects inflation. However, asset prices may also affect inflation via other channels. Direct effects on inflation may be particularly relevant for the exchange rate and house prices via their effect on the price of imported goods and on the cost of housing respectively. The estimated reduced-form equations are in fact nothing but the output gap and the inflation equation from a VAR with exclusion restrictions. In this section we explore an alternative way to estimate FCI weights on the basis of impulse responses of inflation to asset price shocks in an identified VAR. For this purpose we estimate a VAR including the same set of variables that appeared in the Phillips and IS curves: four-quarter inflation, the output gap, the short-term real interest rate, the real exchange rate gap, the real house price gap and the real share price gap. The shocks were identified using a standard Cholesky factorization, with the ordering output gap, CPI inflation, real house prices, real exchange rate, real interest rate and real share prices for the Continental European countries. For all the other countries we reversed the ordering of the real exchange rate and the real interest rate. The ordering of the first two variables is fairly standard in the monetary transmission literature: the output gap can affect inflation contemporaneously and neither variable reacts immediately to shocks of any of the other variables. House prices are ranked third since house prices are also rather sticky. Share prices are ranked last, since share prices are flexible and can thus be assumed to react immediately to all other variables. The difficult point is the ordering of the interest rate and the exchange rate, since there is a potential problem of simultaneity between the two variables.[8] We ordered the exchange rate before the interest rate for the continental European countries, because these countries were usually engaged in some fixed exchange rate arrangement, so that it seems more appropriate to assume that the exchange rate enters the monetary policy reaction function contemporaneously but reacts with a lag to interest rate shocks. Since this argument does not hold for all the other countries, the exchange rate was ordered after the interest rate there, assuming that interest rates do not respond contemporaneously to exchange rates in those countries. Changing the ordering of interest rates and exchange rates, however, did not significantly affect the impulse responses.

The lag order of the VAR was selected by adopting a general-to-specific strategy, allowing for a maximum lag order of 5. A lag order of 3 was chosen for Canada, Germany, Japan and the UK, for the US 2, for Italy 4 and for France 5. The current and the one-period lagged change in the world price of oil were included as exogenous variables in the VAR. We also included the set of dummy variables from the reduced-form equations and the lagged OECD-output gap in the VARs for Germany and Italy, given its high significance in the reduced-form output-gap equations in these countries.[9] Figure 3.2 shows the impulse responses of the output gap and the inflation rate to a one-standard-deviation shock to each asset price in a two-standard-error band. *gap* is the output gap, *dcpi* is CPI inflation, *rhp* is real house prices, *rex* is the real exchange rate and *rir* the real short-term interest rate, and *rsp* is real share prices.

The impulse responses reveal that the effect of interest rate shocks on the output gap and CPI inflation is always significant. The responses seem to confirm the theoretical prior that monetary policy shocks first affect the output gap, where the maximum impact is reached after five quarters on average, and then inflation, where the maximum impact is reached after 12 quarters on average. Thus, our results are strongly in line with prior theoretical beliefs about the transmission of monetary policy. The results for the other asset prices are mixed. The impulse responses for the exchange rate are always correctly signed, but we obtain significant output-gap responses only for Japan, France and the UK and

[8] The problem of potential simultaneity between exchange rates and interest rates has not yet been resolved convincingly in the empirical VAR literature, nor is it clear whether the problem is empirically relevant: see Bagliano *et al.* (1999).

[9] Including the impulse dummies from the reduced-form equations proved to be necessary to obtain significant impulse responses for the output gap and the inflation rate. In the Italian VAR the inclusion of the OECD-output gap significantly improved the impulse responses.

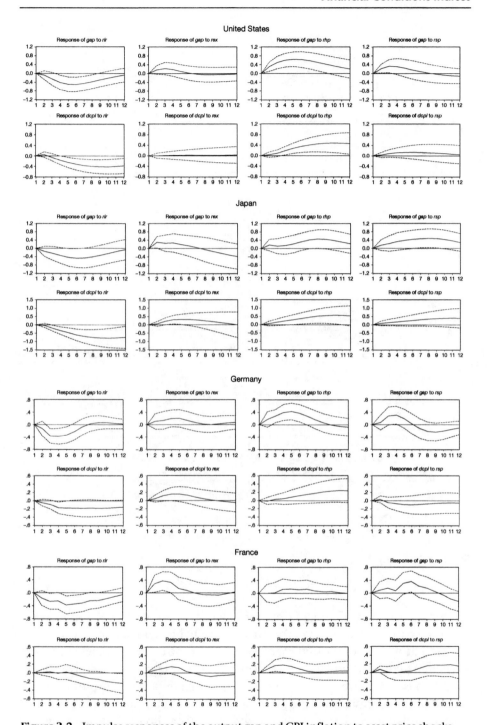

Figure 3.2. Impulse responses of the output gap and CPI inflation to asset price shocks

Note: The graphs show impulse responses to one-standard-deviation shocks in a two-standard-errors band. The deviation from the baseline scenario of no shocks is on the vertical axis; the periods after the shock are on the horizontal axis.

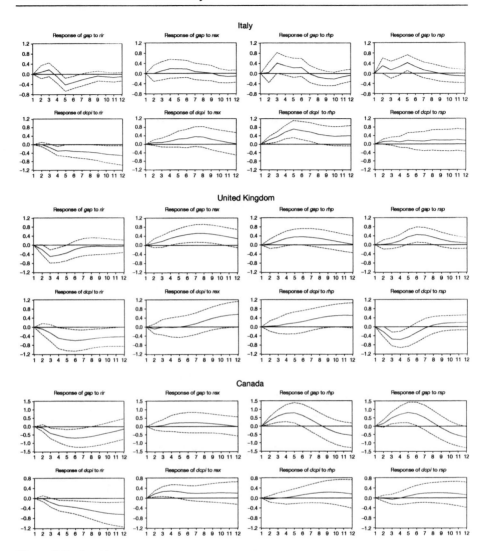

Figure 3.2. (*cont.*)

significant inflation responses only for Japan, Germany, the UK and Canada. With the exception of France, the effect of exchange rate shocks on inflation seems to be more pronounced than the effect on the output gap, which can be attributed to the additional direct effect on the CPI via import prices. For shocks to real house prices we also obtain correctly signed impulse responses throughout, which are also significant except for the output-gap response in France and the CPI inflation response in Germany and Canada. Except for Germany and Canada the effect of house prices on inflation seems to be more pronounced than the effect on the output gap.

Thus, house prices also seem to have a significant direct effect on prices in addition to the indirect effect via the output gap. That result does not come as a surprise, since house prices influence the price of housing, which directly enters the CPI. The results for real share prices are a bit puzzling. We obtain significant positive impulse responses for the output gap in all countries. However, the response of CPI inflation is significantly positive only in Italy. In Germany the response is negative but insignificant, and in the UK the response is even significantly negative. These results are hard to interpret. The only possible explanation we could think of is that there is in fact a forward-looking component driving share price shocks. If stock markets expect lower inflation in the future, they also expect lower future interest rates. This could outweigh the positive effect of higher share prices on consumer prices via the output gap.

Another interesting issue is the response of asset prices to interest rate shocks, which are displayed in Figure 3.3. The findings however, are, rather mixed.

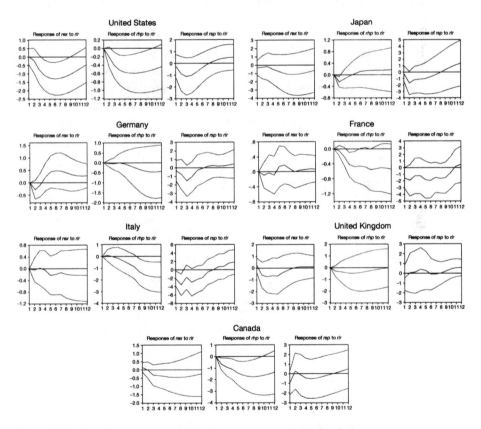

Figure 3.3. Impulse responses of asset prices to interest rate shocks

Note: The graphs display impulse responses to a one-standard-deviation shock to the ex-post short-term real interest rate in a two-standard-errors band. The deviation from the baseline scenario of no shocks is on the vertical axis; the periods after the shock are on the horizontal axis. *rex* is the effective real exchange rate, *rhp* the real house price index, *rsp* the real share price index.

We obtain no significant impulse responses for real exchange rates, and only three for share prices (Japan, France and Italy). Only for house prices are the results reasonably satisfactory, with five significant (negative) impulse responses.

3.3.3 Deriving FCI weights

Given the estimated coefficients in the IS equation and the VAR impulse responses we can now derive weights for the Financial Conditions Indices. For the FCI based on the reduced-form estimates we calculate the weight of asset price x by dividing the sum of the absolute value of the estimated coefficients of asset price x by the sum of the absolute value of the estimated coefficients of all four asset prices. The weights for the VAR-based FCI are calculated on the basis of the average impact of a one-unit shock to each asset price on inflation over the following 12 quarters. The resulting weights are displayed in Table 3.4.

In comparison with the weights obtained from the reduced-form estimates, we find that house prices get a higher weight and consequently all other asset prices a lower weight in the VAR-based FCI. The most straightforward explanation for the higher weight of house prices in VAR-based FCI would seem to be the additional direct effect on the CPI via the price of housing. We have seen that in most countries the effect of house price shocks on CPI inflation is more pronounced than the effect on the output gap. However, when looking at the impulse responses it becomes clear that most of the higher weight of house prices in the VAR-based FCI comes from the relatively stronger effect of house prices on the output gap in the VAR. Figure 3.4 displays the derived FCIs for each country. With the possible

Table 3.4. FCI weights

	Interest rate	Exchange rate	House prices	Share prices
Canada	0.42	0.22	0.18	0.18
	0.59	0.28	0.10	0.04
France	0.54	0.19	0.18	0.09
	0.41	0.04	0.51	0.04
Germany	0.61	0.12	0.18	0.09
	0.43	0.08	0.46	0.03
Italy	0.52	0.19	0.16	0.13
	0.54	0.13	0.29	0.03
Japan	0.42	0.08	0.44	0.06
	0.43	0.04	0.48	0.05
UK	0.46	0.25	0.14	0.15
	0.45	0.17	0.35	0.03
USA	0.54	0.00	0.30	0.16
	0.37	0.02	0.58	0.03
Average	0.50	0.15	0.23	0.12
	0.46	0.10	0.40	0.04

Note: The top figure in each cell is the weight derived from the reduced-form estimates; the lower figure is the weight derived from the VAR-impulse responses.

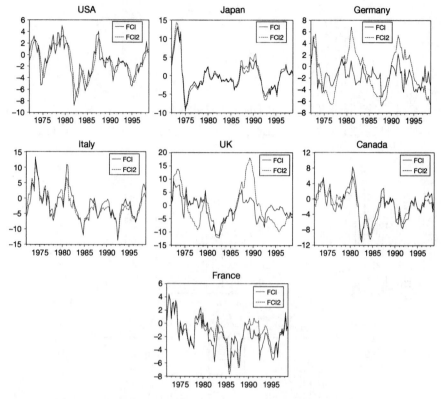

Figure 3.4. Financial Conditions Indices for the G7, 1972–1999

Note: FCI is the FCI derived from the reduced-form estimations; FCI2 is the FCI derived from the VAR-impulse responses.

exception of Germany and the UK, the reduced-form-based and the VAR-based FCI are very similar.

3.4 Financial conditions and future inflation

3.4.1 In-sample evidence

Having derived Financial Conditions Indices, we have to check whether they are of any use to predict future inflationary pressures. As a first, simple exercise we look at dynamic correlations of the FCIs with future inflation. The results are shown in Figures 3.5 and 3.6 and summarized in Table 3.5, which shows for each country the maximum of the dynamic correlations of the FCIs with future inflation, with the respective quarter in brackets. The correlation with future inflation is generally quite high, with a maximum G7-average correlation coefficient of 0.55 (0.59) with a lead of seven (three) quarters over inflation. The correlation of

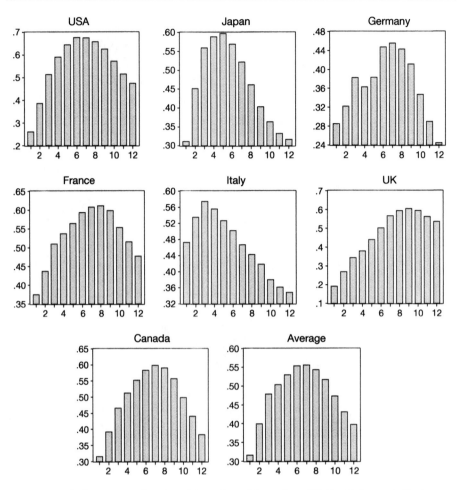

Figure 3.5. Dynamic correlations of the reduced-form-based FCI with future inflation

Note: The graphs display the correlation coefficient between the FCI and the respective lead of inflation.

the VAR-based FCI with future inflation is thus somewhat higher but peaks at an earlier quarter than the FCI based on the reduced-form estimates. Thus, the FCIs seem to be useful indicators for future inflation at horizons that are most relevant for policy-makers.

As an additional in-sample exercise we estimate a bivariate VAR with CPI inflation and each of the two FCIs, do Granger causality tests, and compute impulse responses of inflation to FCI shocks. When carrying out a Granger causality test we examine whether lagged values of the FCI help to predict current CPI inflation, controlling for the information already contained in lagged inflation terms. Table 3.6 reports the results. The null of no causality is rejected at the 1% level in all cases, so that we conclude that the lagged FCIs contain significant

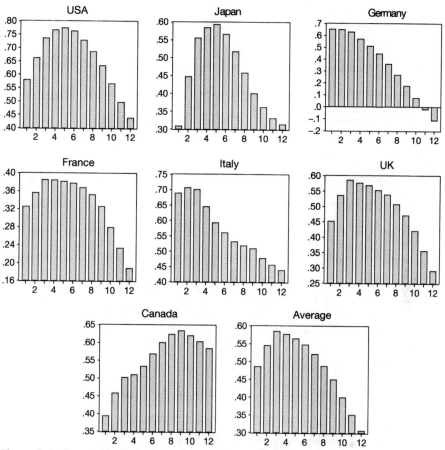

Figure 3.6. Dynamic correlations of the VAR-based FCI with future inflation

Note: The graphs display the correlation coefficient between the FCI and the respective lead of inflation.

Table 3.5. Maximum correlation of FCIs with future inflation

	USA	Japan	Germany	France	Italy	UK	Canada	Average
FCI	0.68 (5)	0.60 (5)	0.46 (7)	0.61 (7)	0.57 (3)	0.61 (9)	0.60 (7)	0.56 (7)
FCI2	0.77 (5)	0.59 (5)	0.65 (1)	0.39 (3)	0.71 (2)	0.59 (5)	0.63 (9)	0.59 (3)

Note: The table shows the maximum dynamic correlation of the FCI with inflation leads, with the respective lead displayed in brackets.

Table 3.6. Granger causality test for the FCIs

	USA	Japan	Germany	France	Italy	UK	Canada
FCI	5.71	9.88	6.77	6.49	4.91	6.58	4.19
FCI2	4.47	5.96	7.03	5.11	8.84	4.18	4.79

Note: Test statistics are based on a regression including five lagged inflation and FCI terms. The 1% critical value is 3.20.

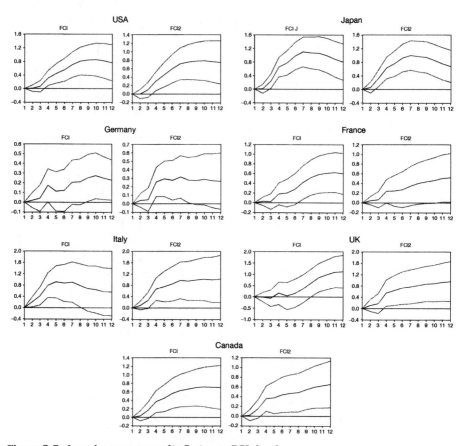

Figure 3.7. Impulse responses of inflation to FCI shocks

Note: The graphs display the response of CPI inflation to a one-standard-deviation FCI shock in a two-standard-errors confidence band.

information for future inflation over and above the information already contained in lags of inflation itself.

Figure 3.7 displays the impulse responses of CPI inflation to FCI shocks based on bivariate VARs with a uniform lag order of 5. The FCI shock was identified on the basis of a standard Cholesky factorization, ordering CPI inflation first. For both FCIs we find strong and highly significant shock impulse responses of inflation.

3.4.2 Out-of-sample evidence

Thus, the in-sample evidence implies that FCIs could be quite useful as indicators for future inflation. But how do they perform out of sample? It is a common finding in the literature on inflation indicators that good in-sample fit does not guarantee a good performance in out-of-sample forecasting (see e.g. Cecchetti 1995).

We calculate out-of-sample forecasts for the four-quarter inflation rate two years ahead and compare the forecasting performance of the FCIs with that of a purely autoregressive inflation forecast and a random-walk or no-change forecast.[10] Following Stock and Watson (1999, 2003) we choose the h-step-ahead projection approach to forecast inflation eight quarters ahead for the time period 1983:1–1998:4. We consider two approaches to model the autoregressive component of the forecasting equation, an autoregressive model and a random-walk model:

$$\Delta cpi_{t+8} = \alpha + \gamma \Delta cpi_t + \beta(L)FCI_t + \varepsilon_{t+8} \quad \text{Autoregressive model} \quad (3)$$

$$\Delta cpi_{t+8} = \Delta cpi_t + \beta(L)FCI_t + \varepsilon_{t+8} \quad \text{Random–walk model} \quad (4)$$

Δcpi is four-quarter inflation, FCI is the Financial Conditions Index and $\beta(L)$ is a lag polynomial. Out-of-sample forecasts for the period 1983:1–1998:4 were calculated by recursively re-estimating the model every period over the sample period starting in 1975:1. The order of the lag polynomial was also updated every period on the basis of the Schwarz–Bayes information criterion. On the basis of the 64 forecasts we calculated root-mean squared errors (RMSEs) to assess the forecasting performance of the FCIs, shown in Table 3.7. The forecasts obtained from adding an FCI to each of the two models are contrasted with the forecasts obtained from the purely autoregressive model and the no-change forecast. RMSE statistics that are lower than the RMSEs from the benchmark models are in bold.

The table reveals that the Financial Conditions Index based on the reduced-form estimates generally performs better out of sample than the FCI based on the VAR-impulse responses. Except for Italy, the reduced-form FCI always outperforms the autoregressive forecast, though in most cases only at very small

Table 3.7. Root-mean-squared errors for inflation forecasting two years ahead

	USA	Japan	Germany	France	Italy	UK	Canada
AR	3.63	2.092	2.137	3.451	5.092	6.131	3.882
AR + FCI	**2.683**	**2.022**	**2.135**	**3.101**	5.446	**4.64**	**3.328**
AR + FCI2	**2.853**	**1.959**	2.458	3.968	5.172	**5.93**	**3.298**
RW	2.176	1.681	2.022	2.222	2.891	3.232	2.659
RW + FCI	**2.113**	**1.639**	2.236	**2.184**	3.361	**3.206**	**2.453**
RW + FCI2	**2.038**	**1.62**	2.156	2.375	3.102	3.249	2.876

Note: AR is the autoregressive model for inflation forecasting, RW is the random-walk forecasting model. FCI is the Financial Conditions Index obtained from the reduced-form estimates, FCI2 is the Financial Conditions Index obtained from the VAR-impulse responses. The forecasting sample period is 1983:1–1998:4.

[10] This is of course not a real out-of-sample forecasting exercise, since the FCI weights and the gap measures for output and asset prices were obtained from in-sample analysis. For these reasons the out-of-sample forecasting results should be taken with caution.

margins. The VAR-based FCI outperforms the autoregressive forecast only in four cases. But all autoregressive forecasts are clearly dominated by the random-walk or no-change forecast. Thus, simply taking this year's inflation rate as the forecast of inflation two years ahead did better than estimating a forecasting model with lagged inflation rates and FCIs every period. However, if the FCIs are integrated in the random-walk framework, we find that the reduced-form FCI can improve the random-walk forecast in five countries, while the VAR-based FCI can do so only in two countries. Thus, the out-of-sample forecasting performance of the FCIs is rather disappointing, since we do not clearly outperform the simple no-change forecast. This finding confirms the conclusion of previous studies (Stock and Watson 1999, 2003; Cecchetti 1995) that inflation is very hard to forecast out of sample.

3.5 Conclusions

In this chapter we have extended the MCI concept to a concept of financial conditions by adding house and share prices to the analysis. We analysed the predictive power of asset prices for future output gaps and CPI inflation in the G7 countries for the post-Bretton Woods period on the basis of a simple, reduced-form model of the economy and an identified VAR. Prior to the estimation, asset prices were de-trended using standard de-trending techniques in order to obtain stationary regressors. The results from the reduced-form regressions reveal that all asset prices significantly affect the output gap except for the real exchange rate in the US. From the identified VAR we obtained significant impulse responses for the output gap and CPI inflation in all cases for the interest shock and in the majority of the cases for the house price shocks. For the exchange rate, impulse responses are always correctly signed, but significant only in about half of the cases. The responses to equity price shocks are rather puzzling, being always significant for the output gap, but generally insignificant or even wrongly signed for CPI inflation. This puzzling result might possibly be due to a forward-looking element in share price movements.

From the estimated coefficients of the reduced-form model and the impulse responses of inflation to the asset price shocks in the VAR we derived two Financial Conditions Indices for each country. The main difference between the two indices is the significantly higher weight for house prices in the VAR-based FCI. It appears that both FCIs are fairly useful for predicting future inflation in sample—a finding however, that is, not fully confirmed out of sample.

4

The Phillips curve, the IS curve, and Monetary Transmission

4.1 Introduction

In its simplest form, the New Keynesian model, which has recently been the most popular model for the analysis of monetary transmission and monetary policy, reduces the economy to a two-equation system: an aggregate supply or Phillips curve, which links the price inflation rate to expected future inflation, lagged inflation and the output gap; and an aggregate demand or IS curve, which links the output gap to the expected future output gap, the lagged output gap, and the short-term real interest rate.[1] From a monetary-policy perspective, the central parameters in this baseline New Keynesian model are (1) the strength and significance of the links in the monetary transmission process, i.e. (a) the link between the output gap and inflation in the Phillips curve and (b) the link between the short-term real interest rate and the output gap in the IS curve, and (2) the relative importance of forward-looking and backward-looking terms in the Phillips and IS curves. The empirical literature has produced quite diverse and often conflicting evidence on both issues. The evidence on the strength of the links in the monetary transmission process is inconclusive. While Rudebusch and Svensson (1999) find it to be strong and highly significant, Goodhart and Hofmann (2005a) find exactly the opposite. The same holds true for the evidence on the importance of forward-looking expectations. For example, while Galí and Gertler (1999) find that inflation is mainly driven by expected future inflation, Fuhrer (1997) finds lagged inflation to be much more important than expected future inflation.

In this chapter we assess both the significance of the links in the monetary transmission process and the role of forward-looking elements in a baseline New Keynesian representation of the economy for the US and the euro area. For this

---

[1] Basic references for the foundations of the New Keynesian model are Clarida *et al.* (1999); Goodfriend and King (1997); McCallum and Nelson (1999a, b); and Rotemberg and Woodford (1999).

purpose we estimate both standard and extended specifications of both the purely backward-looking and the hybrid version of the New Keynesian model. In the standard specification only those variables are included which are directly suggested by theory. In the extended specification other variables which may affect inflation and output are included, i.e. raw material prices in the case of the Phillips curve and property prices in the case of the IS curve. The inclusion of these variables in the estimating equations here is ad hoc, but could be rationalized by appropriate extensions of the basic theoretical model. Examples are Blanchard and Galí (2005) for the Phillips curve and Iacoviello (2004) for the IS curve.

4.2   The Phillips curve and the IS curve: overview

On the supply side, the New Keynesian framework is based on the assumption of intertemporally optimal price-setting by forward-looking, monopolistically competitive firms (Taylor 1980; Rotemberg 1982; Calvo 1983), which yields a purely forward-looking Phillips curve. For example, the commonly used Calvo price-setting model yields a Phillips curve where goods price inflation (π_t) is a positive function of next period's expected inflation ($E_t\pi_{t+1}$) and the output gap (y_t). The modelling of the demand side in the New Keynesian framework is based on the assumption of intertemporally optimizing households, which yields a purely forward-looking IS curve, where the output gap depends on the expected future output gap and the ex-ante short-term real interest rate (r). The New Keynesian baseline model of the economy is therefore given by the following two-equation system:

$$\pi_t = \beta E_t\pi_{t+1} + \lambda y_t + \varepsilon_t \tag{1}$$
$$y_t = E_t y_{t+1} - \delta r_t + \eta_t \tag{2}$$

The coefficient β is the time discount factor of price-setters, which is close to 1 in magnitude, so that there is no exploitable long-run Phillips curve trade-off. The theoretical output gap (y_t) is defined as the deviation of output from its flexible price level, which is unobservable. In empirical applications, conventional measures of the output gap, measured as the deviation of output from a filtered trend, are often used as a proxy, which may give rise to a measurement error of unknown severity in the estimation. To avoid this problem, empirical Phillips curves are also commonly specified using unit labour costs instead of an output gap measure (e.g. Galí and Gertler 1999).

4.2.1   Forward-looking vs backward-looking specifications

A critical issue in the empirical specification of the New Keynesian model is the modelling of expectations. The purely forward-looking specifications of the Phillips and IS curves, with inflation depending only on its own leads and the output gap, and the output gap depending only on its own leads and the real interest rate, have proved unable to match the lagged and persistent response of output and inflation to demand and supply shocks. Hybrid specifications of the New Keynesian model allowing for both forward-looking and backward-looking expectations, or even fully backward-looking specifications, are typically preferred by the data. Backward-looking expectations are inconsistent with the pure theoretical model in (1) and (2) and have to be introduced in an ad hoc way. A simple way to introduce backward-looking terms into the Phillips and IS curves is to assume that expectations are partly based on the experiences of the past, so that the expected future values of inflation and the output gap can be partly approximated by lag polynomials. For example, Galí and Gertler (1999) assume that a fraction of price-setters apply a rule-of-thumb price adjustment rule and simply adjust their prices to past prices and inflation. An alternative approach to introducing backward-looking terms into the IS curve is to assume habit persistence in consumption, so that household utility also depends on lagged consumption (Fuhrer 2000).

The introduction of backward-looking terms in the Phillips and IS curves yields hybrid relations of the form:

$$\pi_t = \gamma^f E_t \pi_{t+1} + \gamma^b \pi_{t-1} + \lambda y_t + \varepsilon_t \tag{3}$$

$$y_t = \alpha^f E_t y_{t+1} + \alpha^b y_{t-1} - \delta r_t + \eta_t \tag{4}$$

In the New Keynesian framework, monetary policy first affects output via the IS curve and then inflation via the Phillips curve. Monetary transmission depends on the strength of link between the policy instrument and output and inflation, i.e. on the size of λ and δ, as well as on the degree of forward-looking behaviour, i.e. on the size of γ^f and γ^b and α^f and α^b. The empirical evidence on the strength and significance of the links in the monetary transmission process as well as on the relative importance of forward-looking and backward-looking behaviour is mixed. While the estimation of larger-scale New Keynesian DSGE models[2] generally yields the finding that the transmission parameters are significant and that both forward-looking and backward-looking behaviour matters for inflation and output determination, the evidence from estimating the baseline system (3) and (4) or only one of the two structural equations is rather diverse. Lindé (2005) estimates the hybrid two-equation system (3) and (4) for the US complemented by a standard Taylor rule and obtains significant estimates for λ and δ. Rudebusch and Svensson (1999) and Peersman and Smets (1999) estimate backward-looking Phillips curves and IS curves for the US and the euro area respectively and also find a significantly positive output-gap elasticity in the Phillips curve and a significantly negative real interest-rate elasticity in the IS curve. On the other

---

[2] See Christiano *et al.* (2005) for the US and Smets and Wouters (2003) for the euro area.

hand, Goodhart and Hofmann (2000b), who estimate backward-looking Phillips and IS curves for a sample of 17 industrialized countries, are able to establish a significant positive link between the output gap and CPI inflation, but fail to find a significant negative effect of the real interest rate on the output gap in all but one case.

Galí and Gertler (1999) and Galí *et al.* (2001) find, on the basis of hybrid specifications of the Phillips curve, that both for the US and the euro area the conventional measures of the output gap appear to be negatively rather than positively correlated with inflation, and they prefer for this reason a Phillips curve specification with unit labour cost instead of a conventional output-gap measure. They also find that expected future inflation is a significant determinant of current inflation and is more important than lagged inflation. Mehra (2004) argues that both the absence of a significant output-gap coefficient in empirical hybrid Phillips curves and the dominant role of expected future inflation are due to the omission of supply shock proxies from the empirical model. He shows that the significance of the output gap in the US Phillips curve can be restored if the effect of supply shocks, such as import price shocks or price controls, are controlled for in the estimation of a hybrid Phillips curve. Furthermore, he also finds that the coefficient on lagged inflation becomes significantly larger than the coefficient on expected future inflation when supply shock proxies are included in the model.

While there is an enormous and rapidly expanding empirical literature on the New Keynesian Phillips curve, there are far fewer studies on the empirical performance of the IS curve. Nelson (2001, 2002) fails to find a significant effect of the real interest rate on the output gap in the US and the UK in backward-looking specification of the IS curve and refers to this finding as the IS puzzle. Goodhart and Hofmann (2005a) estimate backward-looking and hybrid IS curves for the G7 countries and also fail to find significant interest rate elasticities. They show, however, that given an ad hoc extended specification of the backward-looking IS curve, including the change in property prices, a significantly negative interest rate coefficient can be obtained.[3] Fuhrer and Rudebusch (2004) estimate a battery of hybrid IS curves for the US using various model specifications by conventional Generalized Method of Moments (GMM) and Maximum Likelihood (ML). They argue that the conventional GMM estimator exhibits small-sample bias which yields an upward bias in the estimated weight on future expected output, while the ML estimator is unbiased. Their empirical results in fact show that the ML estimator yields a significantly lower weight on future expected output and also appears to be

---

[3] Goodhart and Hofmann (2005a) also consider other additional variables besides the change in property prices, such as the real exchange rate, the change in share prices and money growth. The general pattern, however, is that only the short-term real interest rate and the change in real residential property prices enter significantly into the IS curve.

more successful in establishing a significant link between the real interest rate and the output gap.

4.2.2 An omitted-variable problem

Goodhart and Hofmann (2005a) argue that the insignificance of the interest rate in the IS curve might be due to the omission of other determinants or indicators of aggregate demand, such as asset prices, from the estimating equations. By the same token, the insignificance of the output gap in standard specifications of the Phillips curve may also be explained by the omission of other determinants of inflation, like the supply shock proxies suggested by Mehra (2004). For purely backward-looking models, this argument can be illustrated on the basis of a simple analytical framework used by Woodford (1994) to explain the insignificance of non-standard indicators for monetary policy in simple forecasting regressions. Suppose a very simple backward-looking model of the inflation rate or the output gap given by

$$y_t = \beta_1 z_{t-1} + \beta_2 x_{t-1} + v_t \qquad (5)$$

where y is respectively the inflation rate or the output gap, z is respectively the output gap or the short-term real interest rate, and x is respectively another determinant or indicator of inflation or the output gap, such as the change in commodity prices in the case of the inflation rate or house prices in the case of the output gap.

If we omitted variable x from the estimating equation (5), the OLS estimate of the interest rate elasticity β_1 would be given by

$$\hat{\beta}_1 = \beta_1 + \beta_2 cov(z_t, x_t)/var(z_t)$$

Thus, the omission of x from the regression would give rise to a bias in the estimate of the coefficient of interest, but the direction of the bias is unclear, depending on the sign of the covariance between z and x. The oil or commodity price shocks of the past were often associated with economic downswings and negative output gaps, suggesting that empirically, the correlation between the supply shock proxies and the output gap may well have been negative. Thus, omitting oil prices, commodity prices or import prices from the empirical Phillips curve may give rise to a downwards-biased estimate of the output-gap coefficient, which may explain Mehra's (2004) finding that the significance of the output gap can be restored when supply shocks are included in the empirical model.

The correlation between the monetary policy instrument and other potential determinants/indicators of aggregate demand, such as asset prices, is commonly assumed to be negative. Higher interest rates are assumed to give rise to falling asset prices and an appreciating exchange rate so that $cov(z_t, x_t) < 0$

and the OLS estimate of the interest rate coefficient would be biased upwards.[4] However, if monetary policy responds in an offsetting way to movements in x, i.e. $cov\,(z_t, x_t) > 0$, the OLS estimate of β_1 would be biased towards zero. The consequences of such an offsetting response of monetary policy to other determinants or indicators of aggregate demand were noted by Woodford (1994)[5] and may provide an explanation for Goodhart and Hofmann's (2005a) finding that on the basis of an extended specification of the IS curve, including the change in property prices, a significantly negative interest rate coefficient can be obtained.

4.3   Empirical analysis

The selective overview in the previous section suggests that the literature on the empirical performance of the New Keynesian model appears to be quite diverse and inconclusive both on the strength and significance of the monetary transmission process and on the role of forward-looking expectations. In this section we assess the empirical performance of the New Keynesian Phillips and IS curves by estimating various different specifications for the US and the euro area over the sample period 1982:1–2001:4. The choice of the sample period was due to data availability with regard to the property price data used in the estimation of the IS curve, but it also avoids changes in the monetary policy regime, which occurred in the early 1980s, to affect the estimation results.

---

[4] For example, Rudebusch and Svensson (1999: 4) argue that the standard backward-looking specification of the IS curve with the real interest rate as the sole determinant of the output gap 'is a simple representation of the monetary transmission mechanism, which, in the view of many central banks, likely involves nominal interest rates (e.g., mortgage rates), ex-ante real short and long rates, exchange rates, and possibly direct credit quantities as well'. This statement implies that they also think that other variables besides the real interest rate affect aggregate demand, but that the estimated interest rate coefficient also serves as proxy for the transmission of monetary policy via these other variables. In other words, the correlation between the interest rate and the other omitted variables is assumed to be negative.

[5] Woodford (1994) has argued that the usefulness of indicators for monetary policy cannot be judged from forecasting regressions, as their predictive power crucially depends on whether or not monetary policy is taking these indicators into account. Woodford's point is that if we were interested in the predictive power of x and were to assess it on the basis of a simple forecasting regression of y on x instead of estimating an extended forecasting regression like equation (5), the OLS estimator of β_2 would be given by $\hat{\beta}_2 = \beta_2 - \beta_1 cov(z_t, x_t)/var(x_t)$. This shows that if monetary policy takes the predictive power of x for y into account and thus responds in an offsetting way to movements in x, i.e. $cov(z_t, x_t) > 0$, the OLS estimate would be biased towards zero.

4.3.1 The backward-looking model

We begin by estimating baseline specifications of purely backward-looking Phillips and IS curves suggested by Rudebusch and Svensson (1999):

$$\pi_t = \sum_{i=1}^{m} \gamma_i \pi_{t-i} + \lambda y_{t-1} + \varepsilon_t \tag{6}$$

$$y_t = \sum_{j=1}^{n} \alpha_j y_{t-j} + \delta r_{t-1} + \eta_t \tag{7}$$

π is quarterly inflation in the consumer price index, measured as the quarter-to-quarter percent change in the CPI, y is the percent gap between real GDP and potential real GDP, and r is an ex-post measure of the short-term real interest rate. Following Rudebusch and Svensson (1999) we use a four-quarter moving average of the difference between the short-term nominal money market rate and the quarterly rate of change in the CPI. The data for the US were taken from the St Louis FRED database, except for the potential real GDP series, which originates from the CBO. For the euro area the data were taken from the area-wide model (AWM) database, which also provides a series for potential real GDP.

Equations (6) and (7) were estimated by Seemingly Unrelated Regressions (SUR). The lag order of the lagged endogenous variables was determined by retaining all lags up to the last significant lag, allowing for up to four lags. The estimation results are presented in Table 4.1, where we report coefficient estimates with standard errors in parentheses. The results reveal that on the basis of the standard backward-looking specification we cannot establish a significant transmission from the monetary policy instrument to inflation. Neither the interest rate coefficient in the IS curve nor the output-gap coefficient in the Phillips curve are significantly different from zero.

Thus, our findings are not consistent with those of Rudebusch and Svensson (1999) for the US and Peersman and Smets (1999) for the euro area. In the case of the US the inconsistency is most likely due to differences in sample period, as Rudebusch and Svensson estimate their model over a much longer sample period, starting with the early 1960s.[6] Peersman and Smets estimate their model over a slightly shorter sample than we do and base it on a Kalman filter approach, modelling the output gap as an unobservable variable, so that the inconsistency here may be due to both differences in sample period and econometric methodology.

As we discussed in the previous section, many studies, e.g. Roberts (1995) and Mehra (2004), also include measures of supply shocks, such as an oil price or import price variable, in the Phillips curve, while Goodhart and Hofmann

---

[6] Nelson (2001) also finds that the estimated interest rate elasticity in the US is much lower than the one obtained by Rudebusch and Svensson and insignificant when the IS curve is estimated over a shorter, more recent sample period.

Table 4.1. Estimates from the backward-looking model

	Standard specification									
	Phillips curve					IS curve				
	γ_1	γ_2	γ_3	λ	$\bar{R}^2$ Q(4)	α_1	α_2	α_3	δ	$\bar{R}^2$ Q(4)
USA	**0.235**	−0.03	**0.354**	0.065	0.15	**1.26**	−0.064	**−0.287**	−0.023	0.95
	(0.107)	(0.101)	(0.098)	(0.079)	0.83	(0.098)	(0.16)	(0.097)	(0.033)	0.41
Euro area	**0.194**	0.133	**0.495**	0.125	0.83	**0.883**	—	—	−0.06	0.80
	(0.097)	(0.099)	(0.098)	(0.089)	0.50	(0.049)	—	—	(0.031)	0.78

	Extended specification										
	Phillips curve						IS curve				
	γ_1	γ_2	γ_3	λ	μ	$\bar{R}^2$ Q(4)	α_1	α_2	α_3	δ	κ	$\bar{R}^2$ Q(4)
USA	**0.224**	0.008	**0.355**	0.104	**0.031**	0.22	**1.148**	−0.001	**−0.30**	**−0.069**	**0.082**	0.95
	(0.102)	(0.097)	(0.094)	(0.077)	(0.011)	0.87	(0.099)	(0.152)	(0.092)	(0.034)	(0.026)	0.55
Euro area	**0.266**	**0.203**	**0.381**	0.106	**0.011**	0.87	**0.692**	—	—	**−0.057**	**0.048**	0.76
	(0.087)	(0.089)	(0.088)	(0.079)	(0.002)	0.76	(0.069)	—	—	(0.028)	(0.013)	0.21

Note: The table reports the results obtained from estimating equations (6) and (7) as the standard specification and (8) and (9) as the extended specification by SUR. Standard errors are in parentheses. Coefficients significant at least at the 5% level are in bold. Q(4) is the p-value of a Ljung–Box test of serial correlation up to order 4.

(2005a) show that house prices enter significantly into an extended specification of backward-looking IS curves and help to restore a significant interest rate coefficient. We therefore proceed to estimate extended versions of the backward-looking model, including measures of supply shocks in the Phillips curve and the change in real residential property prices[7] in the IS curve. More specifically, we estimate an extended specification of the Phillips curve, including the quarter-to-quarter rate of change in primary commodity prices,[8] and an extended specification of the IS curve, including, as in Goodhart and Hofmann (2005a), the lagged four-quarter rate of change in real house prices. Commodity price indices for the US and the euro area were respectively taken from the Commodity Research Bureau (CRB) and the Area Wide Model (AWM) database. Residential property price data for the US were taken from the US Office of Federal Housing Enterprise Oversight (OFHEO). The series for the euro area originates from the ECB and is a weighted average of national residential property price series. The nominal house price series were converted to real terms by deflation with the consumer price index.

[7] As in Goodhart and Hofmann (2005a), we also considered other variables as additional regressors in the IS curve such as the change in real share prices or money growth. However, it turned out that no other variable was significant at conventional significance levels.

[8] We also experimented with the change in oil prices and import prices but found the specification with commodity prices to work best.

The extended specifications of the backward-looking Phillips and IS curves take the following forms:

$$\pi_t = \sum_{i=1}^{m} \gamma_i \pi_{t-i} + \lambda y_{t-1} + \mu \Delta cp_t + \varepsilon_t \tag{8}$$

$$y_t = \sum_{j=1}^{n} \alpha_j y_{t-j} + \delta r_{t-1} + \kappa \Delta hp_{t-1} + \eta_t \tag{9}$$

where Δcp is the change in the commodity price index and Δhp is the change in real house prices. Equations (8) and (9) were again estimated by SUR, retaining all lags of the lagged endogenous variables up to the last significant lag, allowing for up to four lags. The estimation results are also presented in Table 4.1, where again we report coefficient estimates with standard errors in parentheses. The results suggest that, on the basis of the extended specification, we can establish a significant link from the monetary policy instrument to the output gap in both the US and the euro area. For the output gap coefficients in the Phillips curve we now also obtain larger estimates and higher t-statistics, but the estimates remain insignificant. The additional variables which have been introduced to the model come out highly significant. In the Phillips curve, the change in commodity prices is significant at the 1% level and the change in real house prices in the IS curve is also in both cases significant at the 1% level. These results are consistent with the findings of Mehra (2004) on the importance of supply shock proxies in the US Phillips curve and of Goodhart and Hofmann (2005a) on the importance of house prices in G7 IS curves.

4.3.2 The hybrid model

The problems arising in the estimation of the standard backward-looking model may also be due to the omission of forward-looking expectations terms, which may give rise to omitted variable biases in the estimation. As the next step we therefore estimate a standard hybrid specification of the Phillips and IS curves. The standard hybrid model takes the following forms:

$$\pi_t = \gamma^f E_t \pi_{t+1} + \sum_{i=1}^{m} \gamma_i^b \pi_{t-i} + \lambda y_{t-1} + \varepsilon_t \tag{10}$$

$$y_t = \alpha^f E_t y_{t+1} + \sum_{j=1}^{n} \alpha_j^b y_{t-j} + \delta r_{t-1} + \eta_t \tag{11}$$

We estimate equations (10) and (11) for the US and the euro area by system GMM, using a standard set of instruments including four lags of inflation, the output gap and real unit labour costs[9] in the case of the Phillips curve and four lags of the

---

[9] Real unit labour costs are measured as the ratio of total compensation to employees to nominal GDP.

output gap, the real interest rate and real GDP growth in the case of the IS curve. An eight lag Newey–West estimate of the variance–covariance matrix was used to control for serial correlation in the error terms. The results are shown in Table 4.2, where we report the coefficient estimates with standard errors in parentheses and the result of a J-test of the overidentifying restrictions for the estimated systems. The estimates suggest that, on the basis of the standard hybrid specification, we are also not able to establish a significant transmission channel for monetary policy. In the US and the euro area, the transmission coefficients λ and δ are both clearly insignificant. The results also suggest that in both the Phillips and the IS curve the forward-looking terms are highly significant and obtain a higher weight than the backward-looking terms. The insignificance of the output-gap coefficient with the standard hybrid specification of the Phillips curve is consistent with the findings of Galí and Gertler (1999) and Mehra (2004). The finding of

Table 4.2. Estimates from the hybrid model (GMM)

	Standard specification with standard instrument set								
	Phillips curve					**IS curve**			**J-test**
	γ^f	γ_1^b	γ_2^b	γ_3^b	λ	α^f	α^b	δ	(*p*-value)
USA	**0.602**	**0.233**	**−0.281**	**0.279**	0.036	**0.588**	**0.441**	−0.011	0.78
	(0.113)	(0.047)	(0.061)	(0.058)	(0.029)	(0.019)	(0.018)	(0.007)	
Euro area	**0.945**	−0.077	**−0.379**	**0.508**	0.019	**0.517**	**0.486**	−0.006	0.93
	(0.163)	(0.108)	(0.109)	(0.076)	(0.035)	(0.024)	(0.018)	(0.004)	

	Standard specification with extended instrument set								
	Phillips curve					**IS curve**			**J-test**
	γ^f	γ_1^b	γ_2^b	γ_3^b	λ	α^f	α^b	δ	(*p*-value)
USA	**0.603**	**0.243**	**−0.301**	**0.294**	**0.05**	**0.583**	**0.445**	**−0.013**	0.78
	(0.073)	(0.031)	(0.033)	(0.035)	(0.018)	(0.011)	(0.011)	(0.006)	
Euro area	**0.521**	**0.067**	**−0.147**	**0.476**	**0.059**	**0.481**	**0.514**	**−0.009**	0.99
	(0.094)	(0.046)	(0.064)	(0.038)	(0.026)	(0.016)	(0.012)	(0.004)	

	Extended specification									
	Phillips curve						**IS curve**			**J-test**
	γ^f	γ_1^b	γ_2^b	γ_3^b	λ	μ	α^f	α^b	δ	κ	(*p*-value)
USA	**0.553**	**0.23**	**−0.243**	**0.299**	**0.10**	**0.038**	**0.572**	**0.447**	**−0.02**	**0.01**	0.93
	(0.078)	(0.025)	(0.042)	(0.046)	(0.02)	(0.009)	(0.01)	(0.011)	(0.007)	(0.004)	
Euro area	**0.402**	**0.137**	−0.017	**0.399**	**0.065**	**0.011**	**0.408**	**0.524**	**−0.016**	**0.011**	0.94
	(0.079)	(0.037)	(0.02)	(0.026)	(0.017)	(0.001)	(0.03)	(0.016)	(0.004)	(0.003)	

Note: The table reports the results obtained from estimating equations (10) and (11) as the standard specification, once with the standard instrument set and once with the extended instrument set, and (12) and (13) as the extended specification by system GMM. The standard instrument set includes four lags of CPI inflation, the output gap, and real unit labour costs for the Phillips curve, and four lags of the output gap, the real interest rate, and real GDP growth for the IS curve. The extended instrument set also includes four lags of the change in commodity prices for the Phillips curve and four lags of the change in real property prices for the IS curve. The extended instrument set is also the instrument set for the extended specification. Standard errors are in parentheses. Coefficients significant at least at the 5% level are in bold. J-test reports the *p*-value of a J-test of the overidentifying restrictions.

an insignificant interest rate coefficient in the standard specification of the IS curve is also consistent with the GMM-based evidence for hybrid IS curves reported in Goodhart and Hofmann (2005a).

For the backward-looking specification we found that a significant effect of monetary policy on output and inflation can be restored on the basis of an extended specification of the Phillips curve and the IS curve. If the backward-looking model is seen as a reduced form of the structural hybrid relationships, this finding does not necessarily imply a causal effect of these variables on inflation and output. It may simply reflect the fact that these variables are useful indicators of future inflation and output, which would suggest that they should be included as instruments but not necessarily as regressors in the hybrid models. For this reason we first re-estimated by system GMM the standard specification given by (10) and (11) with an extended instrument set, consisting of, in addition to the standard instruments stated below, four lags of the quarterly change commodity prices in the case of the Phillips curve and four lags of the four-quarter rate of change in real property prices in the case of the IS curve. The results are reported in Table 4.2 and suggest that, on the basis of the extended instrument set, we obtain a significant link from the output gap to the inflation rate and from the real interest rate to the output gap. Including the additional instruments therefore clearly improves the empirical performance of the standard specification. The estimates of the output-gap coefficient in the Phillips curve and the interest rate coefficient in the IS curve turn out to be very similar for the US and the euro area. However, while statistically significant, the estimated real interest rate coefficients remain rather small. In the case of the euro area, the inclusion of the change in the commodity price index in the instrument set also reduces substantially the weight on the expected inflation term in the Phillips curve.

In order to assess whether the additional variables found to be significant in the backward-looking model retain their significance in the hybrid model and how their inclusion affects the coefficient estimates of the other variables we estimate an extended specification of the hybrid model:

$$\pi_t = \gamma^f E_t \pi_{t+1} + \sum_{i=1}^{m} \gamma_i^b \pi_{t-i} + \lambda y_{t-1} + \mu \Delta c p_t + \varepsilon_t \tag{12}$$

$$y_t = \alpha^f E_t y_{t+1} + \sum_{j=1}^{n} \alpha_j^b y_{t-j} + \delta r_{t-1} + \kappa \Delta h p_{t-1} + \eta_t \tag{13}$$

(12) and (13) are again estimated by system GMM. The instrument set is the same as the extended instrument set for the standard specification described below. These results are also reported in Table 4.2. We find that both additional regressors come out highly significant. The links in the monetary transmission chain all remain statistically significant at the 1% level. Including the two additional regressors yields larger estimated transmission parameters, but the real interest

rate coefficients still remain very small. For the euro area, the extended specification also yields somewhat smaller estimated coefficients for the forward-looking terms.

So far the evidence suggests that the inclusion of commodity prices in the Phillips curve and of house prices in the IS curve improves the strength and significance of the estimated monetary transmission chain and, in the case of the hybrid model, reduces the weight on the forward-looking terms. These findings are consistent with the evidence reported in Goodhart and Hofmann (2005a) for the IS curve and Mehra (2004) for the Phillips curve. However, the validity of the use of GMM to estimate forward-looking or hybrid models has recently been questioned. Fuhrer and Rudebusch (2004) argue that the conventional GMM estimator exhibits small-sample bias while the Maximum Likelihood (ML) estimator is unbiased. This result suggests that it might be more appropriate to use an ML estimator to estimate hybrid models than a conventional GMM estimator. But there are also caveats associated with the use of an ML estimator, most importantly the need to specify an estimating equation for all variables included in the model. Misspecification in one equation may then affect all parameter estimates in the model. Furthermore, when a large number of parameters is estimated and/or the sample period is small, the optimization algorithm may be unstable or produce implausible estimates. Also for this reason, the recent empirical literature increasingly resorts to the use of Bayesian estimation, which essentially reweights the likelihood function of the model by a prior density of the model parameters.

In order to check the robustness of our GMM-based findings we therefore re-estimate the hybrid Phillips and IS curve using Bayesian techniques. For the estimation the model is complemented by a standard Taylor rule of the form

$$i_t = \rho i_{t-1} + (1-\rho)(\omega^\pi E_t \pi_{t+1} + \omega^y y_t) \tag{14}$$

which is jointly estimated with the Phillips and IS curve. For the estimation of the extended specification the model was further complemented by VAR equations for the change in commodity and real house prices. Tables 4.3 and 4.4 report the chosen (industry-standard) prior distributions of the model parameters and the estimated mean with a 90% confidence interval of the posterior distribution. The posterior distribution of the parameters was obtained on the basis of a Metropolis–Hastings sampling algorithm with 100,000 draws.[10] The results are generally consistent with but not as sharp as the GMM-based evidence reported before. In both specifications, all parameters are estimated to be significantly different from zero. Thus, while the additional regressors are also estimated to be statistically significant, their inclusion is no longer crucial to obtaining a

---

[10] The estimations were performed with Dynare 3.02 (available at <www.cepremap.cnrs.fr/dynare>).

Table 4.3. Estimates from the hybrid model, standard specification (Bayesian estimation)

		Prior distribution			Posterior distribution					
		Mean	Standard	Type	US			Euro area		
					Mean	5%	95%	Mean	5%	95%
Phillips curve	γ^f	0.5	0.15	beta	0.361	0.212	0.519	0.392	0.266	0.543
	γ_1^b	0.2	0.10	beta	0.235	0.107	0.374	0.226	0.097	0.341
	γ_2^b	0.1	0.05	beta	0.084	0.022	0.145	0.097	0.026	0.163
	γ_3^b	0.2	0.10	beta	0.268	0.150	0.390	0.263	0.160	0.372
	λ	0.1	0.05	norm	0.077	0.022	0.141	0.098	0.032	0.152
IS curve	α^f	0.5	0.15	beta	0.313	0.183	0.442	0.302	0.171	0.434
	α^b	0.5	0.15	beta	0.653	0.546	0.763	0.639	0.540	0.744
	δ	−0.1	0.05	norm	−0.028	−0.002	−0.054	−0.029	−0.001	−0.059
Taylor rule	ρ	0.9	0.05	beta	0.908	0.859	0.954	0.909	0.868	0.951
	ω^π	1.5	0.20	norm	1.608	1.285	1.903	1.465	1.181	1.725
	ω^y	0.5	0.20	norm	0.512	0.201	0.828	0.680	0.375	0.977

Note: The table reports the prior distributions of the model parameters and the estimated mean with a 90% confidence interval of the posterior distribution. The posterior distribution of the parameters was obtained on the basis of a Metropolis–Hastings sampling algorithm with 100,000 draws.

Table 4.4. Estimates from the hybrid model, extended specification (Bayesian estimation)

		Prior distribution			Posterior distribution					
		Mean	Standard	Type	US			Euro area		
					Mean	5%	95%	Mean	5%	95%
Phillips curve	γ^f	0.5	0.15	beta	0.374	0.216	0.521	0.428	0.292	0.568
	γ_1^b	0.2	0.1	beta	0.232	0.099	0.359	0.219	0.082	0.334
	γ_2^b	0.1	0.05	beta	0.086	0.020	0.142	0.109	0.027	0.192
	γ_3^b	0.2	0.1	beta	0.267	0.163	0.395	0.231	0.126	0.320
	λ	0.1	0.05	norm	0.079	0.021	0.140	0.066	0.021	0.116
	μ	0.01	0.005	norm	0.014	0.007	0.022	0.009	0.006	0.011
IS curve	α^f	0.5	0.15	beta	0.243	0.133	0.363	0.235	0.113	0.366
	α^b	0.5	0.15	beta	0.679	0.585	0.760	0.566	0.485	0.655
	δ	−0.1	0.05	norm	−0.055	−0.019	−0.090	−0.036	−0.005	−0.065
	κ	0.1	0.05	norm	0.052	0.018	0.091	0.031	0.014	0.047
Taylor rule	ρ	0.9	0.05	beta	0.903	0.853	0.948	0.901	0.864	0.940
	ω^π	1.5	0.2	norm	1.627	1.328	1.950	1.447	1.183	1.700
	ω^y	0.5	0.2	norm	0.507	0.187	0.800	0.697	0.433	1.001

Note: The table reports the prior distributions of the model parameters and the estimated mean with a 90% confidence interval of the posterior distribution. The posterior distribution of the parameters was obtained on the basis of a Metropolis–Hastings sampling algorithm with 100,000 draws.

significant monetary transmission chain. However, the estimated effect of the real interest rate on the output gap is again larger in the extended specification. In accordance with Fuhrer and Rudebusch (2004) we also find that ML-based estimation yields a lower weight on the forward-looking expectation terms than does the GMM-based estimation.

4.4 Conclusions

The baseline New Keynesian model, consisting of a Phillips curve to describe the supply side of the economy and an IS curve to describe the demand side, has become a popular tool for the assessment of monetary transmission and the analysis of monetary policy in general. From a monetary policy perspective, the central parameters in the baseline New Keynesian model are (1) the strength and significance of the links in the monetary transmission process, i.e. (a) the link between the output gap and inflation in the Phillips curve and (b) the link between the short-term real interest rate and the output gap in the IS curve, and (2) the relative importance of forward-looking and backward-looking expectations in the Phillips and IS curves. The empirical literature has produced quite diverse and often conflicting evidence on both issues.

In this chapter we assessed the empirical performance of the baseline New Keynesian model of the economy with a special focus on these two central issues. For this purpose we estimated both standard and extended specifications of both the purely backward-looking and the hybrid version of the New Keynesian model for the US and the euro area over the sample period 1982–2001 using quarterly data. In the standard specification only those variables are included which are directly suggested by standard theory. In the extended specification other variables which may affect inflation and output are included, i.e. raw material prices in the case of the Phillips curve and property prices in the case of the IS curve. The results suggest that on the basis of the standard specifications of the purely backward-looking as well as the hybrid model, it is often not possible to establish a significant link between the monetary policy instrument and output and inflation, while we are generally able to restore a significant monetary transmission chain with the extended specifications.

Both in the backward-looking and the hybrid formulation of the model, commodity prices are found to enter significantly the Phillips curve and property prices are found to enter significantly the IS curve. In the backward-looking model, and in the hybrid model when estimated by GMM, including these two additional variables in the model proves necessary to obtain a significant transmission chain of monetary policy. Furthermore, the inclusion of these additional variables is found to reduce the estimated weight on the forward-looking expectation terms in the hybrid model. When we estimate the hybrid model using Bayesian techniques, the results are generally consistent with but not as sharp as the GMM-based evidence, as a significant, though weaker, transmission chain of monetary policy can also be established on the standard specification of the model.

5

Goods and Asset Price Deflations

5.1 Introduction

5.1.1 *Deflation under a commodity base money*

Deflation ought not to be a serious monetary problem; yet it has apparently become so (Bernanke 2003). Deflation should be most likely to occur under a commodity money regime, e.g. the gold standard, when it will reflect the relative shortage of the monetary base commodity vis-à-vis all other commodities. Ceteris paribus, one might expect a roughly equal probability of comparative surpluses and deficits in the monetary base commodity, and during the gold standard century before 1914 there were roughly an equal number of years of price declines and increases. In the UK, for example, between 1815 and 1913 (using the Overall Index from the Rousseaux Price Indices, Mitchell 1962: 471–3), there were 41 years in which prices rose, 45 years of price declines and 13 years of no change; and from 1873 to 1913 there were 16 years of rising prices, 17 years of falling prices and 8 years of no significant change.

5.1.1.1 AUTOCORRELATION OF INFLATION UNDER A COMMODITY MONEY

But prices should not follow a random-walk path under a commodity money standard. A rise in the general price level is the equivalent of a decline in the relative value of the commodity money, so less of it will be produced. Hence, over the longer run, depending on the speed of reaction of the supply of the monetary base commodity to changes in its relative value, one would expect the price level to revert to the mean, unless there is some technological or institutional reason for a differing trend in the supply of the commodity monetary base, relative to all other goods and services.

Such mean-reversion, however, will probably be relatively sluggish, since the effect of changes in the relative price of the commodity base (e.g. gold) will be slow-acting, and also much affected by idiosyncratic supply-side shocks. It may take a century for such mean-reversion to become apparent. In fact, the Overall Index, annually from 1816 to 1913, is marginally stationary. The Dickey–Fuller test statistic was −3.128, compared with a 5% critical value of −2.892 and a 1% critical value of −3.513. In the mean time there may well be trends, perhaps gentles in price levels,

Table 5.1. Inflation autoregressions, 1873–1913

	USA	UK	Germany	France
AR (1) coefficient	0.25	0.21	0.15	−0.12
	(0.16)	(0.16)	(0.16)	(0.16)
Standard error of equation	2.75	2.69	3.88	1.33

Note: Standard errors of the AR(1) coefficients are in parentheses.

depending on underlying shifts in the demand or supply of the monetary base (relative to changes in the supply of all other goods and services). Such trends will be overlain with short-term seasonal, annual or cyclical fluctuations in the economy.

This is, indeed, what we observe. In the years 1873–1913, which is one of the periods on which we focus, and which was the heyday of the gold standard, Dickey–Fuller tests show that the CPI was mildly trended I(1) in the UK, France and Germany, but mean-reverting in the USA. The test statistics were respectively −1.93, −1.59, −0.162 and −3.87 against a 10% critical value of −2.61.

Against this background what is, perhaps, surprising about the gold standard era is how low the short-run first-order autocorrelation of inflation, e.g. from year to year, actually was. One might have expected longer-term changes in the supply of gold, relative to all other commodities, to have imparted some shorter-run persistence in price levels.

One possible reason for the low first-order autocorrelation of inflation in these years was that, at this stage of development, a large proportion of production and consumption was agricultural. The harvest is dependent on the weather; there is considerable fluctuation in the weather from year to year and place to place, and hence in the volume of non-monetary goods. In addition there were a variety of other idiosyncratic shocks, which had varying degrees of commonality between countries (see §5.3 below and Morgenstern 1959). For all such reasons there was no significant autocorrelation between inflation in the previous year and in the current year. Although the shocks to the inflation rate, as measured by the standard error of the error term in the autoregressions reported in Table 5.1, were large, a rational forecaster would have assumed, on this basis, that inflation in the year ahead would be zero.

5.1.1.2 EXPECTATIONS AND REAL INTEREST RATES UNDER A COMMODITY MONEY SYSTEM

One of the main concerns about deflation, at least currently, is that it may force real interest rates above their equilibrium level, given the lower bound to nominal interest rates (abstracting from Gesell-type policies; see Buiter and Panigirtzoglou 1999 and 2003).[1] This syndrome is worsened when deflation is

---

[1] See for example Coenen (2003) and Klaeffling and Lopez Perez (2003) and the many references on this subject cited by them.

autocorrelated, since expectations of past deflation then lead to expectations of future deflation.

There is a great problem with assessing expectations under the gold standard, and indeed probably until 1939. Over the very long run, perhaps a century, a commodity base money should deliver price stability, i.e. a mean-reverting I(0) series; over medium-run periods there will normally be some trending, an I(1) series, as shocks and readjustments occur; over short-run periodicities, quarterly and annual, there was much (largely random) fluctuation. In such circumstances, deflating nominal variables by ex-post inflation will give a poor estimate of ex-ante real interest rates, though this is still commonly done (e.g. Meltzer 2003); this is not to state that a measure of ex-post real interest rates may not be of some considerable relevance, e.g. to existing debtors and creditors; but it is worthwhile to distinguish between the concepts, and effects, of ex-ante and ex-post real interest rates, especially under a commodity base system.

To try to get some handle on ex-ante real interest rates under the gold standard, we turn to a brief study of short and long interest rates. According to the expectations theory of the term structure, the yield of an n-period bond is equal to the average of one-period bonds over the n-periods plus a term premium:

$$i_t^n = \frac{1}{n} \sum_{i=0}^{n-1} E_t i_{t+i}^1 + \theta_t$$

The Fisher equation decomposes the short-term interest rate into an ex-ante real interest rate and an inflation expectations term:

$$i_t^1 = r_t + E_t \pi_{t+1}$$

Combining the expectations hypothesis and the Fisher equation yields the n-period Fisher equation:

$$i_t^n = \frac{1}{n} \sum_{i=0}^{n-1} E_t r_{t+i} + \frac{1}{n} \sum_{i=0}^{n-1} E_t \pi_{t+i+1} + \theta_t$$

or

$$i_t^n = \frac{1}{n} i_t^1 + \frac{1}{n} \sum_{i=1}^{n-1} E_t r_{t+i} + \frac{1}{n} \sum_{i=1}^{n-1} E_t \pi_{t+i+1} + \theta_t$$

If we follow Fama (1975), and assume that the equilibrium real interest rate is constant in the long run and also that the risk premium is constant in the long run, then we should be able to back out movements in inflation expectations from the residuals of the regression:

$$i_t^n = \alpha + \beta i_t^1$$

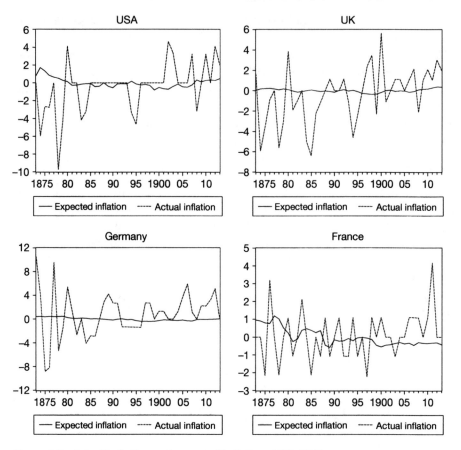

Figure 5.1. Actual inflation and expected inflation, 1873–1913

We ran this regression for the US, the UK, Germany and France. In Figure 5.1 we plot actual CPI and expected CPI inflation given by the residuals of these regressions. The graphs suggest that inflation expectations were in fact rather flat over the sample period, except perhaps for France. Given that really long-run price inflation was zero, we can then assume that during these decades ex-ante real interest rates were roughly the same as nominal interest rates. Since nominal interest rates never came close (for long) to the zero bound, we can be reasonably confident that real interest rates also remained clearly positive during these years.

5.1.2 A fiat monetary system

The main alternative to a commodity money system has been a fiat money system, in which the growth of the monetary base is the (usually indirect) outcome of a series of policy decisions on interest rates, the financing of the government deficit, etc. The tendency for such a fiat system to be inflationary is well documented (Bernholz 2003); this tendency arises largely from the fact that government expenditures are popular and taxation unpopular. So the government is usually a debtor, like other well-organized pressure groups, e.g. business and home-owners with mortgages, and easy money is beneficial to debtors.

5.1.2.1 AUTOCORRELATION OF INFLATION UNDER A FIAT SYSTEM

In such circumstances the persistence and severity of deflation will be accentuated by the greater autocorrelation of inflation under fiat money regimes. This increased persistence between the late 1960s and the 1990s is shown in Table 5.2.

Just as we might have expected more such autocorrelation under the gold standard, quite why such first-order autocorrelation was allowed to rise so high under a fiat money regime is, perhaps, something of a puzzle but we do not have time to pursue that now. It does not seem to us to be a necessary feature of a fiat money system. Indeed, since inflation targetry has been adopted in the UK, from 1993 onwards, such autocorrelation has once again become insignificant: see Figure 5.2 (taken from Benati 2003: fig. 3, p. 41).

So if deflation takes hold, under our current monetary regime, with our standard operating procedures, it will normally be expected to continue. That, of course, means that real interest rates will be above nominal interest rates.

5.1.3 Why do we have occasional deflation under a fiat money system?

It is remarkable that, under a fiat money system, there should be any worry about deflation at all. Under this system the authorities can, in principle, create an

Table 5.2. Time-varying inflation persistence, 1870–2002

	US	UK	Germany	France	Japan
1870–90	0.08 (0.23)	0.13 (0.23)	0.13 (0.23)	−0.16 (0.22)	0.11 (0.24)
1891–1913	0.23 (0.21)	−0.01 (0.22)	0.40 (0.20)	0.01 (0.22)	−0.11 (0.22)
1920–39	0.30 (0.19)	0.32 (0.22)	— —	0.25 (0.22)	—
1925–39	0.59 (0.22)	0.63 (0.21)	0.50 (0.20)	0.40 (0.25)	0.73 (0.26)
1950–1965	−0.21 (0.26)	0.22 (0.27)	−0.30 (0.17)	0.19 (0.27)	−0.34 (0.13)
1966–1979	0.70 (0.23)	0.71 (0.20)	0.77 (0.18)	0.80 (0.16)	0.50 (0.26)
1980–1989	0.75 (0.18)	0.69 (0.21)	0.80 (0.21)	0.94 (0.15)	0.62 (0.27)
1990–2002	0.70 (0.20)	0.68 (0.18)	0.47 (0.27)	0.73 (0.15)	0.84 (0.18)

Note: The table reports the AR1 coefficient with standard errors in parentheses (estimate of AR(1) model for the inflation rate: $\pi_t = \alpha + \beta\pi_{t-1}$). Estimation for 1920–39 was not possible for Germany and Japan because of the German hyperinflation in the early 1920s and unavailability of data for Japan, so the sample was reduced to 1925–39.

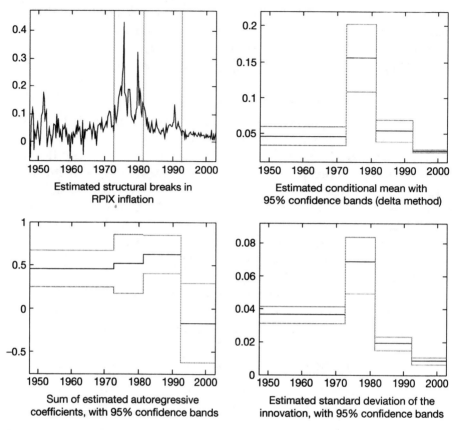

Figure 5.2. Time-varying inflation persistence in the UK, 1947:1–2002:3

Notes: RPIX inflation, estimated structural breaks in the mean, innovation standard deviation, and AR coefficients. Taken from Benati (2003), Figure 3, p. 41.

unlimited amount of (base) money by buying anything that they choose. So unwanted deflation should be inconceivable under such a system.[2]

Nevertheless such deflation has occurred. Much of the deflation outside the USA in the inter-war years was due to the attempt of countries to cling to the restored gold standard (Eichengreen 1992). While there is some debate about how far, and on what occasions, the availability of gold reserves limited the freedom of action of the US authorities (Friedman and Schwartz 1963; Meltzer 2003), the general consensus is that such constraint was slight, and could have been overcome, given sufficient willingness to do so. So the US experience from 1929 to 1933 counts as an example of unwanted deflation in a fiat monetary system.

---

[2] Countries which have chosen to fix their exchange rate to that of another country are in a monetary regime more akin to a commodity monetary system than to a fiat monetary system.

An even more obvious case is that of Japan since 1992. There have been no constraints on its actions from limited foreign exchange reserves, or from trying to prop up a devaluing currency—rather the reverse. Admittedly the extent of deflation in Japan has been mild, but how could it have happened?

5.1.3.1 A PARTIAL EXPLANATION?

There are, perhaps, at least four elements in the attempt to explain unwanted deflation in the USA and in Japan, which should never have happened. These are:

1. The deflation was *not* entirely unwanted, certainly initially.
2. The authorities imposed on themselves strict limits on the set of assets that the central bank was allowed to buy.
3. When nominal interest rates on the assets in this limited set had been driven to zero (ZIRP in Japan), this was regarded as representing the furthest possible extent of the conduct of monetary policy.
4. Prior to the deflation, monetary policy had been run in a manner that raised the autocorrelation between inflation in the past year and current inflation. So now, unlike before 1914, a rational forecaster, having experienced deflation, would forecast future deflation.

We will discuss each of these elements in turn, starting with the possibility that such deflation was not entirely unwanted.

5.1.3.2 (ASSET) PRICE DEFLATION WAS DESIRED

Both in the USA, after 1929, and in Japan, after the bubble around 1990, there was some feeling that the asset price bubble had been so excessive as to be somewhat immoral. Moreover, the Austrian theory of the trade cycle, and Schumpeter's 'creative destruction' implied that some 'cleansing of the Augean stable' would lead to needed structural reforms, and was indeed inevitable and essential to rid the economy of misallocated capital.

Governor Hayami and other Bank of Japan (BoJ) staff have repeatedly referred to a distinction between 'bad deflation' and 'good deflation' and argued that Japan's was a 'good' type. For instance, Hayami (2001) said that 'at a time when prices decline on account of productivity gains based on rapid technological innovation, a forceful reduction in interest rates with a view to raising prices may amplify economic swings'. Governor Hayami regularly raised concerns that low interest rates were creating a 'moral hazard' problem, as they would delay reforms by the corporate sector (see Kyodo News 2000). According to financial newswires, BoJ Governor Matsushita said that 'prolonged easy monetary policy contributed to the creation of Japan's "bubble economy" of inflated stock and land prices in the late 1980s. Traders said this was interpreted as implying that the bank would raise interest rates to avoid creating another bubble' (Reuters News Services 1996).

The Bank of Japan did not seem much concerned about deflation even as late as 1999, when it claimed that its policies had averted deflation, while at the same time worrying that these 'stimulatory' policies may have slowed 'structural change': Deputy Governor Yamaguchi said in 1999 that 'the decisive monetary easing and active interventions to support the financial system by the Bank of Japan no doubt averted deflation or financial panic in Japan. On the other hand, those policy decisions might have dampened the restructuring efforts at Japanese financial institutions' (Yamaguchi 1999).

The argument that the Bank of Japan consciously accepted deflation as a spur to structural reform has been most forcefully stated by Richard Werner. He writes (2003: 165, but see also 162, 163) that

The media have been frequently reporting that 'Hayami is convinced that Japan needs to undergo radical corporate restructuring and banking reforms before it can recover—and that he has a duty to promote this. . . . . Mr. Hayami's passion for reform also has a flavour of austerity. On paper, most economists—and politicians—think it would be sensible to offset the pain of restructuring with ultra-loose monetary policy. But Mr. Hayami fears that if he loosens policy too quickly, it would remove the pressure for reform' (Tett 2001). In other words, it must be concluded that the central bank is aware that serious monetary stimulation *would* create a recovery, but it has chosen for a decade to avoid this because it would delay its structural reform agenda. Also see Werner (1996, 2002). Adam Posen, an economist at the Institute for International Economics in Washington, D.C., agrees with this conclusion: 'Between a process of elimination, and careful reading of the statements of BoJ policy board members, I am led to the conclusion that a desire by the BoJ to promote structural change in the Japanese economy is a primary motivation for the Bank's passive-aggressive acceptance of deflation' (Posen 2000, p. 22).

Mutatis mutandis, there was originally much the same cast of mind at the Fed. Let us begin with a few quotes from Friedman and Schwartz (1963):

Nonetheless, there is no doubt that the desire to curb the stock market boom was a major if not dominating factor in Reserve actions during 1928 and 1929. Those actions clearly failed to stop the stock market boom. But they did exert steady deflationary pressure on the economy. (290)

They [i.e. most of the governors of the Federal Reserve Banks, members of the Board, and other administrative officials of the system] tended to regard bank failures as regrettable consequences of bad management and bad banking practices, or as inevitable reactions to prior speculative excesses, or as a consequence but hardly a cause of the financial and economic collapse in process. (358)

James McDougal of Chicago wrote that it seemed to him there was 'an abundance of funds in the market, and under these circumstances, as a matter of prudence . . . . it should be the policy of the Federal Reserve System to maintain a position of strength, in readiness to meet future demands, as and when they arise, rather than to put reserve funds into the market when not needed.' He went on to stress the danger that 'speculation might easily arise in some other direction' than in the stock market. (371)

Lynn P. Talley of Dallas wrote that his directors were not 'inclined to countenance much interference with economic trends through artificial methods to compose situations that in themselves grow out of events recognized at the time as being fallacious'—a reference to the stock market speculation of 1928–29. Talley's letter, like some others, reveals resentment at New York's failure to carry the day in 1929 and the feeling that existing difficulties were the proper punishment for the System's past misdeeds in not checking the bull market. 'If a physician,' wrote Talley, 'either neglects a patient, or even though he does all he can for the patient within the limits of his professional skill according to his best judgment, and the patient dies, it is concluded to be quite impossible to bring the patient back to life through the use of artificial respiration or injections of adrenalin.'

W.B. Geery of Minneapolis wrote that 'there is danger of stimulating financing which will lead to still more overproduction while attempting to make it easy to do financing which will increase consumption.' (372)

Similarly, Meltzer (2003) writes:

Carter, Glass and Miller blamed Strong's 1927 policy for the speculative boom and the 1929 collapse. Using a phrase that was repeated many times in the next few years, they described the collapse as an *inevitable* consequence of the preceding expansion. For them, the problem was the violation of real bills by financing speculation. (248)

They ['a substantial body of opinion within and outside the Federal Reserve System'] believed that crises and recessions were inevitable after speculative lending; they had to be endured to re-establish a sound basis for expansion. (290)

5.1.3.3   SELF-IMPOSED LIMITS ON ASSET PURCHASES

As the first quote from Meltzer (2003) indicates, the belief about the inevitability (in some cases the desirability) of the deflation following on after the excesses of the stock market bubble in 1928/9 was intimately intertwined with the real bills doctrine. This had two main elements. The first was a belief that the real economy was essentially self-equilibrating. The second was that the quantum of commercial (real) bills extant was closely correlated with the (sustainable) level of real output at current prices.

Consequently, purchases of assets (expansionary open-market operations) other than commercial bills would not lead to an expansion of real output, but only fuel inflation. Indeed, this was even the case with purchases of government bonds; so, extraordinary as it now seems, the occasions of such purchases were criticised by several Board members and Bank Presidents as inflationary even in the depths of the worst deflationary crisis in modern history.

This is one of the main themes of Meltzer (2003): he argues that this theory, which led to a self-imposed constraint on expansionary open-market purchases, was one of the main causes of the depth and persistence of the US deflation.

The real bills doctrine was most certainly erroneous, and has been abandoned. Nevertheless the view that a central bank should only purchase self-liquidating, riskless, short-dated assets has continued. It was only after deflationary pressures persisted, despite short-term interest rates being brought down close to zero, that the Bank of Japan began to buy sizeable quantities of somewhat longer-dated JGBs.

If the authorities limit themselves to buying very short-dated assets, especially when their interest yield is determined by the initial discount at which they are issued, then their yield can be brought down to zero without necessarily having a significant effect on private sector wealth or expenditures. Indeed, it is perhaps partly this absence of direct wealth effect that makes the asset appear suitable for central bank operations in the first place (see Goodhart 2003). Especially when such a short-dated asset is perceived as safe against default, there may be a quasi-liquidity trap, with investors indifferent between holding this safe asset and money.

Given, however, the existence of longer-dated assets offering a prospective yield—e.g. Consols with a coupon, houses with a rental or a convenience yield, equities with an expected dividend yield—it is impossible to have a general liquidity trap. As the authorities buy up the existing stock of such assets, their price will rise, without any necessary limit, toward infinity. If the authorities make the private sector infinitely wealthy, they are likely to start spending more at some stage!

Of course, as the prices of long-dated government debt, foreign exchange, houses or equities, or whatever else the authorities (dare to) buy rises, so Keynes' speculative motive will increasingly kick in. Private sector holders of such assets will sell, since they cannot believe that such high prices will be maintained. It is at least imaginable that the authorities could buy up the entire stock of private sector holdings of government bonds, or houses, or equities at some finite price. But the magnitudes are such that the monetization of the entire stock of longer-dated government bonds (JGBs), or Tokyo property, could be confidently expected to end deflation.

The two assets—beyond safe short-dated assets, e.g. T-bills—that most commentators have advocated that the Bank of Japan should purchase are foreign exchange (e.g. Svensson 2001; McCallum 2000; Meltzer 1999b, c) and Japanese government bonds (JGBs). This is remarkable, first, because in the case of foreign exchange (FX) purchases this will have potentially adverse effects on other countries' economies, and hence will have constraining political-economy repercussions, and second, because JGBs are exactly those assets most likely to fall in value should the policy of moving from deflation to (low) inflation succeed. Also, should the (Japanese) economy be kick-started by an initial large devaluation, there could be some subsequent appreciation (and hence loss on FX holdings). Indeed, in some proposals such appreciation is desirable in order to encourage interest rates in Japan to remain below foreign interest rates (under UIP). Of course, the counterpart to the capital loss on government bond holdings will be a capital gain to the treasury, so the central bank could be effectively indemnified by a variety of (accounting) procedures. But perhaps this is too unconventional for the authorities, who would rather deflate conventionally than reflate unconventionally.

One argument sometimes raised against any such 'unconventional' policies is that they would be so powerful that the merest attempt to introduce them would turn present deflation into uncontrollable (hyper-)inflation. Indeed, Japan probably does now stand at great risk of such serious inflation, but this is rather because the 'conventional' policies of fiscal expansion have led to such a large deficit and outstanding debt stock that it is hard to see this financed, once nominal interest rates have returned to 'normal' levels, without resort to 'unanticipated' inflation. The longer the authorities in Japan refrain from sufficiently expansionary monetary policy, the worse the ultimate danger of hyperinflation succeeding deflation.

5.1.4   Asset prices and deflation

One of the reasons for at least considering expansionary (open-market) purchases of other domestic assets, e.g. property via Real Estate Investment Trusts (REITs), is that the link between deflation and other such domestic asset prices has been strong, as we shall document later in this chapter. This is partly because of the inter-relationships between such asset price fluctuations and bank credit expansion.

In the past, severe, adverse and persistent deflations have been accompanied by major asset price reversals, fragile banking systems and depressed economic activity (US 1929–39, Japan 1991–2003). In these episodes, the scale of the fall in nominal asset prices greatly exceeded the falls in the CPI, so that there was also a severe contraction in real asset prices. As we have already discussed in the Introduction, housing and equity prices may affect household consumption and firm investment via their effect on households' and firms' wealth. Also, via their effect on borrowers' and banks' balance sheets, asset prices influence the risk-taking capacity of banks and thus their willingness to extend loans. This implies that a major reversal in asset prices may lead to a substantial reduction in the availability of credit. Such a decrease in credit availability depresses economic activity, which in turn feeds back into borrowers' and banks' net worth, so that a self-reinforcing process may evolve. A major asset price reversal which leads to a protracted weakness in economic activity is more likely to lead to deflation and depression when inflation persistence is high. With inflation persistence being reflected in inflation expectations, the incidence of a deflation may become more easily entrenched in expectations. With persistent expectations of a deflation, monetary policy will not be able to reduce real interest rates sufficiently to kick-start the economy again. Even when nominal interest rates are reduced to zero, expectations of a persistent deflation will keep ex-ante real interest rates positive. This will on the one hand have a direct negative effect on aggregate demand, and on the other hand will further weaken asset prices. As a result, demand will continue to be restrained and a depression may evolve.

5.2   Deflations: good and bad

The main thesis of this chapter is that deflation per se is not a serious problem. It is the combination of asset price deflation, together with general (goods and services) deflation, that is so deadly. In this section, we shall focus on three particular episodes of deflation to throw some light on this. The first is between 1873 and 1896 in the main Western developed countries: the USA, the UK, France and Germany. The second relates to the USA in the inter-war period. The third is in East Asia in the last decade, covering China, Japan, Singapore and Hong Kong. In the first and third cases we compare the deflationary period with an adjacent period, roughly equal in length, of rising prices, in the first case subsequently to the deflation (1897–1913) and in the latter case previous to it. We also use econometric techniques in all three instances to examine whether either goods and services deflation and/or asset price deflation had an adverse effect on real growth.

5.2.1 Prologue

Prices go down when supply exceeds demand. A rise in supply is intrinsically beneficial. A fall in demand, however, can be bad if there are, as is generally true, price/wage rigidities in the short run. Such a fall in demand may be particularly bad if it causes deflation, for two main reasons: the zero lower nominal bound to interest rates and the possibility of greater intransigence against wage/price nominal cuts (though this latter explanation is contentious: see for example Yates 1998; recent papers on this subject are Nickell and Quintini 2003; Christofides and Leung 2003; Kuroda and Yamamoto 2003). But there is no general reason to be necessarily concerned about wage/price deflation, especially since under the present fiat money system a central bank can always expand the money stock sufficiently to prevent deflation by buying additional assets whose yield has not already been driven to zero.

This expansion of the money stock is not possible under a commodity, or pegged exchange rate system, where monetary growth is restricted by the convertibility objective. In such cases a decline in the growth rate of the money stock can be forced onto the system. One might then, at first glance, expect deflations to have been more troublesome under such fixed rate systems. In fact, however, this has not been the case.

5.2.2 1873–1913

The longest-lasting trend deflation of prices known in history took place in the developed world between the early 1870s and the late 1890s. How far this was due to demand side factors (e.g. a slowing in the rate of gold production relative to a rise in the demand for monetary gold reserves), as compared with supply side factors (e.g. a rise in agricultural production in the New World combined with improved transport and communication technology, such as steamships and the telegraph), is both debatable and beyond the scope of this chapter.

What we do want to show is that this period of the 'great depression' was, in aggregate, quite beneficial. We do so by comparing this period with the subsequent pre-war period of the late 1890s till 1913. The 'great depression' is commonly dated from 1873 till 1896 (Morgenstern 1959). In order to assess whether there was a significant difference in the economic performance of countries between the 'great depression' (1873–1896) and the following pre-war period (1897–1913) we compare the average growth rates of GDP and average inflation rates, shown in Table 5.3.

The obvious feature of these data is that trend growth rates of real output were not greatly different; growth in the US and UK was slightly lower in the second period, whereas growth was a bit faster in France and Germany. In all four countries the difference in growth rates, however, is not significantly different from zero. In contrast there was deflation in all four countries in the first period, and inflation in the second. The difference between the average rate of price change in the two periods was over 2% for the US and UK and about 2% in Germany, but was less significant in France at 0.57%.

We next assess the effect of deflation on output growth in the US, UK, Germany and France on the basis of simple output growth regressions over the period 1873–1913—regressing output growth on lagged output growth, a proxy for the potentially adverse effect of deflation—and once-lagged interest rates, equity and housing prices. These latter were entered both in nominal and ex-post real terms in different runs of the equations. We report on the best runs using real ex-post asset prices below, but all runs are available from the authors. As it is not clear how best to assess the growth effects of deflation, we tried three different specifications to test for these. In the first specification we include a dummy taking on the value 1 from 1897 onwards (*d1897*). This specification essentially tests whether there was a significant change in the average output growth rate between the deflationary period 1873–96 and the inflationary period 1897–1913. If growth was significantly higher in the latter period the dummy coefficient would be significantly positive. In the second specification we include a dummy variable which takes on the value 1 in years when there was a deflation in the previous

Table 5.3. Average CPI inflation and GDP growth, 1873–1913

	CPI inflation			GDP growth		
	Average 1873–96	Average 1897–1913	Difference	Average 1873–96	Average 1897–1913	Difference
USA	−1.52	1.03	2.55	4.52	4.49	−0.03
	(0.57)	(0.50)	(0.76)	(1.07)	(1.35)	(1.72)
UK	−1.53	1.21	2.74	1.81	1.74	−0.05
	(0.53)	(0.48)	(0.72)	(0.74)	(0.84)	(1.12)
Germany	0.0	1.93	1.93	2.32	2.66	0.34
	(0.96)	(0.44)	(1.06)	(0.76)	(0.63)	(0.99)
France	−0.14	0.43	0.57	1.33	1.72	0.39
	(0.27)	(0.32)	(0.42)	(0.94)	(0.95)	(1.34)

Note: Standard errors are in parentheses.

year (def_{t-1}). If deflation had a negative effect on the next period's output growth this dummy variable would come out significantly negative. Finally, we add the lagged change in the CPI (Δcpi_{t-1}) and lagged CPI deflation (Δcpi_{t-1}^{def}) to the equation. Δcpi_{t-1}^{def} equals the change in the CPI in years of deflation and zero otherwise. If deflation had an adverse effect on growth the deflation variable would come out significantly positive.

We present estimates of the following three output growth regressions (NB long rates and housing prices never appeared significant and were therefore omitted):

$$\Delta gdp_t = a1\Delta gdp_{t-1} + a2rirs_{t-1} + a3\Delta rsp_{t-1} + a4d1897 \tag{1}$$
$$\Delta gdp_t = a1\Delta gdp_{t-1} + a2rirs_{t-1} + a4\Delta rsp_{t-1} + a4def_{t-1} \tag{2}$$
$$\Delta gdp_t = a1\Delta gdp_{t-1} + a2rirs_{t-1} + a3\Delta rsp_{t-1} + a4\Delta cpi_{t-1} + a5\Delta cpi_{t-1}^{def} \tag{3}$$

The regressions were estimated by SUR, both allowing all coefficients to vary across countries and by pooling the observations across countries allowing only the regression intercepts to vary across equations. The results are reported in Table 5.4. One common feature is that there appears to be some short-run negative autocorrelation in changes in GDP (not reported). Good years tend to be followed by bad, and vice versa. Why this is so is not clear to us. Of more importance is the negative result that in all three specifications we find no evidence of a negative effect of deflation on growth. In the second and third specification there is even some slight evidence that years of deflation were followed by higher growth in the UK and Germany respectively. The sole important determinant of output growth appears to be the short-term real interest rate, which is significant at the 5% level for Germany, France and the UK. The real interest rate elasticity is also significant at the 1% or 5% level, depending on the specification, in the

Table 5.4. Output growth and deflation, 1873–1913

	Specification 1			Specification 2			Specification 3			
	$rirs_{t-1}$	Δrsp_{t-1}	$d1897$	$rirs_{t-1}$	Δrsp_{t-1}	def_{t-1}	$rirs_{t-1}$	Δrsp_{t-1}	Δcpi_{t-1}	Δcpi_{t-1}^{def}
USA	0.184	−0.055	0.55	0.207	−0.046	−0.956	−0.236	−0.034	−0.869	0.514
	(0.72)	(−0.88)	(0.31)	(0.79)	(−0.71)	(−0.47)	(−0.70)	(−0.51)	(−1.42)	(0.78)
UK	**−0.475**	−0.063	−1.254	**−0.751**	−0.05	**2.419**	−1.00	−0.08	−0.349	−0.412
	(−2.7)	(−0.93)	(−1.25)	**(−3.27)**	(−0.77)	**(2.03)**	(−1.47)	(−1.12)	(−0.48)	(−0.88)
Germany	**−0.284**	0.017	0.062	**−0.511**	0.002	2.103	**−2.157**	−0.03	**−1.831**	0.018
	(−2.29)	(0.40)	(0.06)	**(−2.99)**	(0.04)	(1.50)	**(−2.74)**	(−0.66)	**(−2.39)**	(0.05)
France	**(−1.38)**	**0.223**	−1.176	**−1.246**	**0.195**	−0.40	−0.166	**0.214**	1.422	0.10
	(−3.59)	**(2.50)**	(−0.94)	**(−2.69)**	**(2.25)**	(−0.27)	(−0.24)	**(2.51)**	(1.60)	(0.09)
Pool	**−0.319**	0.001	−0.375	**−0.414**	−0.001	0.99	**−0.567**	−0.001	−0.269	−0.043
	(−3.40)	(0.01)	(−0.64)	**(−3.35)**	(−0.05)	(1.30)	**(−2.08)**	(−0.05)	(−0.91)	(−0.16)

Note: Equations estimated by SUR. Significant coefficients (10% level) are in bold.

pooled regressions. Except for France, where the change in real share prices is significant at the 5% level, we were not able to find clear, significant effects of equity price changes on real output in this data set.

5.2.3   The inter-war period

In the inter-war period many countries experienced deflations in 1920/1 and then again in the great depression of 1929–33. In view of the deflationary spirals evolving in the US and other countries during 1929 to 1932, Irving Fisher (1933) developed his famous theory of debt deflation, as already noted in §5.1.

In order to test whether the great depression in the USA was driven by goods price deflation or rather asset price deflation, we estimate regression specification 2 and 3 of the previous section, now also including the lagged change in real property prices on the right-hand side of the equation. The results are reported in Table 5.5 and suggest that even in the inter-war period goods price deflation did not appear to have had an adverse effect on output growth. In both specifications the measures of deflation are insignificant. Also the real ex-post interest rate was insignificant. Perhaps more surprising, the change in share prices does not appear to have affected output growth significantly. The main driving force of output growth in the USA in the inter-war period appears to have been the change in real property prices, with an elasticity significant at the 1% level.

5.2.4   East Asia, current experience

By comparison with the 'great depression' of 1873–96, or the collapse in prices in many countries in the inter-war years of 1920/1 and again in 1929–33, the recent deflations in East Asia have, in terms of the movements in CPI, been brief and mild. Japan is regarded as the archetype of current deflationary experience, but in practice, by the end of 2003, the CPI had only fallen by 3.3% from its peak in 1998:4. In contrast, asset price deflation has been much more pronounced. The Nikkei stock price index has fallen from its peak in 1989:4 by 64% and residential property prices have fallen since 1991:1 by 32%.

Table 5.5. Output growth regressions for the USA, 1919–1934

Specification 2				Specification 3				
$rirs_{t-1}$	Δrsp_{t-1}	Δrhp_{t-1}	def_{t-1}	$\Delta rirs_{t-1}$	Δrsp_{t-1}	Δrhp_{t-1}	Δcpi_{t-1}	Δcpi_{t-1}^{def}
−0.445	−0.05	**1.886**	−0.54	−0.753	−0.121	**2.149**	−0.486	0.92
(−1.09)	(−0.61)	**(3.19)**	(−0.11)	(−0.79)	(−0.855)	**(3.00)**	(−0.61)	(0.77)

Note: Equations were estimated by OLS. Significant variables (10% level) are in bold.

So much attention has been paid to Japan that there has been little realization that China, from 1998:1, experienced, prior to 2003, greater deflation than Japan, and a much steeper earlier fall in inflation; in 1994 China's rate of inflation was over 20%, compared with around 1% in Japan in that same year. From 1998:1 the cumulative fall in the Chinese CPI was 6%, almost double that of Japan. China, of course, has had no asset price deflation to accompany the recent period of CPI deflation. Housing prices rose slightly, by 3.6%, since the start of the deflationary period in 1998:1; such prices rose strongly in Shanghai and remained broadly stable in the other main cities sampled, which were Beijing, Guangzhou and Shenzhen. Equity prices were volatile, but rose by 27.5%.

The other Asian countries which are frequently described as subject to deflationary pressures are Hong Kong and Singapore. Hong Kong experienced the sharpest fall in consumer prices of all the Asian countries, with a fall from peak at 1998:4 of more than 16%. Still more pronounced has been the drop in property prices. From their peak in 1997:2 property prices came down by 66%. Over the same period, share prices were volatile and fell by 26%. Singapore, on the other hand, experienced only two brief episodes of deflation in 1998/9 and in 2002/3. However, like Hong Kong, Singapore experienced a rather pronounced asset price deflation. Residential property prices fell from 1996:2 by 38% and share prices fell from 1996:1 by 24%.

In accordance with our exercise for the pre-World War I period, we compared the GDP growth performance of the Asian countries in the deflationary years with the preceding period of similar length. GDP data were available up to 2003:2. For Hong Kong we used only GDP data up to 2003:1, as the second quarter of 2003 was strongly affected by the SARS blip. In order to see whether it is CPI or asset price deflation that matters, this was done both for the period of CPI deflation and for the period of asset price deflation. Exceptions are Singapore, where there is no clear peak in the CPI, so that we analysed only the period of asset price deflation, and China, where there was no asset price deflation, so that we analysed only the period of CPI deflation. The results are reported in Table 5.6.

Table 5.6. Average recent GDP growth in the Asian countries

	CPI deflation			Asset price deflation		
	Deflation period	Preceding period	Difference	Deflation period	Preceding period	Difference
Japan	1.41	1.25	−0.16	1.23	3.94	2.77
	(0.84)	(1.06)	(1.35)	(0.54)	(0.43)	(0.69)
Hong Kong	3.15	2.76	−0.39	2.17	4.97	2.8
	(1.40)	(0.48)	(1.99)	(1.38)	(0.74)	(1.56)
Singapore	—	—	—	3.81	8.85	5.04
	—	—	—	(1.54)	(0.91)	(1.79)
China	7.84	10.10	2.26	—	—	—
	(0.13)	(0.34)	(0.36)	—	—	—

Note: Standard errors are in parentheses.

What is patent from the data is that both the deflationary pressure, and the adverse economic implications for these economies, has come from asset price deflation, not from CPI deflation. For both Japan and Hong Kong the growth performance of the economy is not significantly worse in the period of CPI deflation compared to the preceding period of no deflation, while growth appears to have been significantly slower in the period of asset price deflation. In Singapore there is also clear evidence that growth has been slower in the period of asset price deflation, while China appears to be the only case where the period of CPI deflation has been associated with a significant slowdown in GDP growth.

As the next exercise we ran the same regressions as for the pre-World War I and the inter-war using data sets as long as we could find. The only addition is that, in a world characterized generally by fiat money and floating exchange rates, we have also included the real effective exchange rate as an additional variable (though note that China and Hong Kong both had pegged rates, while that of Japan and Singapore were heavily managed). The results of the regression are reported in Table 5.7.

The sample period covers 1982:1–2003:2 for Japan, 1985:1–2003:2 for Hong Kong, 1986:1–2003:3 for Singapore and 1999:2–2003:2 for mainland China. As it was not entirely clear when to date the start of the deflation regime for each country, we restricted the analysis to specifications 2 and 3. For China we estimated only one regression, including the lagged change in the CPI as there were only negative changes in the CPI over the available sample period. As we were using quarterly data instead of annual data we estimated specification 2 and 3 with a richer lag

Table 5.7. Output growth regressions for the Asian countries, 1980s–2003

	Specification 2					Specification 3					
	rirs	*Δrsp*	*Δrhp*	*rex*	*def*	*rirs*	*Δrsp*	*Δrhp*	*rex*	*Δcpi*	*Δcpi*[def]
Japan	−0.36	**0.021**	**0.295**	0.011	−0.513	−0.266	**0.021**	**0.278**	0.006	0.322	−0.059
(1,5,1,1,1)	(−1.72)	**(1.93)**	**(3.37)**	(0.67)	(−0.66)	(−1.13)	**(1.95)**	**(3.09)**	(0.32)	(1.17)	(−0.71)
(1,5,1,1,1,1)											
Hong Kong	0.122	**0.024**	**0.098**	**0.126**	1.625	−0.19	**0.021**	**0.089**	**0.147**	−0.425	−0.108
(1,4,1,1,1)	(0.52)	**(1.86)**	**(2.76)**	**(1.78)**	(0.58)	(−0.50)	**(1.55)**	**(2.47)**	**(2.00)**	(−1.01)	(−0.16)
(1,4,1,1,1,1)											
Singapore	0.30	**0.032**	**0.134**	**0.163**	−1.493	0.299	**0.032**	**0.137**	0.16	−0.351	1.23
(1,3,4,2,1)	(0.68)	**(2.09)**	**(3.21)**	**(1.67)**	(−0.48)	(0.53)	**(2.10)**	**(3.23)**	(1.59)	(−0.47)	(0.69)
(1,3,4,2,1,1)											
China	—	—	—	—	—	**−0.438**	−0.001	**0.107**	**0.235**	−0.088	—
(3,3,4,1,1)	—	—	—	—	—	**(−2.17)**	(−0.04)	**(3.09)**	**(2.43)**	(−0.47)	—

*Note:*This table reports estimation results for two output growth regression specifications. For China only one specification was estimated, as the sample period covered only periods of deflation. The sample period was 1982:1–2003:2 for Japan, 1985:1–2003:2 for Hong Kong, 1986:1–2003:3 for Singapore and 1999:2–2003:2 for China. *rirs* is the ex-post short-term real interest rate, *Δrsp* is the change in real equity prices, *Δrhp* is the change in real property prices, *rex* is the effective real exchange rate, *def* is a dummy which takes on the value 1 if there was consumer price deflation and 0 otherwise, *Δcpi* is the change in the *CPI* and *Δcpi*[def] is the change in the CPI if there was consumer price deflation and 0 otherwise. In the first column we report the chosen lag structure in parentheses; the numbers refer to the retained lags of each variable in each of the estimated specifications. The other columns report estimated coefficients with *t*-statistics in parentheses. Coefficients which are significant at least at the 10% level are in bold.

structure, allowing up to five lags of each variable to enter the regression equation. A preferred regression specification was derived by eliminating all insignificant lags, retaining at least one lag for each variable. As for the pre-World War I and the inter-war period, we find that measures of CPI deflation do not have a significant effect on output growth. The change in real property prices has a strong and highly significant effect on output growth in all four countries. The change in real share prices comes out significantly in Japan and Hong Kong, the real effective exchange rate in Hong Kong and China. The ex-post real interest rate is found to have a significant effect on output growth in Japan for specification 2 and in China.

5.3   Conclusions

The empirical results of this chapter are starkly simple. There is no innate disadvantage in goods and services price deflation as such; indeed this can often be consistent with continuing strong growth. It is rather when (demand) deflation is accompanied by, or exhibits itself in the guise of, property price deflation that trouble brews. The strength of this relationship (except in 1873–1913, when the data for the US and UK are somewhat dodgy) surprised even us. But property is not only the main component of wealth (in most cases far outdistancing equities, to which exaggerated attention has been devoted), but is also closely associated with bank credit (and hence monetary) expansion. Bank lending is collateralized on, and commonly for purchases of property, much more so than for equities, or other goods and services.

The practical conclusions are also clear. Japan will experience a sustainable recovery when property prices there stop falling, and not before.[3] In the US and UK, the dot.com equity collapse did not lead to a sharp drop in output because easy money led to a housing price boom. If, and when, housing prices subsequently tumble, there may be a much more searching examination of the efficacy of monetary policy.

Our claim that the course of property prices has been of greater importance for output growth than that of goods and services inflation does not, of itself, imply that central banks should target housing prices, instead of, or even as well as, general goods and services prices. But it does suggest that central banks, and others, should be aware of the nexus of relationships tying property prices, credit and monetary expansion, output, and general goods and services inflation together. Moreover, a central bank has not exhausted its armoury when interest rates on short-term (or even longer-term) government debt go to zero. Even when international political-economy (a.k.a. US Treasury) concerns prevent a central bank from buying foreign exchange (US T-bonds), it can always purchase domestic property (via REITs). Unconventional indeed, but then purchases of government debt were unconventional to the true believers in the real bills doctrine.

---

[3] This is a testable hypothesis. Time will tell.

Part II

House Prices and Financial Stability

6

House Prices and Bank Credit

6.1 Introduction

Over the last two decades most industrial countries have experienced episodes of boom and bust in credit markets. These credit cycles have often coincided with cycles in economic activity and property markets. The coincidence of these cycles has already been widely documented in the policy-oriented literature (e.g. IMF 2000; BIS 2001a), but there are only a few studies assessing the relationship between credit aggregates, economic activity and property prices in a formal way. In particular, the role of property prices has not been explored to a large extent. This chapter aims to fill this gap. We analyse the determinants of domestic bank credit to the private non-financial sector from an international perspective. For a sample of 16 industrialized countries we model bank credit[1] as a function of economic activity, interest rates and property prices using quarterly data since 1980.

In the empirical literature, credit aggregates are usually assumed to be mainly demand-determined (Bernanke and Blinder 1988; Fase 1995; Calza *et al.* 2001), depending positively on economic activity and negatively on financing costs.[2] Economic conditions, reflected by the state of economic activity, have a positive effect on consumption and investment demand. As a result, economic activity is expected to have a positive effect on credit demand (Kashyap *et al.* 1993).[3] On the

---

[1] We use bank credit as a short-cut for domestic bank credit to the private non-financial sector.

[2] There is some disagreement on how best to proxy financing costs. Most studies use a lending rate (Fase 1995) or money market and capital market rates (Calza *et al.* 2001). Friedman and Kuttner (1993) argue that the interest rate paid on loans should be adjusted for the cost of funds obtainable from alternative sources, such as securities markets or internal cash flow.

[3] There are also arguments for a *negative* effect of economic activity on credit demand. If an economic expansion is expected to be transitory, households and firms may instead increase saving in order to smooth consumption. Also, in times of an economic upswing

other hand, new theoretical insights about the implications of asymmetric information in credit markets have motivated the development of business cycle models, where credit plays an important role in shaping business cycles by
propagating and amplifying productivity and monetary policy shocks.[4] In the
standard real business cycle model and the standard Keynesian textbook IS-LM
model, credit market conditions do not have any effect on macroeconomic outcomes. This result hinges on the assumption of frictionless credit markets.
Following Brunner and Meltzer (1972), Bernanke and Blinder (1988) show that
relaxing the assumption of perfect substitutability of loans and other debt instruments, such as bonds, gives rise to a separate macroeconomic role of credit in an
otherwise standard textbook IS-LM model. Bernanke and Gertler (1989) and
Kiyotaki and Moore (1997) develop modified real business cycle models with
informational asymmetries in credit markets. Because of these information
asymmetries, firms and households are constrained in their borrowing and can
only borrow when they offer collateral, so that their borrowing capacity depends
upon their net worth. Since borrowers' net worth is procyclical,[5] the borrowing
capacity of households and firms increases in economic upswings and decreases
in downswings. An increase/decrease in credit availability stimulates/depresses
economic activity, which in turn feeds back into borrower's net worth, so that a
self-reinforcing process evolves. This implies that credit is procyclical and
amplifies business cycle fluctuations. The mutually reinforcing interaction
between credit and economic activity is referred to in the literature as the 'financial accelerator'.[6]

Financing costs, represented by market interest rates, are expected to have a
negative effect on credit demand. When interest rates go up, loans become more
expensive and loan demand is reduced. The stance of monetary policy, reflected
by the level of interest rates, may also affect the supply of credit by banks. Such
supply effects may arise from the effect of monetary policy on the creditworthi-
ness of firms and households via its effect on their financial positions, or from a
drain of reserves and thus loanable funds from the banking sector following

the cash-flow position of firms is likely to improve, so that firms may switch from external
to internal finance and thus reduce their borrowing (Bernanke and Gertler 1995). The
empirical evidence rather supports the view that economic activity has a positive effect on
credit demand (Bernanke and Blinder 1988; Fase 1995; Calza *et al.* 2001).

[4] Early works focusing on the macroeconomic role of credit are Fisher (1933),
Kindleberger (1973, 1978), Minsky (1964) and Brunner and Meltzer (1972). For a survey of
this early literature see Gertler (1988).

[5] Borrowers' net worth is procyclical because firms' cash-flow positions and household
income, and the value of collateralizable assets, are positive functions of real output.

[6] For a survey of the literature on the 'financial accelerator' mechanism see Bernanke
et al. (1999).

changes in the stance of monetary policy operated via open-market sales by the central bank.[7]

A potentially important but often disregarded determinant of bank lending is the value of real estate. Property prices may affect credit demand indirectly by stimulating economic activity via wealth effects. Wealth effects may also give rise to a direct effect of property prices on the credit demand of house-owners. According to the life-cycle model of household consumption, house-owners may react to an increase in property prices by increasing their spending and borrowing in order to smooth consumption over the life cycle. On the other hand, an increase in property prices also tends to trigger increases in rents. Renters may react by lowering consumption and borrowing. The overall wealth effect of property prices on consumption and credit demand is therefore theoretically ambiguous. The international empirical evidence on the relationship between property wealth and household consumption is mixed. Kennedy and Andersen (1994) analyse the effect of property prices on household saving in 15 industrialized countries. They find a significantly negative effect of house price movements on household saving in eight countries. In the other seven countries the estimated effect is positive. In a recent paper, Case *et al.* (2001) find a significant and large effect of changes in housing wealth on household consumption both for a panel of 14 industrialized countries and for a panel of US states.

According to Tobin's *q*-theory of investment (Tobin 1969), investment activity depends positively on the ratio of the market value of capital to the costs of acquiring it (Tobin's *q*). For the construction sector this implies that construction activity depends positively on the ratio of property prices to construction costs. This means that, ceteris paribus, an increase in property prices will increase construction activity, which may also lead to an increase in the demand for credit.

Property prices may also affect the willingness of banks to lend via balance sheet effects. Due to financial market imperfections, the borrowing of households and firms may be constrained. As a result, households and firms can only borrow when they offer collateral, so that their borrowing capacity is a function of their collateralizable net worth.[8] Since property is commonly used as collateral, property prices are an important determinant of the private sector's borrowing

---

[7] In the literature, the transmission of monetary policy via credit supply is referred to as the credit channel. The sub-channel working via balance sheets and financial positions is called the balance sheet channel; the sub-channel working via bank reserves and deposits is called the bank lending channel. Surveys of the theoretical and empirical credit channel literature can be found in Bernanke and Gertler (1995) and Kashyap and Stein (1997).

[8] Basic works of this literature are Bernanke and Gertler (1989) and Kiyotaki and Moore (1997). For a survey see Bernanke, Gertler and Gilchrist (1999). An early work is Fisher (1933).

capacity. Property prices also affect the value of bank capital, both directly to the extent that banks own assets, and indirectly by affecting the value of loans secured by property.[9] Property prices therefore influence the risk-taking capacity of banks and thus their willingness to extend loans.

Little formal empirical research has been conducted into the effect of property prices on credit. Goodhart (1995) investigates the determinants of credit growth in the US and the UK over a long sample period (US 1919–91, UK 1939–91). He finds that the change in house prices has a significantly positive effect on credit growth in the UK, but not in the US. Rolling regression estimates suggest that in the UK the relationship between credit and house price has strengthened over the post-war period. Hilbers, Lei and Zacho (2001) find that the change in residential property prices significantly enters multivariate probit-logit models of financial crisis in industrialized and developing countries. Gerlach and Peng (2005) analyse the dynamic interaction of bank lending and property prices in Hong Kong and find that property prices drive bank lending, rather than conversely. Davis and Zhu (2004) come to broadly the same conclusion for the relationship between credit and commercial property prices in a large sample of industrialized countries. Borio and Lowe (2004) show that a measure of the aggregate asset price gap, measured as the deviation of aggregate asset prices from their long-run trend, combined with a similarly defined credit-gap measure, is a useful indicator of financial distress in industrialized countries.[10]

In this chapter we show, on the basis of Johansen's (1988, 1991, 1995) approach to cointegration analysis, that the long-run movements of credit cannot be explained by the standard determinants of credit demand, i.e. real GDP and the real interest rate. But once real property prices, measured as a weighted average of real residential and real commercial property prices, are added to the empirical model, we are able to find long-run relationships linking real credit positively to real GDP and real property prices and negatively to the real interest rate. Credit is in most countries found to adjust significantly to the cointegrating relationship, implying that it represents a long-run relationship linking credit to GDP, property prices and interest rates. Property prices therefore appear to be an important determinant of the long-run borrowing capacity of the private sector, which needs to be taken into account in order to explain the long-run movements of bank lending. The estimated error-correction models are then used to analyse

[9] Chen (2001) develops an extension of the Kiyotaki and Moore (1997) model where an additional amplification of business cycles results from the effect of asset price movements on banks' balance sheets. An early source for this argument is Keynes (1931).

[10] Aggregate asset price indices are calculated as a weighted average of residential property prices, commercial property prices and equity prices. The weights are based on the share of each asset in national balance sheets, which are derived on the basis of national flow-of-funds data or UN standardized national accounts. The index weight of both residential and commercial property prices is on average above 80%, so that property price movements dominate the movements of the aggregate asset price index.

dynamic interactions by computing orthogonalized impulse responses. The impulse responses are generally in line with prior expectations. A rise in real GDP has a positive effect on lending, while a rise in the real rate of interest has a negative effect on bank lending, but the impulse responses are often insignificant. Innovations to property prices, on the other hand, have a strong, highly significant and persistent positive effect on bank lending in most countries. This result suggests that innovations to property prices, potentially reflecting changing beliefs about future economic conditions or speculative activity in property markets, may give rise to significant and persistent cycles in bank lending and are thus a potential explanation for the persistent cycles in bank lending observed in the past.

6.2   Data and some stylized facts

In the following sections we analyse the relationship between aggregate bank credit, aggregate economic activity, interest rates and aggregate property prices in 16 industrialized countries since 1980 using quarterly data.[11] All data are taken from the BIS database and, with the exception of nominal interest rates, are seasonally adjusted. Aggregate bank credit is defined as outstanding credit of domestic banking institutions to the domestic private non-financial sector, i.e. to domestic households and domestic non-financial enterprises. Not included, therefore, are loans to the government, loans to non-bank financial institutions, loans to foreigners, and loans extended by foreign banks. Standardized data for aggregate credit to the private sector are not available, so that the comparability of the credit aggregates is restricted by differences in the national definition of bank credit. Nominal credit aggregates were transformed into real terms by deflation with the consumer prices index. We use real GDP as the broadest aggregate measure of real activity. As a proxy for aggregate real financing costs we use an ex-post short-term real interest rate, measured as the three-month interbank money market rate[12] less annual CPI inflation.[13] With the exception of the real interest rate, all data were transformed into natural logs.

[11]   A sectoral breakdown of aggregate credit was not available for most countries, so that an analysis of the determinants of sectoral credit aggregates was not possible.

[12]   A more accurate measure of aggregate financing costs would of course be an aggregate lending rate. Representative lending rates, however, are not available for most countries. Empirical evidence suggests that short-term and long-term lending rates are in the long run tied to money market rates or policy rates (see Borio and Fritz 1995 for a large sample of industrialized countries, Hofmann (forthcoming) for euro area countries and Hofmann and Mizen 2004 for the UK), so that money market rates appear to be useful approximations of the financing costs of credit.

[13]   Using quarterly instead of annual inflation rates introduces substantial variability in the real interest rate, giving rise to heteroscedasticity in the residuals of the estimated

Following the approach of Borio *et al.* (1994), we construct aggregate property price indices as a weighted average of residential and commercial property prices. Data on private sector balance sheets from national wealth statistics were available on a quarterly basis for the US and Australia and on an annual basis for Japan, Germany, Canada and the UK. For Sweden and Norway annual data on the stocks of residential and commercial buildings could be obtained from UN Standardized National Accounts (SNA). The annual wealth data were interpolated to obtain a quarterly series of weights. For all other countries, neither national flow-of-funds data nor data from the UN SNA were available. Following Borio *et al.* (1994) we assume that the relative share of residential and commercial property in private sector balance sheets in France, Italy, Spain, Switzerland, Belgium and the Netherlands is the same as in Germany, that in Ireland the share is the same as in the UK, and that in Norway it is the same as in Sweden.

The balance sheet weights were then applied to residential and commercial property price series to obtain a series of aggregate property prices. A detailed description of the property price data can be found in Table 6.1. We use residential property price indices representing country-wide developments. The exception is Germany, for which we use an average of residential property prices in Berlin, Frankfurt, Hamburg and Munich. Country-wide measures for commercial property prices were only available for the US, Japan, Switzerland and Ireland. For the other countries we had to use commercial property price indices for single cities. Residential property prices were only available on an annual basis for Germany and on a semi-annual basis for Italy and Japan. Except for the US, Canada, Australia and Switzerland, commercial property price indices were only available in annual frequency (Japan semi-annually). In these cases quarterly indices were constructed by linear interpolation.

Nominal property prices were deflated with the consumer price index in order to obtain a measure of real property prices. Figure 6.1 shows the real residential and commercial property price indices and the real aggregate property price indices for the period 1980–98. Commercial property price data for Italy, Canada and Ireland were only available from 1983, 1985 and 1983 respectively, reducing the sample for the aggregate property price index accordingly. The figures show

---

systems in §6.3. Investment and saving decision are determined by the ex-ante real interest rate, which is given by the nominal interest rate less inflation expectations over a corresponding time horizon. Data on inflation expectations are not available for a sufficient number of countries over a sufficiently long period of time, so that we use an ex-post real interest rate as a proxy. For short-term real interest rates this is a valid approach, since inflation is highly persistent, and the inflation rate of the current quarter will be a useful approximation of inflation expectations for the coming quarter. For inflation expectations over longer horizons the current inflation rate may not be such a good proxy, so that ex-post long-term real interest rates can be misleading guides for ex-ante long-term real rates. For this reason we do not consider long-term real interest rates in the analysis.

Table 6.1. Property price data for industrialized countries

	Residential property prices	Commercial property prices
Australia	Established house price index Source: Central Bank	Sydney commercial property price index (CPPI) Source: Central Bank
Belgium	Index of house prices Source: Stadim, Antwerp	Brussels CPPI Source: Jones Lang LaSalle, London (JLL)
Canada	Average house price index Source: Central Bank	Ontario CPPI Source: Frank Russel Canada
Finland	National house price index Source: Central Bank	Helsinki CPPI Source: Central Bank
France	Residential house price index Source: Central Bank	Paris CPPI Source: JLL
Germany	Average sales price of owner-occupied dwellings in Frankfurt, Munich, Hamburg and Berlin Source: Ring Deutscher Makler	Frankfurt CPPI Source: JLL
Ireland	Average prices of new houses for which loans were approved by all lending agencies Source: Department of the Environment	National CPPI Source: Investment Property Databank, London
Italy	National house price index Source: Central Bank	Milan CPPI Source: JLL
Japan	Nationwide residential land price index Source: Japan Real Estate Institute	Nationwide commercial land price index Source: Japan Real Estate Institute
Netherlands	Price index for existing dwellings Source: Central Bank	Amsterdam CPPI Source: JLL
Norway	Sales price index for one-family houses Source: Central Bank	Oslo CPPI Source: JLL
Sweden	Single-family house price index Source: Central Bank	Stockholm CPPI Source: JLL
Switzerland	National residential property price index Source: Central Bank	National CPPI Source: Central Bank
Spain	National house price index Source: Central Bank	Madrid CPPI Source: JLL
United Kingdom	All-dwellings price index Source: Department of the Environment	London CPPI Source: JLL
United States	Single-family house price index Source: OFHEO and National Association of Realtors	National CPPI Source: NCREIF

that commercial property prices are substantially more volatile than residential property prices. This may indicate that there is more speculative activity in commercial property markets. But the validity of this conclusion is certainly limited by the fact that for most countries commercial property price indices represent price movements in only one or a few large cities and not the country as a whole.

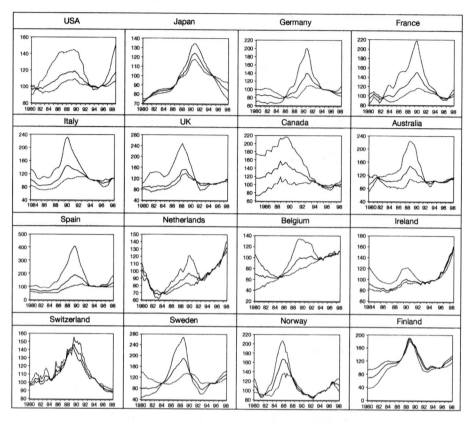

Figure 6.1. Property prices in industrialized countries, 1980–1998 (1995 = 100)

Note: The broken line is the residential property prices index; the dotted line is the commercial property price index. Both indices are measured in real terms, i.e. the nominal indices are deflated with the consumer price index. The solid line is the real aggregate property price index (1995 = 100), constructed as a weighted average of the residential and the commercial property price index. The weights are based on the respective share of residential and commercial property in private sector wealth. A detailed description of the data can be found in Table 6.1.

In Figure 6.2 we display the credit-to-GDP ratio (solid line) and the real aggregate property price index (dotted line) for the 16 countries under investigation over the period 1980–98. The graphs reveal that credit has been characterized by rapid growth, which is on average higher than the growth rate of real GDP, so that credit-to-GDP ratios were upward-trending in most countries. The common explanation for the observed upward trend in credit-to-GDP ratios across countries is the far-reaching process of liberalization and deregulation of credit markets in industrialized countries since the early 1980s.[14] By easing financial

[14] See BIS (1999) for a compilation of articles reviewing the development of financial sectors in industrialized countries since the 1980s. A thorough description of the characteristics of credit markets in developed countries is provided by Borio (1996).

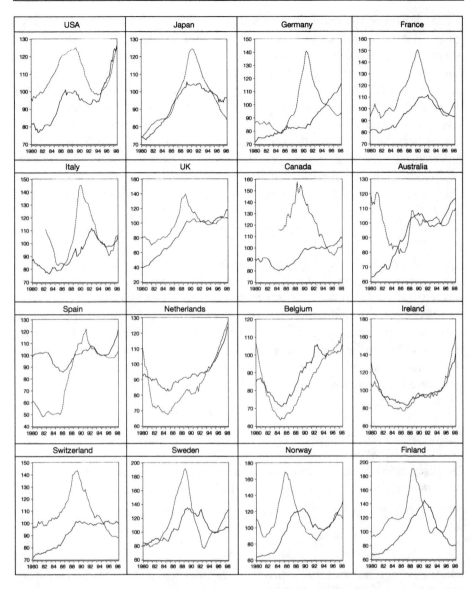

Figure 6.2. Credit-to-GDP ratios and property prices in industrialized countries, 1980–1998
Note: The solid line is the credit-to-GDP ratio; the dotted line is the aggregate property price index.

constraints and improving the efficiency of the banking system, financial liberalization is assumed to have increased the availability of bank credit to the private sector, which is reflected in upward-trending credit-to-GDP ratios over the 1980s and 1990s.

Another remarkable feature of the development of credit markets over this period is the occurrence of pronounced cycles in the credit-to-GDP ratio in a large number of industrialized countries in the late 1980s and early 1990s.

A comparison of the figures suggests that the severity of these cycles has been quite different across countries. These differences may partly be due to the already mentioned lack of standardized data for credit aggregates. Of particular importance in this respect is the treatment of non-performing loans (NPLs) in national credit aggregates.[15] For instance, in Japan and the Nordic countries, the boom-and-bust cycles in credit markets of the late 1980s and early 1990s caused severe financial distress. The graphs shown in Figure 6.2 suggest, however, that the credit cycles in the Nordic countries were much more violent than in Japan. The credit-to-GDP ratio in Japan declined from its peak in 1989 by merely 10%, compared to a fall from peak of between 45% and 20% in the Nordic countries. The reason for this misleading impression is mainly differences in the treatment of NPLs in the national credit aggregates. While NPLs were quite quickly cleansed from banks' balance sheets in the Nordic countries, this was not the case in Japan.[16]

Several studies (Borio *et al.* 1994; IMF 2000; BIS 2001a) have already documented the close correlation between developments in credit markets and property prices. Figure 6.2 reveals that that there is in fact a close positive correlation between bank credit and property prices in most countries. It appears that movements in property prices may at least partly explain both the upward trend as well as the cycles in the credit-to-GDP ratio in many countries. Whether this visual impression is also supported by formal empirical evidence will be considered in the following sections.

6.3 Long-run relationships

The discussion of the determinants of bank lending in §6.1 suggests that a standard specification of a model explaining the long-run movements of credit would involve a measure of economic activity and of financing costs:

$$C = \alpha + \beta_1 Y + \beta_2 R + \varepsilon \tag{1}$$

where C is (log) real credit to the private sector, Y is (log) real GDP as a broad measure of economic activity and R is the (short-term) real interest rate as a broad measure of real financing costs. Specifications of this kind are commonly used in the empirical literature (e.g. Fase 1995; Calza *et al.* 2001).

The arguments brought forward in the introductory section suggest that property prices may be an important additional determinant of credit. An alternative,

---

[15] For a detailed discussion of this issue see BIS (2001b).

[16] Drees and Pazarbasioglu (1998) provide a survey on the causes and consequences of the banking crises in the Nordic countries. The literature on the Japanese crisis is of course enormous. See Hoshi and Kashyap (1999) for a survey and the references therein.

or extended, specification of the long-run credit relationship may therefore be of the form:

$$C = \alpha + \beta_1 Y + \beta_2 R + \beta_3 P + \eta \tag{2}$$

where P is a measure of (log) real property prices. In standard time-series analysis the importance of property prices would be assessed by running a regression based once on equation (1) and once on equation (2) and testing for the significance of the property price coefficient. However, standard augmented Dickey–Fuller (Dickey and Fuller 1981) unit root tests, which we do not report,[17] suggest that real bank lending, real GDP, the real interest rate and real property prices are all integrated of order 1 over the sample period, so that standard regression analysis and inference is not applicable.[18]

Before estimating any long-run relationship for credit we therefore have to establish that such a long-run, or cointegrating, relationship exists at all. Technically, cointegration means that there exists a stationary linear combination between non-stationary variables, so that they cannot drift apart in the long run. In our case, the question is whether property prices are needed to pin down the long-run movements of credit, i.e. whether the long-run relationship for credit is given by (2), or whether the standard specification (1) is already sufficient to explain credit in the long run. We shall now analyse the relationship between real lending, real GDP, the real interest rate and real property prices using the multivariate approach to cointegration analysis proposed by Johansen (1988, 1991, 1995).[19] The Johansen approach is based on the following VAR model:

$$x_t = B_1 x_{t-1} + \cdots + B_k x_{t-k} + \mu + \varepsilon_t \tag{3}$$

where x is a vector of endogenous variables, μ is a vector of constants, and ε is a vector of error terms, which are assumed to be white noise. In order to assess whether property prices play a significant role in explaining the long-run movements of credit we estimate two econometric models, a standard system

---

[17] The results of the unit root tests can be found in the working-paper version of this chapter (Hofmann 2001).

[18] Granger and Newbold (1974) have shown that standard regression techniques may indicate significant correlations between non-stationary variables even though the variables are completely unrelated. This problem is known as the phenomenon of spurious regressions.

[19] In our application, the Johansen approach is preferable to alternative single-equation estimators because we do not have any a priori reason to assume that any set of variables is weakly exogenous. Estimating a long-run relationship based on single-equation estimation techniques yields inefficient coefficient estimates if the explanatory variables are not weakly exogenous.

consisting only of the log of real credit, the log of real GDP and the real interest rate, and an alternative, extended system also consisting of the log of real property prices. The sample period for the analysis is the first quarter of 1980 till the fourth quarter of 1998.[20] Due to data availability the sample is somewhat shorter for Canada, Italy, Ireland and Spain, starting respectively in 1986:2, 1984:1, 1983:3 and 1981:1.

The Johansen methodology is based on maximum likelihood estimation, so that Gaussian error terms are required. The lag order of the VARs was therefore chosen in order to obtain well-behaved VAR residuals. Centred impulse dummies[21] had to be added to the VARs for Germany (1989:2 and 1991:2, related to German reunification), Australia (1981:4 and 1982:3, related to a severe recession), Italy (1992:3, related to the EMS crisis) and Switzerland (1982:2, related to a severe recession) in order to eliminate a few large outliers, which gave rise to heteroscedasticity. Diagnostic tests for the estimated systems, which are reported in Tables 6.2 and 6.3, suggest that the residuals of the estimated systems are free of serial correlation and heteroscedasticity. In some cases there is evidence of non-normality of the residuals, but Lütkepohl (1993) shows that the Johansen approach does not strictly depend on the normality assumption, so that the violation of the normality assumption in some cases must not be seen as a caveat to our analysis. Recursive Chow breakpoint tests, which we do not report, generally suggested that the systems are also stable over sub-samples.[22]

The VAR model can be reformulated in vector error-correction form:

$$\Delta x_t = C_1 \Delta x_{t-1} + \cdots + C_{k-1} \Delta x_{t-k+1} + C_0 x_{t-1} + \mu + \varepsilon_t \qquad (4)$$

In the estimation, the constant is left unrestricted, allowing for deterministic time trends in the levels of the data. The Johansen methodology is based on a Maximum Likelihood estimation of (4). The cointegration test is based on the rank of the matrix C_0, which indicates the number of long-run relationships between the endogenous variables in the VAR. Intuitively, the Johansen cointegration approach is a multivariate generalization of the augmented Dickey–Fuller unit root test. If the rank of the matrix C_0 is zero, this basically means that the vector of the lagged levels of the variables, x_{t-1}, does not have a

---

[20] The reason for not including more recent observations is the start of EMU in January 1999, which affects half of the countries covered by the empirical analysis. The start of EMU means a new monetary policy regime for these countries, which may have given rise to a structural break in the estimated systems. Since there are still only a few observations for the new regime, the potential structural break will not be detected by breakpoint tests, but may adversely affect the estimation results.

[21] The use of centred as opposed to uncentred dummy variables ensures that the standard critical values for the cointegration test are still valid (Johansen 1995).

[22] The results of the recursive breakpoint tests can be found in Hofmann (2001).

significant effect on the dynamics of the system, so that we are basically left with a VAR in first differences. On the other hand, if the rank of C_0 is positive, this implies that the dynamics of the system are in the long run pinned down by some linear combination of the endogenous variables.

If the cointegration test suggests that there exists a long-run relationship, the matrix C_0 can be factorized as $C_0 = \alpha\beta'$, where α is a matrix of loading or adjustment coefficients and β is a vector of cointegrating vectors describing the long-run link between the endogenous variables. The loading matrix α describes the dynamic adjustment of the endogenous variables to deviations from long-run equilibrium given by $\beta'x$. The loading coefficients can help to assess the economic meaning of the estimated long-run relationship. In our case, if the estimated long-run relationship describes a long-run equilibrium bank credit relationship, we should find that the dynamics of credit are pinned down by this relationship in the long run, i.e. credit should be found to adjust significantly to its long-run equilibrium level.

Table 6.2 shows the test results for the standard system, omitting property prices. The standard Trace test evaluates the null hypothesis of at most r long-run relationships against the alternative of more than r long-run relationships.[23] The test results suggest that there exists a single long-run relationship between credit, GDP and the real interest rate in Germany, Canada, Spain, the Netherlands and Belgium, while no long-run relationship is indicated for any other country. In cases where we could reject the null of no cointegration we report the estimated long-run relationship with asymptotic standard errors in parentheses. The results suggest that real credit (C) is in the long run positively related to real GDP (Y) and negatively to the real interest rate (R). The long-run income elasticity of credit is in all four cases significantly larger than 1. This finding could reflect either a process of financial deepening as a result of financial liberalization since 1980, or the effect of omitted variables, such as property prices, which are captured by GDP. The semi-elasticity of credit demand with respect to the real interest rate is negative and also significant except for Belgium. The adjustment coefficient in the credit equation, which is shown in the last column of Table 6.2, is negative and significant at least at the 5% level except for Germany. This means that credit adjusts to the identified long-run relationship, lending support to the view that it represents a relationship explaining the long-run movements of credit. However, the overall conclusion from estimating the standard system consisting of real credit, real GDP and the real interest rate must be that the long-run movement of credit cannot be explained by the standard system in the large majority of countries in our sample.

Table 6.3 reports the results of the cointegration analysis for the extended system, also comprising the log of real property prices in addition to the log of real

---

[23] For a more detailed technical exposition of the Johansen approach see e.g. Johansen (1988, 1991, 1995); Lütkepohl (1993); Hamilton (1994).

Table 6.2. Cointegration analysis for the standard system

Country (Lags)	Johansen trace test			Long-run relationship	Loading	Diagnostics		
	$r = 0$	$r = 1$	$r = 2$			SC	H	N
USA (4)	20.16	4.25	0.23	no cointegration	—	8.49	121.52	41.52*
Japan (7)	24.46	10.36	2.02	no cointegration	—	1.90	168.05	33.71**
Germany (5)	36.70**	12.16	0.91	C = **1.411Y −0.096R** (0.195) (0.018)	0.005 (0.008)	10.24	129.05	48.24**
France (6)	16.61	4.35	0.39	no cointegration	—	14.47	83.36	17.95**
Italy (3)	19.59	7.85	0.79	no cointegration	—	4.61	137.80	9.28
UK (2)	27.07	10.25	1.04	no cointegration	—	6.23	105.71	7.55
Canada (2)	36.40**	9.68	0.01	C = **1.559Y −0.030R** (0.097) (0.006)	**−0.077** (0.045)	14.92	183.52	16.92**
Australia (3)	19.55	8.77	0.82	no cointegration	—	5.42	208.94	14.89*
Spain (4)	33.52*	8.97	1.26	C = **1.269Y −0.022R** (0.068) (0.005)	**−0.112** (0.023)	12.73	315.75	19.00**
Netherlands (2)	37.48**	11.87	0.01	C = **1.689Y −0.035R** (0.126) (0.007)	**−0.047** (0.012)	8.45	105.87	5.30
Belgium (4)	38.00**	12.57	0.14	C = **2.169Y −0.011R** (0.136) (0.009)	**−0.059** (0.018)	9.95	172.64	11.14
Ireland (2)	25.42	7.64	0.75	no cointegration	—	7.07	201.75	13.09*
Switzerland (3)	25.27	6.65	2.80	no cointegration	—	9.62	202.94	6.14
Sweden (4)	21.59	7.26	0.06	no cointegration	—	13.43	85.91	24.48**
Norway (4)	18.93	3.165	0.025	no cointegration	—	4.08	110.85	10.98
Finland (3)	23.35	7.51	0.18	no cointegration	—	7.98	199.42	15.26*

Note: The table displays the test statistics of the Johansen trace test for cointegration, the identified long-run relationship (if any) and the loading coefficient (α) in the VECM equation for lending (if any); the 5% (1%) critical values for the cointegration test are 29.68 (35.65), 15.41 (20.04), 3.76 (6.65) for $r = 0$, $r = 1$ and $r = 2$ respectively (Osterwald-Lenum 1992). * and ** indicate significance of the cointegration test statistic at the 5% and 1% level respectively. 'Lags' indicates the lag order of the underlying VAR. C represents the log of real credit, Y the log of real GDP and R the real interest rate. Long-run and loading coefficients which are significant at least at the 10% level are in bold. SC is a Lagrange Multiplier test for autocorrelation up to order 5, H is White's test for heteroscedasticity and N is a Jarque–Berra test for normality. All tests refer to the system as a whole. * and ** indicate significance of a test statistic at the 5% and 1% level respectively.

credit, the log of real GDP and the real interest rate. With the exception of Australia, the Trace test indicates the existence of a single long-run relationship for all countries. For Australia the trace test indicates no cointegration, but the test statistic is only marginally below the 5% critical value.

The adjustment coefficient in the VECM equation for real lending growth, which is shown in the last column of Table 6.3, is, with the exception of Japan and Germany, negative and significant at least at the 10% level. Thus, credit adjusts significantly to the identified long-run relationship, supporting the view that it represents a long-run relationship linking real credit to real GDP, the real interest rate and real property prices. While there is quite a lot of variation in the estimated adjustment coefficients, taking the size of the standard errors into account suggests that the speed of adjustment of credit to its long-run equilibrium level is not significantly different across the majority of countries. The adjustment coefficients are quite small, suggesting that credit adjusts rather slowly so that deviations of credit from its long-run equilibrium level can be quite persistent. The average half-life of the reversion of credit back to its equilibrium level is about three to four years. The insignificance of the error correction coefficients in Japan and Germany may in the case of Japan be explained by the fact that the decline in outstanding amounts of bank credit in the 1990s is understated by the official figures because non-performing loans were not cleansed from banks' balance sheets (see §6.2), while it may be due to special factors related to reunification governing the dynamics of credit in the case of Germany.

The cointegration tests therefore suggest that property prices are an important determinant of the long-run borrowing capacity of the private sector which needs to be taken into account in order to explain the long-run movements of bank lending. The estimated long-run relationships suggest that there is a significantly positive long-run correlation between credit (C), real GDP (Y) and real property prices (P) and a significant negative long-run correlation between credit and the real interest rate (R). Except for Finland, real GDP and the real interest rate always enter the cointegrating vector significantly. Property prices always enter the long-run relationship significantly, except for Germany and Spain.

The long-run elasticity of credit with respect to real GDP is not significantly different from 1 at the 5% level in Italy, Australia, Spain, the Netherlands, Belgium, Ireland and Sweden, implying that a 1% change in real GDP gives rise to a 1% change in real bank lending in these countries. The output elasticity of credit is found to be significantly larger than 1 in the US, Germany, France, the UK, Canada, Switzerland and Norway and significantly smaller than 1 in Japan and Finland.

The variation in the long-run elasticity of credit with respect to GDP may reflect differences in wealth effects not accounted for by the empirical model which are proxied by real GDP, such as the effect of rising equity prices. Empirical evidence reported in Boone *et al.* (1998) suggests that equity prices have a substantially stronger effect on private consumption in the US, the UK and Canada compared to Japan, Germany, Italy and France. This finding may therefore provide an explanation for the differences in the estimated long-run output elasticities for the G7 countries. The high elasticity for Germany does not fit into this picture and may again be explained by special factors related to German reunification.

An alternative explanation may be given by cross-country differences in the degree of banking sector liberalization over the sample period. A higher degree of financial liberalization is usually associated with higher debt levels relative to GDP and an increased sensitivity of credit to economic conditions (BIS 2001a). Abiad and Mody (2003) present indices quantifying the degree of financial liberalization for a sample of developed and developing countries. Their sample of countries covers only a few of the countries covered by our analysis, so we can again perform only a limited comparison along these lines. Comparing their

Table 6.3. Cointegration analysis for the extended system

Country (Lags)	Johansen trace test				Long-run relationship	Loading	Diagnostics		
	$r = 0$	$r = 1$	$r = 2$	$r = 3$			SC	H	N
USA (4)	90.90**	27.27	11.67	0.72	$C = 1.550Y - 0.019R + 0.504P$ (0.022) (0.002) (0.032)	−0.135 (0.075)	19.88	364.40	16.56*
Japan (7)	53.10**	23.93	8.97	0.15	$C = 0.661Y - 0.065R + 1.121P$ (0.162) (0.014) (0.161)	0.024 (0.034)	10.75	183.32	30.03**
Germany (5)	52.36**	28.96	10.96	2.68	$C = 1.855Y - 0.063R + 0.129P$ (0.156) (0.015) (0.12)	0.004 (0.012)	12.91	439.01	29.47**
France (6)	50.19*	29.43	12.23	0.36	$C = 1.332Y - 0.014R + 0.778P$ (0.097) (0.004) (0.058)	−0.053 (0.030)	13.60	520.37	31.11**
Italy (3)	49.59**	21.90	5.68	1.78	$C = 1.067Y - 0.069R + 0.409P$ (0.261) (0.020) (0.149)	−0.039 (0.018)	9.00	330.06	24.27**
UK (2)	54.45*	27.40	10.1	5.25	$C = 2.036Y - 0.057R + 1.04P$ (0.324) (0.024) (0.285)	−0.015 (0.008)	17.46	175.36	5.08
Canada (2)	49.51**	21.25	10.99	2.40	$C = 1.834Y - 0.036R + 0.227P$ (0.121) (0.006) (0.077)	−0.076 (0.032)	19.39	165.27	8.36
Australia (3)	46.74	20.37	5.43	0.30	$C = 1.250Y - 0.069R + 1.090P$ (0.188) (0.02) (0.353)	−0.013 (0.006)	10.05	274.33	15.16
Spain (4)	56.93**	25.11	8.14	0.177	$C = 1.178Y - 0.023R + 0.036P$ (0.104) (0.006) (0.062)	−0.079 (0.019)	15.65	342.08	16.70*
Netherlands (2)	49.59**	29.21	11.50	1.34	$C = 1.326Y - 0.050R + 0.736P$ (0.295) (0.011) (0.210)	−0.024 (0.008)	16.04	203.04	12.17

	r=0	r=1	r=2	r=3	Long-run relationship	α			
Belgium (4)	57.58**	25.32	11.33	0.02	$C = 1.269Y - 0.011R + 0.459P$ (0.265) (0.005) (0.152)	-0.062 (0.026)	16.37	371.86	20.78**
Ireland (2)	52.98*	27.96	7.67	0.12	$C = 1.172Y - 0.030R + 0.361P$ (0.110) (0.006) (0.171)	-0.082 (0.036)	18.75	157.73	75.17**
Switzerland (3)	59.11**	24.10	6.57	0.66	$C = 2.487Y - 0.077R + 0.438P$ (0.147) (0.011) (0.100)	-0.026 (0.015)	14.28	251.01	7.88
Sweden (4)	57.99*	26.68	6.37	0.42	$C = 0.973Y - 0.053R + 1.356P$ (0.70) (0.022) (0.248)	-0.056 (0.011)	19.95	175.57	16.22*
Norway (4)	61.77**	26.12	7.61	0.17	$C = 2.369Y - 0.077R + 3.828P$ (0.369) (0.028) (0.606)	-0.01 (0.005)	11.45	179.14	8.72
Finland (3)	76.98**	27.69	10.16	1.41	$C = -0.494Y + 0.009R + 1.681P$ (0.389) (0.011) (0.200)	-0.058 (0.013)	24.68	254.52	10.66

Note: The table displays the test statistics of the Johansen trace test for cointegration, the identified long-run relationship and the loading coefficient (α) in the VECM equation of credit; the 5% (1%) critical values for the cointegration test are 47.21 (54.46), 29.68 (35.65), 15.41 (20.04), 3.76 (6.65) for $r = 0$, $r = 1$, $r = 2$ and $r = 3$ respectively (Osterwald-Lenum 1992). * and ** indicate significance of the cointegration test statistic at the 5% and 1% level respectively. 'Lags' indicates the lag order of the underlying VAR. C represents the log of real credit, Y the log of real GDP, R the real interest rate and P the log of real property prices. Long-run and loading coefficients which are significant to at least the 10% level are in bold. SC is a Lagrange Multiplier test for autocorrelation up to order 5, H is White's test for heteroscedasticity and N is a Jarque–Berra test for normality. All tests refer to the system as a whole. * and ** indicate significance of a test statistic at the 5% and 1% level respectively.

liberalization index numbers with our estimated output elasticities of credit, it turns out that the countries with a relatively higher average degree of liberalization (Canada, Germany, the UK and the US) also have higher long-run output elasticities than countries with a lower average degree of liberalization over the sample period (Japan, France, Italy and Australia).[24]

Finally, the relatively small long-run output elasticities estimated for Japan, Sweden and Finland may be explained by the particularly severe banking and economic crises experienced by these countries in the 1990s. These events are likely to have had particularly negative effects on credit supply and demand, which may also be reflected in the long-run coefficients due to the rather short sample period.

With the exception of Finland, the long-run semi-elasticity of credit with respect to the real interest rate is significantly negative and the size of the estimated semi-elasticities is broadly in line with estimated long-run interest rate semi-elasticities of money demand.[25] The most likely factors influencing cross-country differences in the interest rate semi-elasticity of credit are differences in the strength of the monetary transmission mechanism, but also differences in the maturity structure of credit and the indebtedness of the private sector. Compared to the majority of countries, the interest rate semi-elasticity appears to be significantly higher in the three countries in our sample which are characterized by a German origin of their civil law—Germany, Japan and Switzerland.[26] Cecchetti (1999) has argued, drawing on the work of LaPorta et al. (1997, 1998), that monetary transmission is stronger in countries characterized by a German origin of civil law, because of a weaker protection of shareholder and debtor rights, which gives rise to a stronger transmission of monetary policy via the credit channel. Thus, the high interest-rate semi-elasticities in Germany, Japan and Switzerland may be explained by a particularly strong transmission of monetary policy in these countries.

Among the rest of the countries, interest semi-elasticities are also relatively high in Italy, the UK, Australia, the Netherlands, Norway and Sweden. An explanation for this finding may be the relatively high share of short-term lending in the case of Italy, the UK and Australia (see Borio 1996: table 1), which is likely to increase the sensitivity of bank credit to movements in the short-term real interest rate, and the relatively high indebtedness of the private sector in the case of the Netherlands, Norway and Sweden (see Borio 1996: table 2), which may reinforce the effect of interest rate changes on credit via wealth effects. Private sector

[24] The liberalization index of Abiad and Mody (2003) ranges from 0 (full repression) to 18 (full liberalization). Over the period 1980–1996, which roughly corresponds to our sample period, the average value of the liberalization index is 10 for Australia, 17 for Canada, 11 for France, 18 for the UK, 16 for Germany, 10 for Italy, 10 for Japan and 16 for the US.

[25] For example, von Hagen and Hofmann (2003) estimate a long-run interest rate semi-elasticity for euro area M3 demand of 0.03.

[26] See LaPorta et al. (1997, 1998).

indebtedness is also rather high in Germany, Japan and Switzerland, which may be an alternative or additional explanation for the rather high estimated interest-rate semi-elasticities in these countries.

The long-run elasticity of credit with respect to real property prices is, with the exception of Germany and Spain, significantly positive, but varies widely across countries. For example, the coefficient estimates imply that a 1% change in property prices gives rise to a 3.83% change in bank credit in Norway, compared to a mere 0.23% change in Canada. The differences in the estimated long-run property price elasticities may reflect differences in the long-run effect of property prices on the collateral constraints faced by households and firms, reflected by the importance of real estate collateral in total lending. Survey data reported in Borio (1996: table 1) suggest that the share of loans backed by real estate collateral is rather high in the UK, the US, Canada, Sweden and Switzerland. Data for Japan are not available, but Borio points out that there are indications that the share of loans secured by real estate may also be relatively high there. Also not available are data for Norway and Finland, but given the strong similarities in economic structure, one may conjecture that these countries are similar to Sweden in this respect, so that the role of real estate collateralization may also be rather important in these countries. The high estimated property price elasticities for Japan, the UK and the three Nordic countries are consistent with the relatively high importance of real estate in total lending in these countries, but real estate collateralization is also high in Canada, for which we have estimated a rather low long-run property price elasticity. Also, the long-run elasticity is rather high in Australia, where real estate collateralization does not appear to be particularly important.

Differences in home ownership, measured by the share of households owning their home, may provide an alternative explanation for the cross-country differences. As we have already discussed in §6.1, an increase in property prices will have a positive wealth effect on home-owners, but a negative wealth effect on renters, so that the wealth effects arising from changes in property prices will be stronger the higher the share of home-owners. It turns out that relatively high shares of home ownership may partly explain the high property price elasticities in Australia, the UK, Japan and the Nordic countries, while the low share of home-owners may explain the unimportance of property prices for credit in Germany.[27] However, home ownership is very high in Ireland, Italy and Spain, where we find rather low long-run property price elasticities.

An alternative explanation is that, owing to the rather short sample period, the estimated long-run property price elasticities also partly reflect the interlinkages between credit and property prices over the boom–bust cycles in

[27] Data on home ownership are reported in *The Economist* (2002) and Kennedy and Andersen (1994) and in Chapter 1 of this book.

credit and property prices experienced by some countries. In fact, the countries with the highest estimated long-run property price elasticities, the Nordic countries, Japan, the UK and Australia, are also the countries which experienced the most pronounced boom–bust cycles in credit and property markets over the sample period.

6.4 Credit dynamics

In this section we analyse, on the basis of the vector error-correction models estimated in §6.3, the dynamic effect of innovations to real GDP, real interest rates and real property prices on bank lending by computing orthogonalized impulse responses. In order to recover the structural shocks from the reduced-form system in (2) we use a standard Cholesky decomposition (Sims 1980). A Cholesky decomposition involves a recursive ordering of the variables. The ordering adopted here is the following: real GDP, real property prices, real bank lending and the real interest rate. We therefore assume that real GDP does not respond contemporaneously to innovations to any of the other variables, but may affect all other variables within the quarter. This assumption is fairly standard in the monetary policy transmission literature. We further assume that real property prices are rather sticky, so that they are not affected contemporaneously by credit and interest rates. Money market interest rates are also rather flexible, so that they are allowed to respond within a quarter to innovations to economic activity, property prices and credit. The chosen ordering also reflects the common assumption that interest rate changes are transmitted to the economy with a lag. The chosen ordering of the variables, in our view, has the most intuitive appeal and also yields plausible impulse responses. The results are generally not sensitive to a reordering of the variables. The exception is the ordering of the real interest rate and bank lending. Allowing for an immediate effect of interest rates on lending often yields an implausible positive response of bank lending to a positive interest-rate shock.

Figure 6.3 displays the impulse response of credit to one-standard-deviation shocks to real GDP, the real interest rate and real property prices together with 10% confidence bounds. As expected, the general picture is that credit responds positively to GDP and property price shocks and negatively to the real interest rate shock. The response to GDP shocks is statistically significant in ten countries. Insignificant responses are obtained for the US, Japan, the UK, the Netherlands and Sweden. An innovation to the real interest rate triggers a statistically significant negative response of bank lending in nine out of the 16 countries under investigation, namely the US, Japan, Germany, Italy, Canada, Spain, the Netherlands, Ireland and Switzerland.

Innovations to property prices are found to have a highly significant and persistent positive dynamic effect on bank lending. In 14 out of 16 countries the

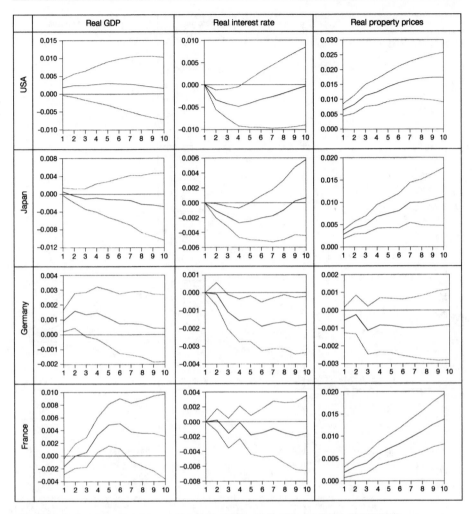

Figure 6.3. Impulse responses of credit in industralized countries, 1980–1998

Note: The graphs display impulse responses of bank lending to one-standard-deviation shocks in a 10% confidence band. The deviation from the baseline scenario of no shocks is on the vertical axis; the periods after the shock are on the horizontal axis.

impulse response of credit to a property price shock is positive and significant at the 10% level. Only in Germany and Italy does the response appear to be not significantly different from zero. This finding suggests that innovations to property prices, possibly reflecting changing beliefs about future economic conditions or speculative activity in property markets, may give rise to significant and persistent cycles in bank lending and are thus a potential explanation for the persistent financial cycles observed in the past.

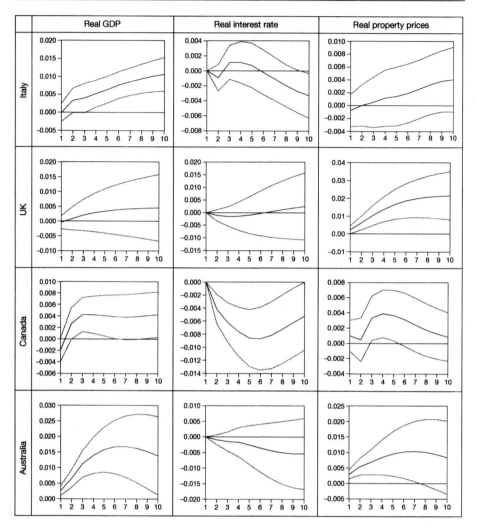

Figure 6.3. (*cont.*)

6.5 Conclusions

Over the last two decades most industrialized countries have experienced pronounced boom-and-bust cycles in credit markets, often ending in economic distress and financial crises. These credit cycles have often coincided with cycles in economic activity and property markets. The coincidence of these cycles has already been widely documented in the literature, but there are only a few studies addressing the issue in a formal way. The role of property prices in particular has not been explored to a large extent. This chapter has attempted to fill this gap.

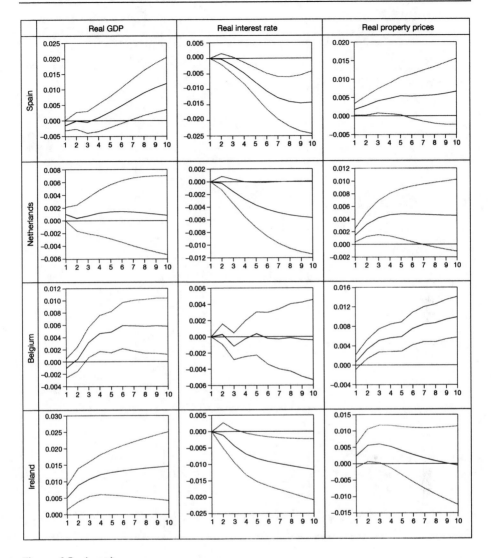

Figure 6.3. (*cont.*)

On the basis of a cointegrating VAR we analysed the determinants of credit to the private non-bank sector in 16 industrialized countries over the period 1980 till 1998 using quarterly data. Cointegration tests suggest that the long-run movements of credit cannot be explained by standard credit demand factors, i.e. real GDP and the real interest rate. But once real property prices, measured as a weighted average of real residential and real commercial property prices, are added to the system, we are able to find long-run relationships linking real credit positively to real GDP and real property prices and negatively to the real interest rate. Property prices therefore appear to be an important determinant

111

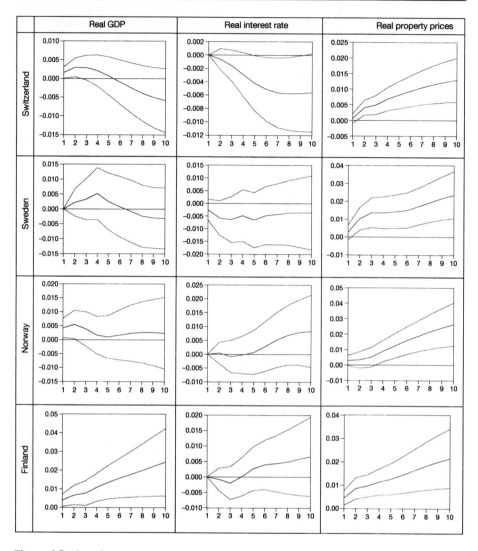

Figure 6.3. (*cont.*)

of the long-run borrowing capacity of the private sector which needs to be taken into account in order to explain the long-run movements of bank lending.

The adopted multivariate approach enabled us also to analyse the dynamic effect of innovations to real GDP, the real interest rate and real property prices on bank lending. The impulse response paths reveal that, as expected, innovations to real GDP have a significantly positive effect on bank lending, while shocks to the real interest rate trigger a decline in credit. Innovations to real property prices appear to have a strong positive, highly significant, and persistent effect on bank lending. The response of credit to real property price shocks also appears to be more significant than the response to real GDP and the real interest rate. This suggests that innovations to property prices, possibly reflecting changing beliefs about future economic conditions or speculative activity in property markets, may give rise to significant and persistent cycles in bank lending and are thus a potential explanation for the persistent cycles in bank lending observed in the past.

Taken together, these findings suggest that property prices are an important driving force of bank lending. This implies that boom–bust cycles in property markets may also be transmitted to credit markets, possibly causing severe financial imbalances which may pose a risk to macroeconomic and banking system stability. This, in turn, seems to suggest that monetary policy should respond actively to fluctuations in credit and asset markets, both for the sake of financial stability and long-run price stability.[28] Our impulse response analysis suggests that innovations to the real interest rate have significantly negative effects on real lending. Evidence reported in Goodhart and Hofmann (2004a) and in Chapter 8 of this book suggests that interest rate changes also have a significantly negative effect on property prices. These findings could be interpreted as supporting the view that monetary authorities may, via their leverage over short-term interest rates, be able to smooth or even prevent the occurrence of financial cycles by responding actively to movements in credit and property prices.

However, the finding that central banks may influence credit conditions and asset prices does not guarantee that this instrument is and can be used in the right way to smooth financial cycles. Bordo and Jeanne (2002) set up a small stylized model with collateral constraints to investigate this issue and found that whether a response of monetary policy to asset price movements is warranted depends in a highly non-linear way on economic sentiment. Goodhart and Hofmann (2004a) argue, on the basis of the experiences of the US Fed in 1929 and the Bank of Japan in 1989/90, that the effects of interest rate movements on asset prices and bank lending may be a highly non-linear function of economic sentiment as well. During booms, general euphoria may lower the sensitivity of asset valuations and lending to interest rate hikes. Once market sentiment changes, investors may realize how high interest rates have gone, which may trigger a sharp reversal in asset prices. Spreading pessimism may then again render interest rate cuts ineffective. Given that the driver of the potential non-linearities, economic sentiment, is unobservable, the usefulness of interest rate policy as an instrument to safeguard financial stability is in doubt.

A probably less controversial policy implication of our empirical findings is that regulatory measures should be taken in order to limit the exposure of the banking system to fluctuations in property prices. This can be achieved by imposing regulatory limits on the direct or indirect exposure of the banking sector to

---

[28] Borio and Lowe (2004) argue forcefully along these lines.

the property market. Examples of such an approach are Hong Kong, where the HKMA guidelines on property lending include a maximum loan-to-value ratio on property loans,[29] and Ireland, where guidelines require banks to observe a maximum ratio of loans to funds in their lending to single sectors or to two sectors facing similar economic risks.

---

[29] Gerlach and Peng (2005) show that the effect of property prices on bank lending in Hong Kong was significantly reduced after banks started to apply the maximum loan-to-value ratio guideline.

7

Bank Regulation and Macroeconomic Fluctuations

7.1 Introduction

Macroeconomic cycles have been changing in recent decades, since the end of the Bretton Woods system, and now involve more asset price volatility (boom–bust cycles) and financial fragility. In the face of more frequent banking crises, regulators have moved to reinforce individual bank capital adequacy ratios, for example through the Basel I and II Accords. But bank regulation is inherently procyclical; it bites in downturns, but fails to restrain in booms. The more 'sophisticated' and 'risk-sensitive' the regulation, the greater the scope for procyclicality to become a problem, particularly in view of the changing nature of macroeconomic cycles. The main purpose of this chapter is to explore this nexus, and the policy problems thereby generated.

With price stability (inflation targets) being the primary responsibility of the monetary authorities, the instrument of short-term interest rates is, correctly and properly, allocated to this task. So a central bank has hardly any usable instruments for countering financial volatility on its own. This problem is enhanced in a large and diverse currency region, such as the euro area. Asset price movements can differ sharply between regions; think of the varying experiences of housing price inflation of Ireland and Spain on the one hand and Germany and Austria on the other. Large capital flows in, and possibly out of, the relatively small Accession States can provide yet another problem. Within a wide currency union, there is little that the Eurobean Central Bank can do.

We begin this chapter, in §7.2.1, by recording the particular nature of the post-World War II business cycle. In the decades immediately following World War II, 1945–71, demand was kept high, and one means of limiting the inflationary consequences of that was by keeping the banking system under tight credit controls. So there were virtually no banking crises, and, consequently, bank regulation was light.

After the stagflation of the 1970s, and particularly after Arthur Volcker's monetary policy shift in October 1979, the monetary authorities gradually learnt how to use a market-oriented monetary policy to maintain price stability. On the other hand, liberalization of banking sectors since the early and mid-1970s had increased the scope for risk-taking and leverage and thus the procyclicality of the financial system. This combination of stable consumer prices and liberalized banking sectors was accompanied by a reversion of the business cycle in some respects to the kind of pattern seen, for example, in the decades up till 1913, when again consumer prices remained stable. In this new pattern, real shocks often tended to generate fluctuations in asset prices, which frequently led to asset-price and lending booms and busts, in which latter case banks would often become fragile and fail.

In this context there was a need to strengthen financial regulation, not only nationally but also internationally, given the extent of global competition in financial intermediation. This is described in §7.2.2, where we focus particularly on the key role of the Basel Committee on Banking Supervision in enabling a coordinated international response to a global problem.

Nevertheless the Basel approach has several weaknesses. The first is that regulation is inherently procyclical. Banks are weaker in recessions and when asset prices decline. The more that regulation is based on current assessed riskiness and current market valuations, the more procyclical the regulatory system will become. The second is that supervision is, almost necessarily, focused on the individual financial institution. But actions and procedures that may appear obvious and straightforward at the individual level may be damaging at the aggregate systemic level, especially if regulation reinforces herd activity. So in §7.2.3, we consider not only the likely extent of procyclicality, but also steps that might be taken to mitigate it.

Section 7.2 approaches this subject at a fairly high level of generality. So we have chosen to support this overview with three more focused empirical exercises. In the first of these, §7.3.1, we analyse the procyclical effects of financial liberalization. We show how the relationship between liberalization and a subsequent asset price boom/bust has been a common phenomenon, common to Western as well as Asian countries, to developed as well as developing countries, and that financial liberalization appears to have strengthened the financial accelerator mechanism by increasing the sensitivity of bank lending to property price fluctuations.

In our main analysis, in §7.2, we suggest that an increase in required bank capital during downturns may exacerbate the recession. We seek to support that hypothesis, in §7.3.2, by looking (again) at the experience in the USA of the 'credit crunch' in the recession of 1990/1, when required bank capital adequacy ratios were being hoisted in the aftermath of the first Basel Accord in 1988.

Finally, in §7.3.3, we try to do a counterfactual simulation to see how banking capital adequacy requirements would have changed over recent history for a 'typical' bank in three countries, Mexico, Norway and the United States, using three different regulatory approaches. These are:

(i) the Basel II standardized approach

(ii) the Basel II Foundation Internal Ratings Based (IRB) approach

(iii) an Improved Credit Risk Method

What we show is that the introduction of the Basel II IRB approach may well have considerably accentuated the procyclicality of the regulatory system.

7.2 General considerations

7.2.1 The changing nature of cycles and the role of asset prices

The characteristics of trade cycles, of crises, and of financial regulation have all changed over time. Eichengreen and Bordo (2003) and Bordo *et al.* (2001) divide up the 120 years since 1880 into four main periods: 1880–1913, 1919–39, 1945–71 and 1973–97. It is the third period that stands out as unique in several respects. First, inflation not only continued, but accelerated; this had never happened before during peacetime. Second, in the developed world, output and productivity growth were much higher than previously, or (with a few exceptions) subsequently, and unemployment was low and stable. Third, there were no banking crises (see Eichengreen and Bordo: table 3.5, reproduced here as Table 7.1; the same data are shown diagrammatically in Figure 7.1, taken from Bordo *et al.* 2001), and, no doubt largely in consequence, bank supervision and regulation remained generally light.[1] In most countries, at least until the end of this period, bank lending to the private sector was not only directly constrained by credit controls in aggregate, but also directed towards the preferred sectors of exporting and manufacturing companies.

Demand was generally kept high enough, primarily through expansionary fiscal policies, to keep unemployment below its 'natural' rate, so that inflation tended to accelerate from peak to peak. The monetary authorities would then

Table 7.1. Financial crisis frequency, 1880–1997 (annual probability, %)

Year	Banking crises	Currency crises	Twin crises	All crises
1880–1913	2.30	1.23	1.38	4.90
1919–39	4.84	4.30	4.03	13.17
1945–71	0.00	6.85	0.19	7.04
1973–97 (21 countries)	2.03	5.18	2.48	9.68
1973–97 (56 countries)	2.29	7.48	2.38	12.15

Source: Eichengreen and Bordo (2003: table 3.5).

[1] For an account of the changing structure of bank regulation in the UK, see Goodhart (2004).

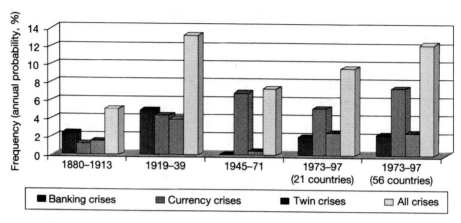

Figure 7.1. Financial crisis frequency, 1880–1997
Source: Bordo *et al.* (2001: fig. 1, p. 56).

raise interest rates to check inflation and also the balance of payments/currency crises that attended the comparatively more inflationary countries. It was said that every boom in the USA during these decades was killed off by the Federal Reserve System. Thereafter, during the Stop intervals of the Stop–Go cycles of the time, interest rates would be lowered out of a wish to hold down the cost of public sector indebtedness and to encourage private sector investment. The increases in interest rates, sharp though they sometimes were, caused relatively little financial fragility, since the banks' assets were primarily short-dated government securities and loans to large (and generally safe) private sector (manufacturing) companies.

The economically disastrous decade of the 1970s, with stagflation, brought about a reconstruction of the policy mix. In particular there was a maintained shift away from direct, central (government) controls towards market mechanisms. There was a similar shift from using fiscal policy, primarily to target a desired level of unemployment, to using monetary policy, primarily to target a (low and stable) level of inflation.

The banking system, owing to its central role in the economy, had been a focus for such prior controls: controls on interest rates, on credit allocation, on international financial flows (via exchange controls). So controlled were such commercial banks that they were seen as akin to public utilities, not commercial entities: boring, uninnovative, but safe. The main task of bank managers/loan officers was to say 'no' to requests for loans from prospective borrowers in less-favoured sectors. Risk analysis and risk management atrophied in such circumstances.

It has therefore not been surprising that one facet of the liberalization of banking systems around the world has been a subsequent lending boom and subsequent bust. As we document in §7.3.1, this has occurred in country after country, starting perhaps in the UK, where the liberalization of 'Competition and Credit Control', Bank of England, 1971, was shortly followed by the Fringe Bank

Crisis in 1973/4 (see Reid 1982). One common aggravating feature was that prior to the liberalization, part of the business of the controlled commercial banks had often been taken by new intermediaries whose *raison d'être* was essentially to avoid such controls (with, or without, the blessing of the authorities). Once liberalized, there was a grab for market share by the commercial banks to recover previously lost business and by the non-bank intermediaries to hold on to it. Stir in the lack of experience with risk management, and the shift of the largest and safest borrowers to the capital markets, and the result was the danger of a boom–bust cycle. As noted in §7.3.1, this became the experience in Scandinavia in the early 1990s, Japan in the 1990s, and much of East Asia in 1997/8; much the same syndrome may await India and China when they eventually liberalize.

This experience, though general, was not, however, universal. Several major European countries, notably Germany, avoided any such experience. In the German case this may be attributed to their banking system being re-established, after World War II, on a relatively liberalized basis from the outset.[2] Even so, the dangers of enhanced financial instability in the immediate aftermath of liberalization indicate the need for ensuring that financial supervision and risk management skills are improved at the same time.

Liberalization of banking systems has been one of the most potent progenitors of boom–bust cycles, but it has not been the only factor. Once the large companies, to whom the banks had primarily lent in Eichengreen and Bordo's third period (1945–71), had migrated to capital markets, banks increasingly began to lend to small and medium enterprises (SMEs) and to persons. Such smaller borrowers were, in general, somewhat riskier, and the costs of acquiring information on a large number of idiosyncratic small borrowers were greater. So banks placed increasing weight on collateral as a basis for lending. But this gave rise to the likelihood of enhanced dynamic instability, in the guise of the financial accelerator mechanism (see for example Bernanke, Gertler and Gilchrist 1999) or the cyclical mechanism of Kiyotaki and Moore (1997).

Essentially an upturn may be triggered by some good shock, e.g. to productivity or trade; profits increase, asset values rise; lending increases because collateral becomes more easily available; enhanced lending raises investment, profits and asset values. This goes on until the rise in the capital stock becomes so large that profit margins crumble. Then, of course, everything goes into reverse.

---

[2] Kaminsky and Schmukler (2003) provide a comprehensive chronology of financial liberalization for a large sample of industrialized and developing countries. Their chronology shows that the German banking sector was liberalized much earlier than the banking sectors in other industrialized countries. Ceilings on interest rates were abolished in 1967. In most other countries the removal of interest rate ceilings occurred in the 1970s or even the 1980s. The liberalization index constructed by Abiad and Mody (2003), which also takes into account other dimensions of financial liberalization, indicates that the German financial system could be characterized as already fully liberalized in the early 1970s.

An interesting feature of such booms is that they are often characterized by stable real-unit labour costs (held down by productivity gains), stable prices (often held down by currency appreciation, partly owing to capital inflows), and seemingly prudent, or even robust, fiscal policies (with rising tax revenues and declining social expenditures)—a markedly different profile from the earlier period.

Besides greater lending to SMEs, banks also increasingly muscled into the business of mortgage lending to households, territory which had previously been confined to specialized (and often cartelized) mortgage lenders. Again, a similar nexus between some favourable initial shock leading to higher housing prices, providing a stronger collateral basis for bank lending, with such lending tending to cause yet higher housing prices and so on, could be discerned on numerous occasions in a variety of countries, though more so in Anglo-Saxon countries, where home-ownership is prized, than in continental Europe, especially where accommodation is more commonly rented.

In §7.3.1 we present some formal evidence supporting the hypothesis that financial liberalization has increased the procyclicality of financial systems. We first show that financial liberalizations were generally followed by boom–bust cycles in economic activity, bank lending and asset prices. Using rolling regressions we also demonstrate that liberalizations of banking sectors were associated with an increased sensitivity of bank lending to property price movements, which implies a strengthening of the effect of business cycle fluctuations on bank credit.

Such characteristics, of course, have led to the debate on whether the monetary authorities could, and should, observe and then react to deviations of asset prices from some longer-term fundamental value, i.e. asset price bubbles (see in particular the debate between Cecchetti *et al.* 2000 and Bernanke and Gertler 1999; also see Gertler *et al.* 1998). This debate continues in the aftermath of the dot.com equity bubble and bust, but it is not the remit or purpose of this chapter to discuss macro-monetary policies. Rather it is our objective to discuss how policies with respect to financial regulation and supervision interact with the cycle.

7.2.2   Interaction between regulation and the trade cycle

These changing characteristics of the trade cycle, notably liberalized financial markets combined with sharp asset-price fluctuations, have resulted in a crop of banking crises and twin banking/currency crises. Table 7.1 shows that the frequency of such crises reverted to the previous norm in 1880–1913, though still below that exhibited during the Great Depression in the inter-war years.

The liberalization of financial markets was meant to, and did, enhance competition. Competition led to lower profit margins. A combination of factors led to the assumption of greater risk in loan books, e.g. the migration of larger (and safer) borrowers to capital markets, initial (i.e. post-liberalization) inexperience with risk management, the desire to break into new and unfamiliar markets, and a wish to maintain the return on equity (ROE) despite declining margins for safer business. Riskier business led to a rise in non-performing loans (NPLs) and subsequent write-offs. Declining profit margins and higher NPLs, plus a desire to maintain ROE, led to a trend decline in capital ratios, in turn implying increasing financial fragility.

As this was happening, in the 1970s, the institutions with particular responsibility for maintaining the systemic strength of the banking system were the central banks in the major developed countries. In practice, they had not had much experience of such a role since the middle of the 1930s, but earlier historical developments had left them with that responsibility. As banking crises began to occur in the early 1970s, e.g. Franklin National (1973), Herstatt (1973/4) and Fringe Bank (1973/4), many of the key central bankers became nervous.

Moreover, the growing development of international financial markets, the huge growth of international capital flows (following the removal of exchange controls), and the interpenetration of national financial markets at the wholesale level (and occasionally at the retail level also) by banks and investment houses with an international reach, meant that no single country, even the USA, could maintain higher standards of financial probity unilaterally. The problem was that, absent exchange controls, financial intermediation could just move offshore.

This led to one of the more remarkable institutional developments of our age, the Basel Committee on Banking Supervision (BCBS, initially called the Blunden and then the Cooke Committee, these being the officials from the Bank of England who were its first two chairmen). This committee was established by the conclave of the central bank governors of the G10 meeting under the auspices of the Bank for International Settlements (BIS). It had no formal or legal status, and no governmental support (either international or national). Its pronouncements (Accords) were the softest of soft law. Yet there were sanctions to encourage adherence. The central banks of the countries with the main international financial markets were the leading members of the BCBS. If a country refused to abide by the Accords of the BCBS, the banks of that country could have their branches, and/or subsidiaries, banned from operating in the main financial centres.

As multinational trade flourished and international capital flows multiplied, so the leading banks and investment houses set up subsidiaries and branches in many countries. There was an urgent need to systematize and rationalize international procedures for banking supervision and, above all, to ensure that there was one lead regulator who could oversee the consolidated accounts of the bank as a whole (a need evidenced for example by the Banco Ambrosiano collapse in 1981). The BCBS did much excellent work on this front. But their main concern was to halt and, indeed, to reverse the trend decline in capital ratios. They achieved that objective with the introduction of the Accord on Capital Adequacy Requirements in 1988, now generally known as Basel I.[3] This was a great success for the BCBS, which by now really deserves a proper full-scale historical assessment.

Basel I required internationally active banks to hold capital equal to 8% of their risk-weighted assets, where loans to the private non-bank sector were given a uniform risk weight of 100%. Since the risk-insensitiveness of Basel I gave banks an incentive to move high-quality assets off the balance sheet and also did not reward the use of credit risk-mitigation techniques (see Secretariat of the Basel Committee on Banking Supervision 2001: 12), it was increasingly criticized. One of the main aims of the recently approved new capital accord, Basel II, was thus to increase significantly the risk-sensitiveness of capital requirements. This was achieved by substantially spreading the range of risk weights and making them dependent on external or internal ratings of the borrower.

While the introduction of capital adequacy requirements under Basel I was deservedly hailed as a great achievement, nevertheless it had a number of weaknesses. It is upon these that we shall now mainly focus. First, the decision was made to try to relate banks' capital requirements to the relative riskiness of the assets. That is an understandable, some might say even an obvious, decision. But the measurement of risk is horribly complex (finance academics spend a lifetime on the subject). If the authorities try to lay down risk ratings, they run into a nasty dilemma. On the one hand, they can try to keep their risk measures simple and broad-brush, as in Basel I; but that will mean that such risk measurements will be inaccurate, and hence subject to gaming, arbitrage and avoidance, with unfortunate side-effects, as indeed happened with Basel I. On the other hand, they can try to make their risk measurements as close to state-of-the-art analysis as possible. Since risk measurement is complex, the resulting requirements will similarly become dense and difficult, the more so since analytical logic often has to compromise with national idiosyncrasies. Moreover the state of the art evolves over time—we would hope that it is improving—so that what may be correct today will become inaccurate tomorrow, and hence, perhaps, as subject over time to gaming, arbitrage and avoidance as simpler rules.

Moreover, the more detailed the rules, the more they will tend to require those subject to them, i.e. the banks, to respond in exactly the same way to common shocks. That will enhance herd-like behaviour—one-way markets—that many observers had already seen as a danger even before Basel II. In response to this, the BCBS can rightly state that the Internal Ratings Based (IRB) component of Basel II has been an instrument to induce the banks to improve their own individual modelling of (credit) risk. On this view Basel II is but a temporary phase (or step) in an evolving process whereby individual banks develop their own effective

---

[3] Secretariat of the Basel Committee on Banking Supervision (2001) states on p. 11 'the major impetus for the 1988 Basel Capital Accord was the concern of the Governors of the G10 central banks that the capital of the world's major banks had become dangerously low after persistent erosion through competition.'

proprietary (credit) risk-metric models, preferably with continuing differences and innovation. Then, as has been happening with supervision of the trading/investment book, the supervisors could focus on oversight of bank models, and not to try to specify such models themselves.

One continuing concern, however, is that the modelling needs of bankers differ from those of supervisors. Supervisors are mostly focused on what would happen under extreme adverse events, in the far one-sided tails of probability distributions, whereas bankers need to be concerned about the full distribution of outcomes. Whereas Value at Risk (VaR) models do a good job most of the time, with their assumption of log-normal distributions, and so are suitable for bankers, extreme events occur more often than in a normal distribution (fat tails, kurtosis), and so the bankers' model was not, as it happened, of much use to supervisors.

The second weakness is that the supervision, the analysis, and the modelling focus primarily on the individual banking institution, not on the system as a whole. These two weaknesses are interrelated in the sense that the realization that supervisors could not rely on bankers' own VAR models led to a new generation of stress tests, or scenario simulations, in which individual banks were asked to assess the effect on their own profitability, and capital adequacy, of the onset of certain extreme shocks. But there was no possibility whatsoever, in this attempt to estimate the effect of a macro-shock on each individual micro-institution, of examining dynamic interactions between banks (e.g. if bank A was forced to withdraw funds from the interbank market, what effect would this have on bank B?) or between bank reactions and the wider economy (e.g. if banks cut back on making new loans in the face of an adverse economic shock, would it impart a serious further downwards impulse on the economy?). In short, the macro/micro stress tests go only part of the way to an assessment (and measurement) of systemic fragility.

Of course, the robustness of the system as a whole is related to the strength of the individual members. Given the myriad interconnections between banks, if the individual banks are in poor condition, then the banking system as a whole is also likely to be fragile, and vice versa. Even so, it is perfectly possible to envisage circumstances where liquidity, or solvency, problems in one bank might have a cascade effect on other banks, perhaps via some combination of fund withdrawals and asset price declines, that could, possibly quite rapidly, put initially healthy banks into serious difficulties. It is not possible to analyse and estimate such systemic weaknesses using present techniques.

Some steps have been taken to analyse the systemic implications of one of the most obvious sources of interconnection, i.e. the interbank market. Here there have been various empirical studies (e.g. Elsinger *et al.* 2002; Furfine 2003; Upper and Worms 2004; Wells 2002), and the initial results have been quite reassuring. So long as pro rata payments on their interbank debts can be made quite quickly by failing banks, and/or concern about other banks' position with the failing bank does not trigger secondary (reputational) withdrawals of funds on them, then the first-round, direct effect of interbank linkages, via the interbank market, can almost always be comfortably absorbed.

This analysis underlines one of the problems about trying to analyse financial fragility. Developments in the financial system depend critically on the state of confidence. Given that we are dealing with the aftermath of assumed extreme shocks, which by definition occur very rarely, it is almost impossible to quantify the potential likelihood of such secondary (reputational) effects (though one might be able, at least in theory, to simulate them).

Be that as it may, one of us, along with two colleagues at the Bank of England, is trying to model the systemic effects of extreme shocks (see e.g. Goodhart, Sunirand and Tsomocos 2004a). But that is somewhat separate from the main focus of this chapter, so we shall not pursue that further here.

A common problem in this field is that regulations which are entirely sensible when applied to the individual institution can have unwanted, and often unintended, macro-, aggregate effects. This is particularly so when the individual institutions are all simultaneously affected by a common factor, notably the trade cycle, as we will discuss in §7.2.3. But whenever a common factor affects a large proportion of the intermediaries at the same time, some unfortunate results may occur.

A good example of this occurred in the case of the UK Life Insurance (LI) companies in 2002. In this case the downturn in the equity market, following the dot.com bubble and bust, put pressure on the LI companies' solvency ratios, whereby they have to demonstrate that they can meet their obligations to stakeholders even should (equity) markets continue to decline (by another 25%). The standard way to be sure of meeting such commitments is to match (hedge) the liabilities with assets of the same duration, and with a similar, fixed payment stream. So the downturn in the equity market, interacting with the prudential requirements for solvency, forced the LI companies into selling equity onto a falling market, while buying long-dated (government) bonds on a rising market, thereby exacerbating both market trends. Moreover, their predicament was obvious to others, who could attempt to benefit by front-running speculation.

7.2.3 The procyclicality of regulation

The main common factor to affect banks, and most other financial intermediaries, is the trade cycle, i.e. generalized fluctuations in the economy. Regulation is inherently procyclical. Borrower and bank profits rise during booms; new capital is easier to raise; asset prices are higher. Per contra, in a downturn, non-performing loans, failures and write-offs increase. Prudential regulations bite harder during periods of economic weakness because the individual banks are more fragile. So the more accurately the value, and relative riskiness, of each bank is measured at any point of time, the greater will be the procyclicality of the prudential regime. Thus Basel II will be more procyclical than Basel I; fair-value accounting methods more than historic cost; point-in-time ratings more than those averaged through the cycle; and advanced internal risk-based assessments (IRB) more than foundation IRB (especially so since Loss Given Default (LGD) is to be treated as constant over time in the foundation method, whereas almost all empirical studies have found LGD to be strongly cyclical, perhaps as much as, or more than, the procyclicality of default (PD), e.g. Acharya *et al.* 2003; Altman 2002; Altman *et al.* 2002).

This proposition, that the greater the accuracy of current valuation, the greater the resulting procyclicality of prudential regulation, is generally accepted. A much more problematic question is what the practical, empirical scale of this relationship may be, and how important the resulting macroeconomic consequentials may have been. We examine these issues in two studies in §7.3. In §7.3.2 we reconsider whether, and how far, the requirement for additional capital, in order to satisfy the newly imposed capital adequacy requirement (CAR) of Basel I, exacerbated the recession of 1991/2, especially in the USA, where most of the empirical studies were carried out.

The second exercise, which we undertake in §7.3.3, is to simulate the comparative effect of Basel II, relative to Basel I, on CARs over the course of the cycle. For this purpose we use data sets from Mexico, Norway and the USA, and comment on some other empirical exercises in the literature.

This procyclicality of prudential regulation tends to exacerbate the trade cycle itself. We have already mentioned the example of the solvency regulations on Life Insurance companies enhancing the boom–bust experience on the London Stock Exchange. By the same token if banks, in aggregate, are subject to binding prudential constraints on their lending in downturns (constraints which are relaxed during booms), the amplitude of the cycle is likely to be greater.[4]

Of course, if the scale of this problem of procyclicality is small, then we need not worry so much. But the empirical exercises in §7.3.3, though as always inconclusive, suggest that the scale could be large. That raises the question of how best to respond.

One approach is to use some kind of averaging of the data over the cycle, to use historic cost accounting, or constant PDs (as in Basel I), or constant LGDs (as in the Foundation approach), or through-the-cycle ratings. But this goes against the grain of trying to obtain the best, and most accurate, valuations in order to guide efficient market pricing, investor information and capital allocation.

---

[4] A counter-argument is that, should the binding prudential regulations during downturns succeed in reducing the number and scale of bank failures, then the probability of systemic collapses during the recession will have been lessened. Likewise the greater sophistication of risk-measurement methods may encourage private sector bank managers to curb their own risks in a voluntary manner.

A second possible response is to try to use fiscal, rather than monetary, measures to mitigate such procyclicality. Capital gains taxes may limit the volatility of post-tax returns. In so far as various taxes can be adjusted according to the condition of asset markets, they could be used by the authorities to mitigate procyclicality. But this not only depends on the authorities having somehow better information on 'fundamental' asset prices, but may also introduce other distortions which usually have adverse effects.

A third, and perhaps more promising, approach is to adjust the prudential parameters (to be applied to the most accurately estimated valuations) contracyclically over the cycle (Gordy and Howells 2004). This possibility, however, depends, quite largely, on their being an identifiable cycle, which can be expected to revert back to some (estimated) normal, mean level.

Assume, for example, that there is a recognized tendency for mean-reversion towards some (calculable) price/earnings ratio (P/E) in the equity market. Then the solvency ratio calculations that are prescribed should require that the percentage fall which the LI should be able to withstand should be an increasing function of the current level of the P/E in the equity market. Similarly loan-to-valuation ratios in mortgage and property markets should, in principle, be functions of the deviation of housing/property prices from their equilibrium level.

An obvious problem in this respect, both for the economy as a whole and for the key asset markets, is that mean-reversion is an extremely weak and unreliable force (think of foreign exchange markets) and that the ability to observe a long-run fundamental equilibrium is equivalently weak and doubtful. There is always a possibility that 'there really is a New Economy'. Although this latter is most often a delusion (and in some cases a self-seeking delusion), trends, e.g. in productivity, do change. Estimates of output gaps, and of equilibrium asset prices, will always be extremely unreliable. Nevertheless there is a case that it would be better to tie prudential parameters to such unreliable estimates than to hold them constant over the cycle, which must have adverse effects on procyclicality. Thus it would be possible to require some contra-cyclical variation in minimum CARs, raising these during booms and allowing these to fall back again during recessions.

Many might welcome this idea in principle, but argue that, since the estimate of the deviation from the norm is inevitably somewhat subjective, this should properly come under Pillar 2 of Basel II, as an optional, discretionary add-on for national supervisors, rather than as part of any agreed rule book. And some supervisors may already be attempting to follow this course. There is some force in this argument, but it runs up against the problem that different national authorities will respond in different ways, so that international banks will complain loudly if their national authorities impose unilaterally higher CARs on them during expansions. Note also that minimum CARs will be required by formal regulation, e.g. EU directives, under Pillar 1, so that national supervision will not (at least not officially) be allowed to combine higher ratios during expansions with ratios below the Pillar 1 requirement in recessions. So a draw-back of Basel II is that any national supervisor trying to build in some contra-cyclical effects into their own approach will simultaneously expose their own banks to higher average CARs over time. There will be a clash between the desire for greater stability and the desire to allow their own banks to maintain international competitiveness.

Nevertheless the main problem with this approach lies in the weakness of mean-reversion and the difficulty of observing deviations from fundamentals. Once events have safely become past history, enabling the commentator to draw trend lines, historical cycles come to appear immediately obvious. If, however, one allows for changing trends, and other breaks in the time series (and these have happened before), then the estimates of current deviations (from 'funda-mental' norms) become a matter of hot, and difficult, argument. Perhaps the strongest argument for Alan Greenspan not raising interest rates to constrain the dot.com bubble was that this would have been extremely difficult to justify to the US Congress and the American people, the more so since there were many siren voices, and gullible investors (see Brennan 2004), who did not see the run-up in equity values as an unsustainable bubble. If it is too difficult for those in charge of monetary policy to assess deviations from fundamental equilibrium,[5] why should financial regulators and supervisors be better endowed with economic insight?

A somewhat simpler alternative to relating regulatory parameters to deviations from the norm is to relate them to rates of change, relative to past average rates of change. These latter are easily calculated (though the length of the window over which the average is to be calculated is somewhat arbitrary and can, at times, be substantively important). The rate of growth of bank lending to the private sector has, in the past, been a good predictor of financial crises, i.e. it is unusually high before crises. Again, bubbles in asset prices tend to be characterized by accel-erating prices as the peak, and resulting crisis/collapse, is reached. If solvency requirements, loan-to-value requirements, etc. were related to prior rates of change, that should help to avoid procyclicality.

All this discussion, however, is reminiscent of the long-past discussion on ways to stabilize the macro-trade cycle via e.g. derivative or integral stabilization. Much of that got washed away in the general attack on fine-tuning, and the belief that demand management is better focused on long-term rules, such as achieving an inflation target and sticking to a set of 'golden' fiscal rules.

---

[5] A counter-argument is that monetary policy-makers already aim to assess deviations from long-run equilibrium in the guise of the output gap, so why should they not be willing to assess similar deviations from equilibrium elsewhere in the economy, e.g. in the housing market? Against this it can be replied that the aggregate economy is generally more stable, and more predictable, than individual asset markets such as housing, or equities, or foreign exchange.

By the same token one can ask whether it is the purpose of regulatory policy to concern itself with the amplitude of cyclical swings. Perhaps not, but then it is surely the purpose of regulatory policy to avoid systemic crises, rather than to prevent all individual failures. At present, the focus of financial regulation and supervision is on the individual institution, not on the system as a whole. Through the indirect effects of procyclicality, it is at least possible that the current, and prospective, methods of individual institutional supervision could have damaging implications for the system as a whole.

7.3 Empirical analysis

7.3.1 Financial liberalization, credit cycles, and the changing role of asset prices

Since the early to mid-1970s there have been extensive efforts to liberalize banking systems in both developed and developing economies.[6] The trend towards financial liberalization was motivated by theoretical and empirical findings that higher financial development leads to higher economic growth and that financial liberalization was in turn a precondition for financial development. Theoretically, by easing financial constraints and improving the efficiency of the banking system, banking sector liberalization stirs higher and more efficient investment in both physical and human capital and thus spurs faster long-run growth.[7] Empirically, this hypothesis appears to be supported by the data (see e.g. Leahy et al. 2001).

In recent years, however, the perception of financial liberalization has become more critical, owing to the recurrence of violent boom–bust cycles in credit creation, economic activity and asset markets in the wake of financial liberalization. These boom–bust cycles often ended in outright systemic crisis in the banking sector. A central finding of the large and growing literature on the causes of banking crises is that financial liberalization significantly increases the probability of a banking crisis. Various studies (Demirgüc-Kunt and Detragiache 1998; Kaminsky and Reinhart 1999) have shown that indicators of financial liberalization help to explain the occurrence of banking crisis in large samples of developing and developed countries.

Tornell et al. (2004), amongst others, argue that the occurrence of occasional crises does not overturn the general result that financial liberalization is beneficial for long-run growth. They show that in a sample of developing

---

[6] For a chronology of financial liberalization in developed and developing markets see Kaminsky and Schmukler (2003).

[7] See Levine (1997) for a survey of the relationship between financial development and growth.

countries the fastest-growing countries are also those that experienced boom–bust cycles. They also present a theoretical model where financial liberalization leads to both higher long-run growth and higher financial fragility. However, there are also noteworthy counter-examples to this conclusion. Japan, for example, certainly grew at a slower pace after the boom–bust cycle which followed the liberalization of the mid-1980s than before. Thus, even if financial liberalization generally remains beneficial for growth after also controlling for the damaging effects of financial fragility, the potential occurrence of boom–bust cycles in the wake of financial liberalization remains a concern.

Rather surprisingly, only a very few studies have tried to derive stylized facts for the development of key macroeconomic and financial variables in the wake of financial liberalization.[8] Anecdotal evidence, e.g. Drees and Pazarbasioglu (1998) for the Nordic countries and Collyns and Senhadji (2002) for the East Asian countries, suggests that financial liberalization is followed by boom–bust cycles in bank lending, economic activity and asset prices, especially real estate. In order to assess whether this finding also holds on a broader basis of financial liberalization episodes we looked at the development of real GDP, bank lending, property prices and share prices in the wake of financial liberalization for a sample of 16 OECD countries: Australia, Belgium, Denmark, Finland, France, Ireland, Italy, Japan, Korea, New Zealand, Norway, Spain, Sweden, Switzerland, the UK and the US.[9]

Figure 7.2 shows the unweighted country average (solid line) of the development of real GDP growth, the change in real bank lending, the change in real property prices and the change in real share prices (four-quarter growth rates) in the ten years following financial liberalization together with upper and lower

---

[8] Reinhart and Tokatlidis (2001) derive stylized facts for the long-run effects of liberalization for a large sample of developed and developing countries. They analyse the development of key macroeconomic variables, national account aggregates, monetary and credit aggregates, and interest rates before and after dates of financial liberalization in order to assess whether the pre- and post-liberalization mean of each indicator is significantly different. Kaminsky and Schmukler (2003) focus on the effects of financial liberalization on the volatility of stock prices. They find that liberalization leads to more pronounced boom–bust cycles in the short run, but more stable stock markets in the long run.

[9] Financial liberalization dates for the post-Bretton Woods period were identified on the basis of information provided in Abiad and Mody (2003), Kaminsky and Schmukler (2003), Glick and Hutchison (1999) and Drees and Pazarbasioglu (1998). The dates of liberalization for the individual countries are 1985 for Australia, 1986 for Belgium, 1981 for Denmark, 1986 for Finland, 1985 for France, 1981 for Italy, 1985 for Japan, 1988 for Korea, 1985 for New Zealand, 1983 for Norway, 1981 for Spain, 1983 for Sweden, 1989 for Switzerland, 1981 for the UK and 1982 for the US. Note that the date taken for the UK from this literature differs from that specified earlier in §7.2.1, which was 1971. This indicates both that liberalization can proceed through several waves (so there may be several valid dates for a single country), and that such dating inevitably involves some potentially fallible, subjective judgement.

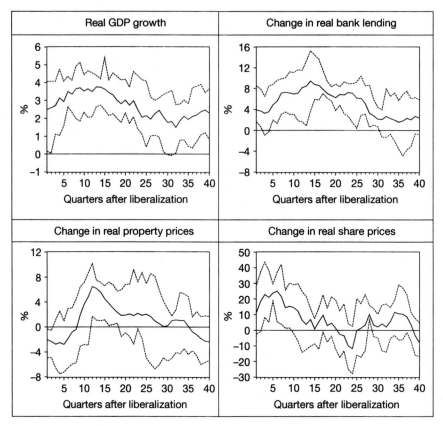

Figure 7.2. Post-liberalization cycles

Note: Solid lines are sample averages; dotted lines are upper and lower quartiles.

quartiles (dotted lines). The figures reveal that, on average, financial liberalization is followed by a boom–bust cycle in economic activity, bank lending and asset prices. Real GDP growth starts to rise immediately after liberalization and peaks after about three years. Then real growth gradually declines and falls below its initial value after about five years. Real lending growth starts to rise about five quarters after the date of liberalization and peaks after about three years. Subsequently, the growth rate of real lending declines and falls below its initial value after about seven years. Property prices start to rise one year following liberalization. The increase in property prices peaks after about three years and then gradually declines. After about six years, property prices start to fall. Real share prices appear to be rising at a brisk pace already at the time of liberalization. After liberalization, the increase in share prices further accelerates and peaks after about six quarters. About five years after liberalization, share prices are falling. Thus, the sample averages appear to support the notion that episodes of financial liberalization are followed by pronounced boom-bust cycles.

The upper and lower quartiles, which are also displayed in Figure 7.2, also reveal, however, that there is substantial variation in the movements of the variables across countries. A look at the individual-country-level data, which we do not discuss here for the sake of brevity,[10] suggests that all countries experienced a cycle after financial liberalization, but that there is substantial variation in the timing of the occurrence of the cycle. This may partly be due, however, to unavoidable imprecision in the exact dating of liberalization episodes.

Why do boom–bust cycles evolve in the wake of financial liberalization? Financial liberalization relaxes the borrowing constraints faced by the private sector and therefore has effects similar to a positive, permanent productivity shock to the economy. In models with credit-constrained borrowers,[11] a positive productivity shock gives rise to a boom–bust cycle in lending, economic activity and asset prices. A positive productivity shock leads to an increase in the value of collateralizable assets. As the borrowing capacity of entrepreneurs depends on the value of their collateralizable assets, this gives rise to higher lending, which in turn further fuels economic activity and asset prices, which again increases borrowing capacity, and so on. Eventually, all variables converge back to their steady-state levels and the boom turns into a bust. The result is a credit cycle *à la* Kiyotaki and Moore (1997). Thus, from the perspective of models with credit constraints, the evolution of a boom–bust cycle in the wake of financial liberalization is fully consistent with theoretical models with credit constraints and a financial accelerator.

Financial liberalization is in fact even likely to be associated with a strengthening of the financial accelerator mechanism and thus to give rise to more pronounced boom–bust cycles. As the liberalization of banking systems has usually been accompanied by liberalizations of capital and stock markets, it has become easier for the largest and safest borrowers of banks to raise funds on the capital and stock market.[12] As a consequence, banks have tried to make good the lost business by beginning to lend to small and medium-sized enterprises and persons. These smaller borrowers have been, in general, somewhat riskier and the costs of monitoring these small borrowers have been higher, so that banks place increasing weight on collateral as a basis for lending. As a result, changes in the value of collateralizable assets, predominantly property, are likely to have a stronger impact on lending after liberalization.

In order to test this hypothesis empirically, we performed rolling regressions for a reduced-form credit-growth equation, where we regressed the change in real

---

[10] Individual-country-level data are available from the authors upon request.

[11] The basic works of this literature are Bernanke and Gertler (1989) and Kiyotaki and Moore (1997).

[12] See Kaminsky and Schmukler (2003) for a cross-country chronology of banking-sector and stock-market liberalizations.

bank lending (Δc) on its own lag, the lagged change in real property prices (Δp), the lagged change in real GDP (Δy) and the lagged change in the ex-post short-term real interest rate (Δr):

$$\Delta C_t = \beta_1 \Delta c_{t-1} + \beta_2 \Delta p_{t-1} + \beta_3 \Delta y_{t-1} + \beta_4 \Delta r_{t-1} + \varepsilon_t \qquad (1)$$

Equation (1) was estimated by OLS for a sample of OECD countries over a rolling window of 15 years with quarterly data. In order to have a first coefficient estimate for a sample period covering mainly the pre-liberalization period, availability of all explanatory variables back to the early 1970s was required. This data requirement reduced the sample of countries for this exercise to ten: Australia, France, Italy, Japan, New Zealand, Norway, Sweden, Switzerland, the UK and the US. The estimated rolling property price coefficients are displayed in Figure 7.3 in a 5% confidence band. The graphs appear to support the hypothesis of an increasing effect of property prices on bank lending. Except for Australia and New Zealand, there is for all countries a clear and significant increase in the rolling property price coefficient over the 1990s. A comparison of the first and the last rolling coefficient estimate makes a clear case. The first property price coefficient estimate of the rolling regression, which corresponds to the sample period covering the pre-liberalization period from the early 1970s to the mid-1980s, is insignificant in all countries. In stark contrast, the last property price coefficient estimate of the rolling regression, which corresponds to the sample period 1987:1 till 2001:4, when domestic banking sectors in all countries under investigation were fully liberalized, is significant to at least the 5% level in seven out of ten countries. The rolling regression results therefore clearly support the view that bank lending has become more sensitive to property price movements in the wake of financial liberalization.

7.3.2 Macroeconomic effects of the Basel Accord

As intended by the BCBS, the introduction of the 1988 Basel Accord was followed by a significant increase in average risk-weighted capital ratios in the G10 countries (see Basel Committee on Banking Supervision 1999). What was not intended was that in many countries, including the US, the introduction of the new CARs in the early 1990s coincided with a recession. The introduction of the 1988 Basel Accord may therefore provide a case in point of the potential macroeconomic effect of procyclical CARs.

Risk-weighted capital ratios can increase by increasing regulatory capital (the numerator) or by reducing risk-weighted assets (the denominator). Figure 7.4 shows the development of regulatory capital, risk-weighted assets and the CAR in

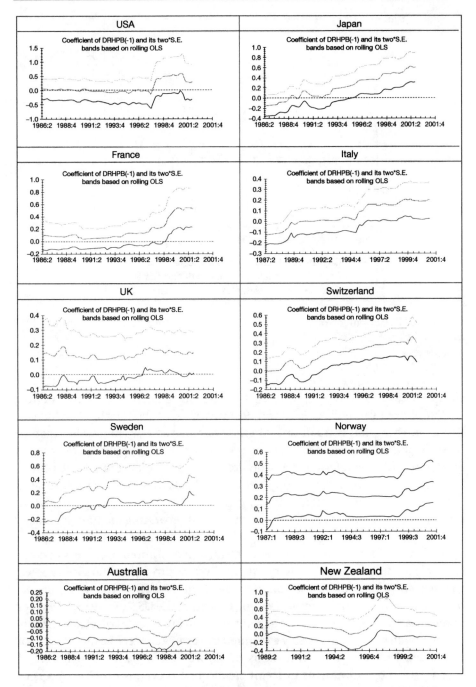

Figure 7.3. Increasing sensitivity of bank lending to property prices, mid-1980s–2001

Note: The graphs report rolling OLS estimates of the property price coefficient in equation (1) over a window of 15 years.

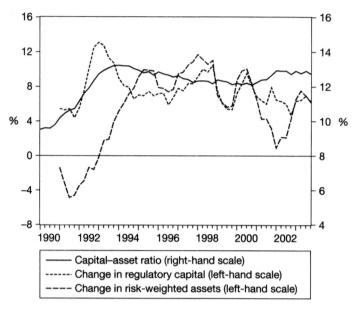

Figure 7.4. Development of capital-to-asset ratio, regulatory capital and risk-weighted assets in the US, 1990–2003

Source: FDIC.

the US since 1990.[13] The graphs reveal that the marked increase of the CAR from 9.5% to above 13% between 1990 and 1993 was brought about by both an increase in regulatory capital and a decrease in risk-weighted assets. This implies that the increase of the CAR may have caused a reduction in the supply of credit to the economy, which is referred to in the literature as a 'credit crunch'. It is often argued that the adverse credit-supply effects of the Basel Accord may have exacerbated the 1990/1 recession. A convincing proof of this hypothesis is still missing, mainly due to the problem with identifying and separating credit demand and credit supply movements.

Movements in real activity influence credit demand and movements in credit supply may influence real activity, which gives rise to a simultaneity problem that has not yet been resolved convincingly. Figure 7.5 shows the development of real GDP growth and nominal lending growth in the US since 1965. The graph reveals that economic activity and credit creation are closely correlated over the cycles, which may be reasonably explained by the effect of economic activity on credit demand. The three recessions of 1974/5, 1980/2 and 1990/1 were all accompanied by slowdowns in credit creation. However, the 1990/1 recession

---

[13] The data were taken from the BIS database. Unfortunately, there was no longer time series available for the US. For other countries, time-series data for risk-adjusted capital ratios and risk-weighted assets, if available at all, do not go back further than the late 1990s.

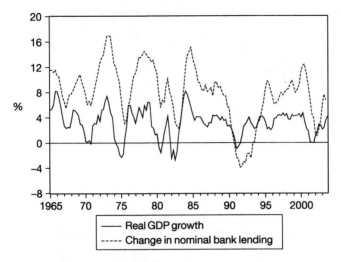

Figure 7.5. Economic activity and credit creation in the US, 1965–2004

was the only case where credit growth turned negative. The downturn in bank lending was therefore stronger than would have been expected from prior experience. This is often taken as evidence that additional adverse supply effects were at work at that time.

Various empirical studies have investigated this question by looking at the significance of credit supply determinants in credit growth regressions (see e.g. Berger and Udell 1994). An alternative strategy, followed e.g. by Walsh and Wilcox (1995), is to take independent movements in the prime lending rate as an indication of changes of credit supply conditions. The prime lending rate (which has never been a market-determined rate) used to be considered the rate at which banks lend to their best corporate customers. In practice, however, the best corporate customers borrow at rates below prime and the prime lending rate is more a benchmark rate used to price loans for smaller firms and for less creditworthy large firms. In the long run, lending rates are set as mark-up over the bank's marginal cost of funds, which in the case of the prime rate is given by the federal funds rate. The mark-up of lending rates over the bank's marginal cost of funds is a function of the additional costs a bank incurs when extending a loan, such as the cost of doing a credit evaluation and, in particular, the cost of raising the capital to meet the capital requirement for the loan. This implies that, given that capital requirements have been tightened by the Basel Accord, the spread of the prime rate over the federal funds rate would be expected to rise, which would be an indication of an adverse supply effect on the credit market. Figure 7.6 shows the development of the prime lending rate and the federal funds rate since 1980. The graph suggests that the spread of the prime rate over the federal funds rate has in fact widened since around 1990/1.

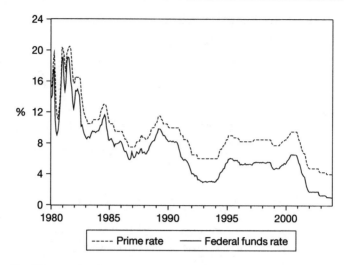

Figure 7.6. The US prime lending rate and the federal funds rate, 1980–2004

The hypothesis of a significantly widening spread of the prime rate over the federal funds rate can be tested more formally based on unit-root tests. Perron (1989) has shown that the presence of breaks in the trend or mean of a time series may give rise to non-rejection of the unit-root hypothesis when not accounted for in unit-root tests. Perron has proposed a consistent testing strategy against breaking trend and means, both for the case of known breakpoints (Perron 1989, 1990) and for the more general case of unknown breakpoints, where the dates of shifts in the mean or the trend are endogenously determined in the testing procedure (Perron 1997).

Table 7.2 shows the result of a standard augmented Dickey–Fuller (ADF) unit-root test (Dickey and Fuller 1981), once allowing for a constant and a trend in the prime rate spread and once allowing only for a constant, and the ADF-type unit-root test allowing for a shift in the mean of the spread at an unknown date, to be determined endogenously by a sequential testing procedure, proposed by Perron (1997). The tests were performed for the spread of the prime lending rate over the federal funds rate using monthly data over the period 1980–2003 taken from the IMF International Financial Statistics. The lag order of the lagged dynamic terms was chosen on the basis of sequential lag-reduction tests starting with a maximum lag order of 12, which suggested retaining the maximum number of 12 lags. In both cases the null of a unit root cannot be rejected. This finding would imply that there is no long-run relationship between the prime rate and the federal funds rate. An alternative interpretation, which is suggested by Figure 7.5, is that there was a shift in the mean of the spread around the time of the introduction of the Basel Accord and that the non-rejection of the unit-root hypothesis merely reflects the failure to take this shift into account in the testing procedure.

Table 7.2. Unit-root tests for the prime lending rate spread

ADF test (constant and trend)	ADF test (constant and no trend)	Perron test (breaking constant)
−2.65	−1.99	−5.03

Note: The 5% critical values are –3.43 for the ADF test with a constant and a trend, −2.87 for the ADF test with a constant but without trend and –4.80 for the Perron test for the innovational outlier model. The endogenously determined breakdate in the Perron test is September 1990.

In order to assess which interpretation is right, we apply Perron's (1997) unit-root test with a break in the mean at an unknown date.[14] The lag order of the lagged dynamic terms was again chosen on the basis of sequential lag-reduction tests starting with a maximum lag order of 12, which suggested retaining ten lags. The break date was endogenously determined by calculating the unit-root test statistic for all possible break dates and then choosing the date that minimizes the unit-root test statistic. The regression results suggest that the mean spread is significantly higher after September 1990. The unit-root test statistic, which is reported in Table 7.2, is given by –5.03, which compares with a 5% critical value of –4.80. Thus, the Perron unit-root test with unknown breakpoint suggests that the spread of the prime rate over the federal funds rate is stationary around a constant mean which breaks in September 1990 and that the mean spread appears to be higher after the break. These results give some indication of potentially lasting supply effects of the introduction of the Basel Accord on the US credit market.

7.3.3 Basel and procyclicality

Under the new Basel Accord (Basel II), two different approaches can be used to measure the riskiness and thus the risk weights of assets, the standardized approach and the internal-rating-based (IRB) approach. The standardized approach is based on external ratings of the credit risk of borrowers, while the IRB approach is based on the banks' internal ratings of their borrowers.

Our procedure here is to try to reconstruct a typical bank portfolio for a country and then, holding the presumed loan book unchanged over time (i.e. replacing failed loans with loans of a similar quality), to examine how the loan ratings would have shifted, and hence how the capital adequacy requirements for the banks would have varied over time under different credit-risk measurement approaches; for other similar exercises see Kashyap and Stein (2004) and Gordy and Howells (2004). To do this we use Moody's data on US corporate bonds, included on Moody's Investors Service, Credit Risk Calculator. We can

[14] Perron terms this model, where only a break in the mean is allowed for, the 'innovational outlier model'. In the second model he proposes, the 'additive outlier model', both the mean and the trend are allowed to break.

only do this exercise for those countries for which Moody's data on credit ratings has a long enough time series. Unfortunately this rules out most large European countries, since adequate Moody's data only goes back to 1988 for the UK, 2001 for Germany, 2002 for France, 2003 for Italy and 2002 for Spain. We used data provided by the Mexican Financial Regulatory Agency and the Norwegian Central Bank on Corporate Loans. The Mexican data incorporate information from 1995 to 2000 and the Norwegian data incorporate information from 1988 to 2001.

This sounds easier to do than it actually is, and a detailed exposition of this exercise has been done separately (Goodhart and Segoviano 2004). Among the problems are how to reconstruct a 'typical' bank portfolio; whether, and how, to deal with the problem of failing loans dropping out of the portfolio; and what consideration to take of the fact that Basel II is a regime change that may make banks alter their 'typical' behaviour. Very briefly, we reconstructed a typical bank portfolio as follows. We assumed that each portfolio consisted of 1,000 loans, each one with equal exposure. From each specific country's data sources, we obtained the *through-time* proportion of assets (bonds for the US or corporate loans for Mexico and Norway) that were classified under each of the reported ratings for a given country. With this information we constructed the *benchmark portfolio* that we used to compute capital requirements at each point in time.

By assuming that the initial bank loan book remains unchanged throughout, this is equivalent to assuming that failed loans are replaced by loans of similar initial quality. This is what Kashyap and Stein (2004) did, and seems natural. Gordy and Howells (2004) argue, however, that banks will aim for a higher-quality portfolio during recessions, and thus will replace failing loans with credits of higher than initial quality. At the macro level, in most countries, it is hard to see where the supply of such higher-quality loans would come from during recessions; in discussion of this point at a BIS conference in May 2004, Michael Gordy noted that in the USA high-quality companies tended to shift their borrowing from capital markets, e.g. the commercial paper market, to banks during recessions. In any case, since risk-spreads widen during recessions, any extra benefit would be slight. So we feel relatively comfortable about this assumption.

The results of this exercise for the three countries examined are stark. We compared the implied capital requirements for our 'typical' bank under three regulatory regimes; first the standardized approach in Basel II (which is close to that applied in Basel I); second, the Foundations IRB approach (i.e. assuming a constant Loss Given Default, since we have no good time series in any country for average LGD); and third, an Improved Credit Risk Method (ICRM). This last uses a Merton approach to model credit quality changes and an indirect approach to model correlations among the individual credits in the overall portfolio. The construction of an ICRM is, however, quite complex, and interested readers should consult our companion paper, Goodhart and Segoviano (2004).

In a nutshell, this latter approach entails deriving the distribution of the possible values that the portfolio of financial assets held by the bank can take. The potential different values that a portfolio could take—and their respective probabilities—are recorded in the so-called profit-and-loss distribution of the portfolio (P&L). For risk management purposes, the Value at Risk measure (VaR), from which economic capital for a bank is defined, is obtained from this distribution. If a bank holds a portfolio of assets, we can then attempt to quantify how the diversification of its assets will affect the value of its portfolio. So, when computing the P&L, the geographical location and industrial activity of the assets held in a portfolio are taken into account. When implementing this approach, we assumed that the benchmark portfolios had loans that were evenly distributed across geographical regions and industrial activities within their respective countries. We then programmed an algorithm that simulated 10,000 different 'quality scenarios' that might affect these portfolios, and so produce a migration of loans between credit-quality bands. Each quality scenario shows a change in the market value of the assets, and therefore the difference between the initial and final credit quality. Once the credit-portfolio quality scenarios were simulated, we computed the losses/gains that come from the difference between initial and final credit qualities. The losses/gains obtained from the simulation process were used to construct a histogram, which summarizes the loss distribution of the credit portfolio. From this distribution a 'value at risk' (VaR) is defined from which we can obtain the amount of unexpected losses from the portfolio. The unexpected losses divided by the total amount of the portfolio represent the percentage that, with a given probability (for example 99.9%), could be lost in an extreme event.

Anyway, we have simulated the time paths of CARs under each of our three approaches—standardized, IRB Foundation (IRB F) and ICRM—for our various countries, and the results are set out in Tables 7.3 to 7.5 and Figures 7.7 to 7.9.

The important result to observe is the much greater variance of the simulated outcomes for the IRB than for the standardized or ICRM approaches. During periods of strong growth, high profits and low NPLs (the USA in the mid-1990s and Norway in 1997), the IRB has a lower CAR than the standardized approach in all our developed countries; whereas in recessions (e.g. USA in 1990/1, Mexico mid-1995/6 and Norway in 1994/5), the CAR is markedly higher for the IRB than in the other two approaches. In Mexico, an emerging market economy (EME), the average quality of loan is lower throughout than in developed countries, so the IRB gives a higher CAR in all years, but, as in developed countries, the variance of the CAR (up in recessions as in 1995/6, and lower during the better years) is greater for the IRB than in the other two approaches.

It follows that the percentage change in the required CAR under the IRB as a country moves from boom to recession (up) and back to boom again (down) will be much more extreme under the IRB than under the other two approaches. This is shown in Table 7.6.

Table 7.3. CARs for the USA, 1982–2003

Period	Standardized	IRB F	ICRM
1982	9.597967	8.591044	8.070189
1983	8.933900	7.185306	6.802057
1984	8.933900	7.624870	7.032411
1985	9.133900	8.024912	7.262765
1986	9.463390	9.989917	8.736384
1987	9.463930	9.824500	8.545390
1988	9.463930	8.659141	6.990717
1989	9.563390	10.804149	6.488127
1990	9.563390	11.677029	7.601025
1991	9.986339	11.434979	7.541649
1992	9.687739	8.064210	6.470195
1993	9.287739	6.468979	4.665018
1994	8.901877	5.395182	3.783256
1995	8.507394	5.561594	4.087216
1996	8.246774	5.646111	4.316443
1997	8.294313	5.940010	4.837646
1998	8.312774	6.508256	5.831926
1999	8.403155	7.810893	6.704727
2000	8.410316	8.126805	7.163834
2001	8.531238	8.245881	7.242604
2002	8.312375	8.180511	6.779526
2003	8.107739	6.603000	6.258685
Average	8.959430	8.016694	6.509627
Variance	0.339964	3.392352	1.945790

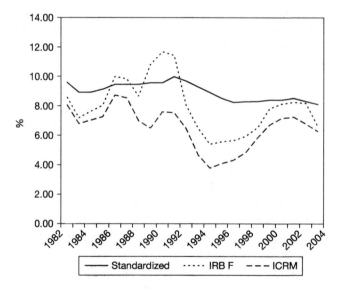

Figure 7.7. CARs for the USA, 1982–2003

The implication of this is that procyclicality may well still be a serious problem with Basel II, even after the smoothing of the risk curves that were introduced between Consultative Papers 2 and 3, produced by the Basel Committee to mitigate this problem. However, there will be other potentially

Table 7.4. CARs for Norway, 1989–2002

Period	Standardized	IRB F	ICRM
1989	9.991635	8.311481	7.580115
1990	10.265155	9.275921	8.127573
1991	10.465155	9.781705	8.675031
1992	10.367155	9.929912	9.034373
1993	10.265155	9.523779	9.186305
1994	10.940239	13.235447	9.821542
1995	11.320031	14.066170	11.082487
1996	10.669155	12.141937	9.722593
1997	10.265155	8.857323	7.317353
1998	10.265155	9.001267	7.422621
1999	10.265155	9.218641	7.527889
2000	10.265430	9.486551	7.930505
2001	10.360916	9.648655	8.333122
2002	10.461360	9.764866	8.343509
Average	10.440489	10.160261	8.578930
Variance	0.113401	2.941614	1.190491

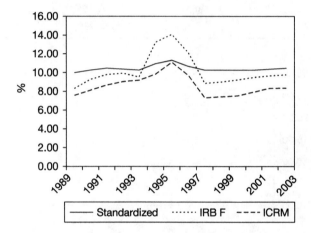

Figure 7.8. CARs for Norway, 1989–2002

offsetting factors. Banks normally keep buffers above the required minimum CARs, both for their protection against sanctions should the minimum be infringed and to satisfy ratings agencies, and these buffers are likely to be raised during booms when IRB CARs may fall to extremely low levels. Note, however, that we have used Moody's data for the USA from 1982 to 2003, for Norway from 1988 to 2001 and for Mexico from 1995 to 2000, which are already supposed to be averaged over the cycle, whereas most commercial banks, so we are told by several of them, are likely to use point-in-time ratings, which could worsen procyclicality yet further.

141

Table 7.5. CARs for Mexico, 1995–1999

Period	Standardized	IRB F	ICRM
March 1995	8.765096	13.864230	10.462123
June 1995	9.221855	16.650790	12.285877
September 1995	9.299730	17.103009	12.714591
December 1995	9.493498	18.151470	12.820000
March 1996	9.251044	17.067542	12.589874
June 1996	9.494958	18.448561	13.248221
September 1996	9.557249	19.415843	14.891864
December 1996	10.303734	24.230942	17.645355
March 1997	9.430354	19.088714	15.153354
June 1997	9.273425	17.500911	13.895955
September 1997	9.396601	18.254201	14.344051
December 1997	8.928781	15.194116	14.796451
March 1998	8.813186	14.397932	13.673818
June 1998	8.851211	14.428160	12.256023
September 1998	9.058278	15.545394	11.622476
December 1998	9.040916	15.456234	11.797630
March 1999	9.052107	15.519282	12.003802
June 1999	8.981783	15.296608	12.251375
September 1999	9.135013	15.979265	12.725803
December 1999	8.968905	15.345409	12.100842
Average	9.215886	16.846931	13.163974
Variance	0.122662	5.644965	2.588205

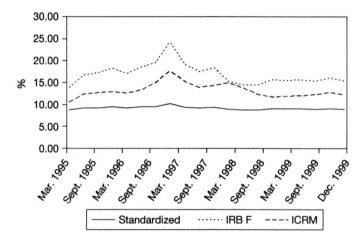

Figure 7.9. CARs for Mexico, 1995–1999

7.4 Conclusions

Over the last two decades, macroeconomic cycles have frequently been associated with boom–bust cycles in bank lending and asset prices, often followed by financial instability. The liberalization of banking sectors since the early to mid-1970s has increased the scope for risk-taking and leverage and thus the procyclicality of

Table 7.6. Maximum percentage change in CARs

A. IRB

	Upwards				Downwards			
	1 period	Date	2 consecutive periods	Dates	1 period	Date	2 consecutive periods	Dates
USA	0.25	1989	0.33	1989/90	−0.29	1992	−0.49	1992/3
Norway	0.39	1994	0.45	1994/5	−0.27	1997	−0.41	1996/7
Mexico	0.25	Dec. 1996	0.30	Sept./Dec. 1996	−0.21	Mar. 1997	−0.30	Mar./June 1997

B. ICRM

	Upwards				Downwards			
	1 period	Date	2 consecutive periods	Dates	1 period	Date	2 consecutive periods	Dates
USA	0.21	1998	0.33	1998/9	−0.28	1993	−0.47	1993/4
Norway	0.13	1995	0.20	1994/5	−0.25	1997	−0.37	1996/8
Mexico	0.18	Dec. 1996	0.30	Sept./Dec. 1996	−0.14	Mar. 1997	−0.22	Mar./June 1997

C. Standardized

	Upwards				Downwards			
	1 period	Date	2 consecutive periods	Dates	1 period	Date	2 consecutive periods	Dates
USA	0.04	June 2005	0.06	1985/6	−0.07	1983	−0.09	1994/5
Norway	0.07	June 2005	0.10	1994/5	−0.06	1997	−0.10	1996/7
Mexico	0.08	Dec. 1996	0.08	Sept./Dec. 1996	−0.08	Mar. 1997	−0.10	Mar./June 1997

the financial system. As we have shown in this chapter, this was reflected in the frequent occurrence of boom–bust cycles in bank lending and asset price and a strengthening of the financial accelerator mechanism by increasing the sensitivity of bank lending to property price fluctuations.

In the face of more frequent financial cycles, regulators have moved to reinforce individual bank capital adequacy ratios, for example through the Basel I and II Accords, in order to mitigate the risk of systemic instability. But bank regulation is itself inherently procyclical; it bites in downturns, but fails to restrain in booms. The more 'sophisticated' and 'risk-sensitive' the regulation, the greater the scope for procyclicality to become a problem, particularly in view of the changing nature of macroeconomic cycles. The simulation exercise performed in this chapter suggests that the new Basel II accord, which deliberately aimed at significantly increasing the risk-sensitiveness of capital requirements, may in fact considerably accentuate the procyclicality of the regulatory system. Since the experience of the past, especially the experience of the US in the recession of 1990/1, which we also discussed in this chapter, suggests that a required hoisting of capital ratios in downturns may be brought about by cutting back lending rather than raising capital, the new capital accord may therefore lead to an amplification of business cycle fluctuations, especially in downturns.

Basel II will be a regime change, and one of the purposes of this is to make bankers more conscious of risk assessment and risk management. It has already succeeded in this. One hope is that it will induce bankers to be more prudent during booms despite declines in CARs. An implication of a move from the standardized to an IRB approach is that the individual bank making this transition will be encouraged to shift its portfolio to higher-quality, higher-rated credits, because it then benefits from a lower CAR. This is good of itself, but the higher the quality of the credit, the steeper is the risk curve (relating quality to required risk ratio); so the procyclicality is likely to be enhanced, even if average quality improves.

When a regime change is introduced, no one in truth can predict its ramifications, certainly not us. Nevertheless these simulations suggest that procyclicality could remain a serious concern. It is even possible that with the advent of a serious downturn, were one to occur, the impact of abiding by the IRB would be too severe for the authorities in some countries to countenance. Perhaps, like the Stability and Growth Pact, it would only be observed in the breach when it began to bite hard. An even greater worry might be that the adoption of Basel II, while not being so adverse as to force reconsideration, might yet exacerbate future capital fluctuations.

Certainly there remains a tension between relating CARs more closely to underlying risks in individual banks, and trying for macroeconomic purposes to encourage contra-cyclical variations in bank lending in aggregate. How to square this circle must, however, be a subject for future research.

8

Default, Credit Growth and Asset Prices

8.1 Introduction

The analytical relationships between financial markets for defaultible financial assets and the real economy remain obscure. This is, perhaps, because the maintained assumption in most macroeconomic theoretical models is that all agents always pay their debts (with probability 1). This then implies that all agents can borrow (lend) an indefinite amount (to maximize their intertemporal utility) at the risk-free rate. So there is consequently no need for financial intermediaries, and there is only one market (for the risk-free asset), where—in such models—the interest rate is, in most cases, set by the reaction function of a central bank, interacting with the expectations of the private sector. Woodford (2003) is the canonical example, in which there are no commercial banks (or any other intermediary), no default and only one financial market.

There are attempts being made to bring default back into mainstream macroeconomic theory, as it should be. Shubik and several of his followers have made a start with developing markets in which the probability of default plays a central note (e.g. Shubik 1973, 1999; Shapley and Shubik 1977; Shubik and Tsomocos 1992; Shubik and Wilson 1997). One of us has been involved in trying to extend and develop the Shubik-type models with the aim of modelling financial fragility in a theoretically rigorous, but empirically tractable form (Goodhart *et al.* 2004a, b, 2005, 2006). Kiyotaki and Moore have also been developing models in which the commitment to repay debt is less then 100% (see Kiyotaki and Moore 2001).

This paucity of theoretical structure has meant that most work in the field of the interaction between financial fragility and real developments (apart from the transmission mechanism via the riskless real interest rate) has been via empirically driven studies. This chapter follows this emprical tradition.

Although some proponents of real business cycle theories argue that real factors, e.g. technological advances, are vastly more important than financial factors, it is hard to look at current developments (Japan since 1985, the Scandinavian boom–bust of the early 1990s, the East Asian crisis of 1997/8, the dot.com bubble, the widespread housing price cycles in evidence today) without believing in the importance of primarily financial factors. Apart, perhaps, from the years 1939–70, when financial freedom was widely repressed, the same has been true historically.

How then should one approach an empirical study of the interaction between financial developments and the real economy? No doubt there are many possibilities. One common starting point has been event studies, notably the event of a financial crisis. This has been very fruitful, notably in many World Bank studies (e.g. Demirgüç-Kunt and Detriagiache 1998, 1999; see also Kaminsky and Reinhart 1999, and Demirgüç-Kunt and Detriagiache 2005 for a recent survey).

But this approach inevitably has certain drawbacks. The exact timing, duration and intensity of a crisis are all measured with uncertainty. Often crises may be averted by preventative prior action; does the study of cases where crises were not averted, but the lack of attention when they were, lead to bias? Study of crisis on its own leads to putting aside the evidence from non-crisis years.

Perhaps the main innovation in this chapter is that we replace crisis events as the main dependent variable by a Merton-type estimate of the probability of default (PoD) of the main banks in each of our sample of countries. As with any empirical approach, this has several deficiencies. In particular, the resultant series, in our view, appear to be too sensitive to factors that affect the aggregate level and variance of the equity market rather than the particular robustness (or fragility) of the banking system. Thus the decline and enhanced volatility of the overall national stock markets, after the collapse of the dot.com bubble in the early 2000s, suggests on this measure a degree of fragility among national banking systems that in many cases (e.g. the UK, Spain, Netherlands) we doubt was really there. For such reasons, we feel that sectoral and company-level estimates of PoDs need to be further enhanced, in order to distinguish nation-wide, sectoral and idiosyncratic influences (via some form of decomposition, which has yet to be done).

Any primarily empirical exercise runs into the difficulty that there is a legion of factors which might influence the variable under consideration (in this case the PoD of the main banks in each country). How does one limit the range of variables, and all their transforms? Inevitably one leans on a combination of theory, stylized facts from the prior literature and one's own earlier work.

Earlier work, notably Goodhart, Hofmann and Segoviano (2004), Goodhart and Segoviano (2004) and Segoviano and Lowe (2002), has indicated the close relationship between asset price fluctuations in the property market (residential and commercial), bank lending to the private sector, and the real economy. On our evidence, the property market is a far more important driver of both banking robustness and—in some part, via the banking system—of the economy than are equity markets, or even—in a surprisingly large number of cases—the foreign exchange market (see in particular Goodhart and Hofmann 2000b, 2005a).

Of course, the interactions between bank credit extension and the property market are two-way. Most prior studies have only considered unidimensional effects. In §8.2 we present some new cross-country and panel evidence of the two-way interactions between the property market, bank lending to the private sector and the real economy.

The institution which has done much of the work on the interaction between asset prices, bank lending and the real economy has been the Bank for International Settlements (BIS), notably in papers by Claudio Borio and his various co-authors (e.g. Borio *et al.* 1994 and Borio and Lowe 2002). What they have typically found is that surges in the ratio of bank lending to GDP are a common indicator of subsequent financial crises. Again, so long as property prices are given due weight, booms in asset prices also generally tend to be followed by busts which impinge on the banking system and the real economy.

Segoviano (2006) has independently analysed these statistical relationships as well. There he confirmed that these two variables did commonly affect banking sector PoDs, and that the relationship was clearer when the variables were entered as a deviation from trend rather than in first-difference form. Thus, building on this prior work, we re-examine in §8.3 the effects of these two main financial variables on banking sector PoDs for a much wider range of countries. One of the problems here is that not only is the lag structure between such developments and banking PoDs quite long (which may be a boon for the authorities' prudential management), but also the lags seem to vary quite widely from country to country.

Besides specifically financial developments, bank PoDs are obviously affected by fluctuations in the real economy. Borrowers fail to repay their debts to the banks (e.g. non-performing loans) in bad times, and asset prices fall. So banks tend to do worse, and have higher PoDs, in cyclical downturns. Consequently, in addition to the financial variables, an assortment of real variables needs to be examined as potential indicators of financial fragility in the shape of bank PoDs.

Given that prior work has suggested a range of leading candidates as variables affecting bank PoDs, we begin by examining the lag structure of their bilateral (correlation) relationship in each country, to allow us, among other things, to see whether we might be able to identify a common lag structure, and thereby run a cross-country, time-series panel exercise, rather than just doing a time-series regression for each country separately.

The results in this section extend and support earlier work, both by Borio and his set of co-authors, and by us, that these two financial variables, i.e. the deviation of bank lending, and of asset prices, from their trend relationship with GDP, have been able to improve prediction of bank PoDs.

8.2   Bank credit and property prices

The coincidence of cycles in credit and property markets has been widely documented and discussed in the policy-oriented literature (IMF 2000; BIS 2001a).

However, the question of the direction of causality between bank lending and property prices has remained a rather unexplored issue. From a theoretical point of view, causality may go in both directions. Property prices may affect bank lending via various wealth effects. First, due to financial market imperfections, households and firms may be borrowing-constrained. As a result, households and firms can only borrow when they offer collateral, so that their borrowing capacity is a function of their collateralizable net worth. Since property is commonly used as collateral, property prices are therefore an important determinant of the private sector's borrowing capacity. Second, a change in property prices may have a significant effect on consumers' perceived lifetime wealth,[1] inducing them to change their spending and borrowing plans and thus their credit demand in order to smooth consumption over the life cycle.[2] Finally, property prices affect the value of bank capital, both directly to the extent that banks own assets, and indirectly by affecting the value of loans secured by property.[3] Property prices therefore influence the risk-taking capacity of banks and thus their willingness to extend loans.

On the other hand, bank lending may affect property prices via various liquidity effects. The price of property can be seen as an asset price, which is determined by the discounted future stream of property returns. An increase in the availability of credit may lower interest rates and stimulate current and future expected economic activity. As a result, property prices may rise because of higher expected returns on property and a lower discount factor. Property can also be seen as a durable good in temporarily fixed supply. An increase in the availability of credit may increase the demand for housing if households are borrowing-constrained. With supply temporarily fixed because of the time it takes to construct new housing units, this increase in demand will be reflected in higher property prices.

This potential two-way causality between bank lending and property prices may give rise to mutually reinforcing cycles in credit and property markets.[4] A rise in property prices, caused by more optimistic expectations about future economic prospects, raises the borrowing capacity of firms and households by increasing the value of collateral. Part of the additional available credit may also be used to purchase property, pushing up property prices even further, so that a self-reinforcing process may evolve.

[1] Data on the composition of household wealth, reported in OECD (2000), show that households hold a large share of their wealth in property.

[2] The lifecycle model of household consumption was originally developed by Ando and Modigliani (1963). A formal exposition of the life-cycle model can be found in Deaton (1992) and Muellbauer (1994).

[3] Chen (2001) develops an extension of the Kiyotaki and Moore (1997) model in which an additional amplification of business cycles results from the effect of asset price movements on banks' balance sheets. An early version of this argument is Keynes (1931).

[4] The possibility of mutually reinforcing cycles in credit and asset markets was already stressed by Kindleberger (1978) and Minsky (1982).

Little empirical research has been done on the relationship between credit and asset prices. Most studies rely on a single-equation set-up, focusing either on bank lending or property prices. Goodhart (1995) finds that property prices significantly affect credit growth in the UK but not in the US. Hilbers, Lei and Zacho (2001) find that the change in residential property prices significantly enters multivariate probit-logit models of financial crisis in industrialized and developing countries. Borio and Lowe (2002) show that a measure of the aggregate asset price gap, measured as the deviation of aggregate asset prices from their long-run trend, combined with a similarly defined credit gap measure, is a useful indicator of financial distress in industrialized countries.

Borio, Kennedy and Prowse (1994) investigate the relationship between credit-to-GDP ratios and aggregate asset prices for a large sample of industrialized countries over the period 1970–92 using annual data. They focus on the determinants of aggregate asset price fluctuations, hypothesizing that the development of credit conditions as measured by the credit-to-GDP ratio can help to explain the evolution of aggregate asset prices. They find that adding the credit-to-GDP ratio to an asset pricing equation helps to improve the fit of this equation in most countries. On the basis of simulations, they demonstrate that the boom–bust cycle in asset markets of the late 1980s to early 1990s would have been much less pronounced or would not have occurred at all had credit ratios remained constant. For a panel of four East Asian countries (Hong Kong, Korea, Singapore and Thailand), Collyns and Senhadji (2002) find that credit growth has a significant contemporaneous effect on residential property prices. On the strength of this finding, they conclude that bank lending contributed significantly to the real estate bubble in Asia prior to the 1997 East Asian crisis. Hofmann (2004, which is Chapter 6 of this book) and Gerlach and Peng (2005) analyse the relationship between bank lending and property prices using a multivariate empirical framework and find that long-run and short-run causality goes from property prices to lending, rather than conversely.

In the following section we analyse the relationship between real aggregate bank lending, real GDP as a measure of aggregate economic activity, real residential property prices and real money market interest rates in 18 industrialized countries: Australia, Belgium, Canada, Denmark, Finland, France, Germany, Ireland, Italy, Japan, the Netherlands, New Zealand, Norway, Spain, Sweden, Switzerland, the UK and the US. The data for the industrialized countries were taken from the IMF International Statistics and the OECD Economic Outlook database. Residential property prices and an aggregate asset price index, which is calculated as a weighted average of equity prices and residential and commercial property prices, were obtained from the BIS. All data except for the nominal interest rate are seasonally adjusted.

Bank lending, which was transformed into real terms by the GDP deflator, is defined as total credit to the private non-bank sector. It should be noted that cross-country comparisons of the development of bank lending are flawed by differences in the definition of total credit across countries. These differences in definition will be reflected in the results of the empirical analysis. Differences exist, for example, with respect to the treatment of non-performing loans (NPLs) in national credit aggregates. A drop in property prices will on the one hand have a negative effect on the extension of new loans. On the other hand it will give rise to an increase in NPLs. The estimated effect of property prices on bank lending will therefore depend on whether or not banks are forced to write off NPLs quickly. For instance, Japan and the Nordic countries experienced severe banking crises in the late 1980s or early 1990s, which were preceded by a collapse in property prices.[5] While NPLs were quite quickly cleansed from banks' balance sheets in the Nordic countries, this was not the case in Japan.[6]

Quarterly residential property price indices were available for all countries except Japan, Italy and Germany. For Japan and Italy, semi-annual indices were transformed to quarterly frequency by linear interpolation. For Germany, a quarterly series was generated by linear interpolation of annual data. In order to obtain a measure of real property prices, nominal property prices were deflated with the GDP deflator. We also consider aggregate asset price indices from the BIS in the empirical analysis, as our measure of bank credit includes bank lending to both households and enterprises, so that residential property prices alone may not fully capture the property price developments which are relevant for aggregate bank lending.

The short-term real interest rate is measured as the three-month interbank money market rate less four-quarter CPI inflation. The short-term real money market rate serves as a proxy for real aggregate financing costs. A more accurate measure would be an aggregate lending rate. Representative lending rates are not available, however, for most countries. Empirical evidence suggests that lending rates are tied to money market rates at least in the long run,[7] so that money market rates may serve as a crude approximation of financing costs.

In the following exercise we use a multivariate modelling approach in order to analyse the relationship between bank lending and house and aggregate asset prices based on the VAR model:

$$x_t = A_1 x_{t-1} + \cdots + A_n x_{t-n} + \mu + \delta t + \varepsilon_t$$

where x is a vector containing the log of the real GDP, the log of real domestic credit to the private sector, the log of real residential property prices, each

---

[5] Drees and Pazarbasioglu (1998) provide a survey on the causes and consequences of the banking crises in the Nordic countries. The literature on the Japanese crisis is of course enormous. See Hoshi and Kashyap (1999) for a recent survey and the references therein.

[6] For a more detailed discussion of this issue see BIS (2001b).

[7] See e.g. Borio and Fritz (1995), Hofmann and Mizen (2004) and Hofmann (forthcoming).

multiplied by 100, and the short-term ex-post real interest rate. *t* is a deterministic time trend. The lag order *n* was in each case determined by consulting sequential likelihood ratio tests and information criteria (Akaike, Schwarz–Bayes). We do not perform an explicit analysis of any potential long-run relationships because of the relatively short sample period and large number of endogenous variables. By doing the analysis in levels we allow, however, for implicit cointegrating relationships in the data.

In order to avoid imposing any untested and questionable restrictions which may bias the results in favour of or against finding causality in one or another direction we adopt a fully astructural approach and simulate one-unit shocks to the reduced-form residuals of the VAR. As our focus is on the dynamic interaction of credit and asset prices we report in Figure 8.1 the impulse responses of credit to asset price shocks and of asset prices to credit shocks in a two-standard-error confidence band. It should be recalled that the VARs were estimated separately, once including the aggregate asset price indices from the BIS (Model 1) and once including a residential property or house price index (Model 2). Our prior considerations suggest that an increase in property or aggregate asset prices should lead to a significant increase in bank credit and that an increase in bank credit might in turn lead to a significant increase in aggregate asset and property prices. The results of the impulse response analysis are summarized in Table 8.1, where we report respectively the number of positive responses and the number of significantly positive impulse responses of each variable. The findings suggest that there is significant positive two-way causality between aggregate asset and property prices and credit. However, only in slightly more than half of the countries do we find the effect of house price or aggregate asset price shocks on bank lending to be statistically significant. On the other hand, in slightly less than half of the countries we also find a significantly positive effect of credit shocks on house prices and aggregate asset prices.

This relatively low number of statistically significant impulse responses might be due to the low power of the significance test as a result of the rather short sample period in combination with the sometimes rather long lag lengths that were chosen on the basis of the lag selection tests. As a tentative attempt to increase the power of the analysis we exploit the rather large cross-section dimension of our country sample and repeat the impulse response analysis based on a fixed-effects panel VAR estimated over the same sample period. The panel VAR was also estimated separately, once including the aggregate asset price indices (Model 1) and once including the house price indices (Model 2). In both cases the lag order was again selected by consulting likelihood ratio tests and various information criteria, which in most cases suggested a lag order of 12, consistent with the long lag orders that were chosen in the individual country VARs.

Figures 8.2 and 8.3 report impulse responses from the panel VARs in two-standard-error bands. Besides the dynamic interaction between bank credit and

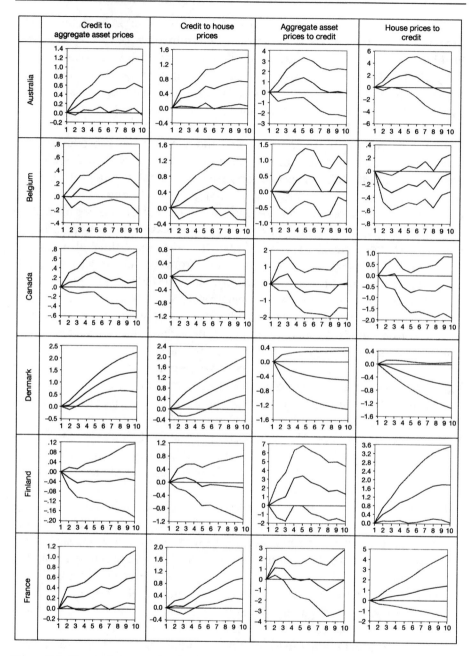

Figure 8.1. Dynamic interaction between credit and asset prices

Note: The graphs display impulse responses to a non-factorized one-unit shock in a two-standard-error confidence band. The deviation from the baseline scenario of no shocks is on the vertical axis; the periods after the shock are on the horizontal axis.

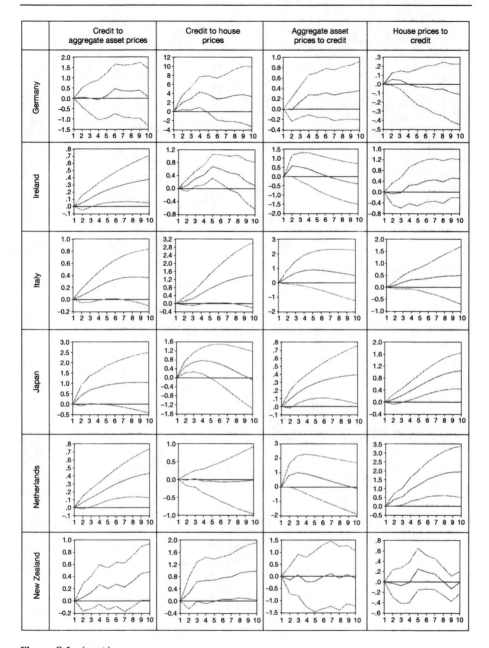

Figure 8.1. (*cont.*)

asset prices, we also investigate the dynamic effects of GDP and the real interest rate on bank credit and asset prices as well as the dynamic effects of increases in asset prices, bank credit and real interest rates on real GDP. Again, we do not venture to impose any restrictions on the contemporaneous interaction of the

153

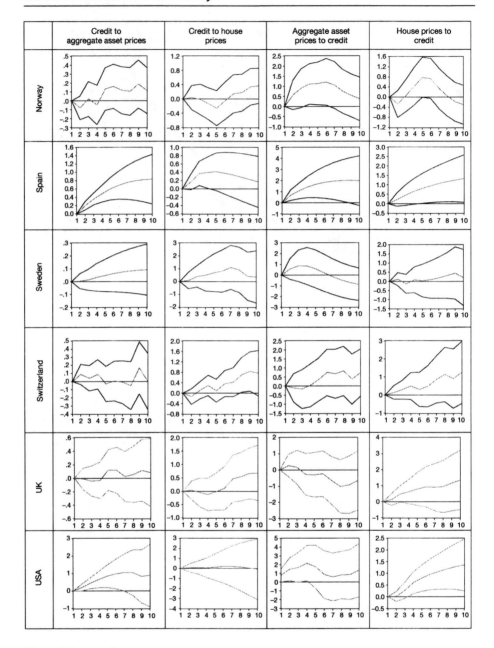

Figure 8.1. (*cont.*)

variables and instead simulate non-factorized one-unit shocks of the residuals of the reduced-form VAR equations. On the whole, the results confirm the findings from the individual-country VARs of a significant two-way relationship between credit and asset prices. Bank credit significantly increases after an

Table 8.1. Summary of impulse response analysis for credit and asset prices

	Model 1 (aggregate asset prices)		Model 2 (house prices)	
	Asset prices ↓ Bank credit	Bank credit ↓ Asset prices	House prices ↓ Bank credit	Bank credit ↓ House prices
Positive responses	17	15	14	13
Significant responses	10	8	11	7

Fixed-effects panel VAR: Model 1 (aggregate asset prices)

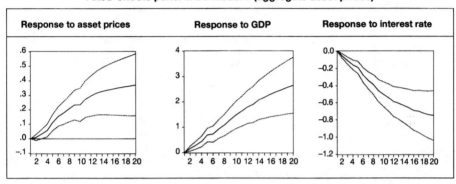

Fixed-effects panel VAR: Model 2 (house prices)

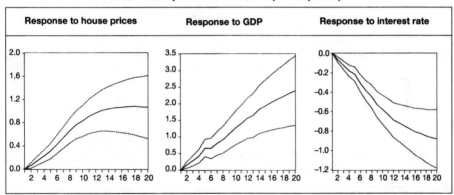

Figure 8.2. Credit dynamics

Note: The graphs display impulse responses to a non-factorized one-unit shock in a two-standard-error confidence band. The deviation from the baseline scenario of no shocks is on the vertical axis; the periods after the shock are on the horizontal axis.

increase in both aggregate asset prices and residential property prices (Figure 8.2), while both asset price variables give a significant positive response to an increase in bank credit (Figure 8.3). The impulse responses also reveal that an increase in real GDP has a strong and significant positive effect on bank credit (Figure 8.2)

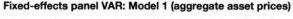

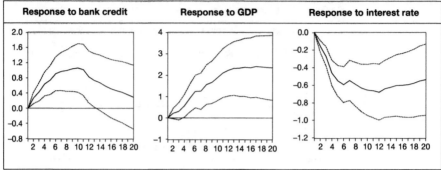

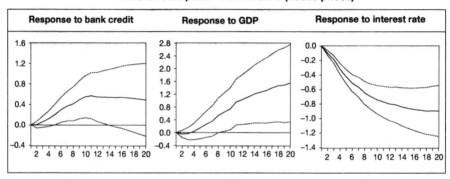

Figure 8.3. Asset price dynamics

Note: The graphs display impulse responses to a non-factorized one-unit shock in a two-standard-error confidence band. The deviation from the baseline scenario of no shocks is on the vertical axis; the periods after the shock are on the horizontal axis.

and asset prices (Figure 8.3). Real GDP (Figure 8.4), in turn, displays a significantly positive response to increases in bank credit and asset prices, suggesting that there might even be a mutually reinforcing relationship involving bank credit, asset prices and economic activity. Finally, the impulse responses suggest that an increase in real interest rates leads to a significant decline in bank credit, asset prices and real GDP.

8.3 Default, credit growth and asset prices

In this section we analyse the interaction between default, credit growth and asset prices in 17 developed and developing countries: Argentina, Canada, Denmark, Finland, France, Germany, Italy, Japan, Korea, Mexico, the Netherlands, Norway, Spain, Sweden, Thailand, the UK and the US. The data were taken from the IMF

Fixed-effects panel VAR: Model 1 (aggregate asset prices)

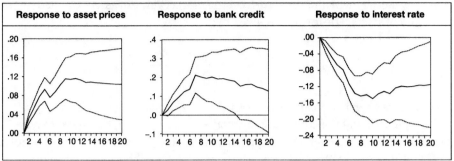

Fixed-effects panel VAR: Model 2 (house prices)

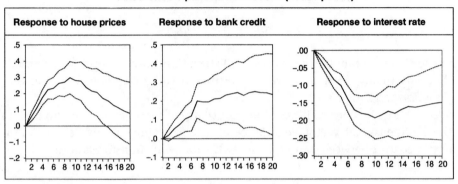

Figure 8.4. GDP dynamics

Note: The graphs display impulse responses to a non-factorized one-unit shock in a two-standard-error confidence band. The deviation from the baseline scenario of no shocks is on the vertical axis; the periods after the shock are on the horizontal axis.

International Statistics and the OECD Economic Outlook database. The aggregate asset price indices, which are calculated as weighted averages of equity prices and residential and commercial property prices, were obtained from the BIS. All data except for the nominal interest rate are seasonally adjusted.

The dependent variable that is used in this section is a transformation of the distance-to-default (DD) indicator reported in the Financial Systems Trends (FST), which is prepared by the Monetary and Financial Systems Department of the Financial Surveillance Policy Division in the IMF. The DD indicator is used in the FST to gauge banking sector soundness. The variables to calculate the DD indicator are obtained from information contained in bank equity prices and balance sheets of some of the largest financial institutions for each country under analysis. In a standard valuation model, the distance to default, DD, is determined by: (a) the market value of a firm's assets, V_A; (b) the uncertainty or volatility of the asset value (risk), σ_A; and (c) the degree of leverage or the extent of the firm's contractual liabilities, measured as the book value of liabilities at time t, D_t (with maturity T).

The DD indicator is computed as the sum of the ratio of the estimated current value of assets to debt and the return on the market value of assets, divided by the volatility of assets. The formula is given by:

$$DD_t = \frac{\ln(V_{A,t}/D_t) + (\mu - (1/2)\,\sigma_A^2)T}{\sigma_A^2\sqrt{T}}$$

where μ measures the mean growth of V_A.

Using market data of equity and annual accounting data, the market value V_A and the volatility of assets σ_A are typically estimated using the Black and Scholes (1973) and Merton (1974) options pricing model. Once the DD is computed, the theoretical probability of default (PoD) is obtained as:

$$PoD_t = N(-DD_t)$$

where N is the cumulative probability distribution function (*cdf*) for a variable that is normally distributed with a mean zero and a standard deviation of 1 (Vassalou and Xing 2002).

The theoretical probabilities of default (PoD_t) at each period t are grouped in the T-dimensional vector PoD. Since each observation in the vector PoD is restricted to lie between 0 and 1, we make the following transformation:

$$Y = N^{-1}(PoD) + 5$$

where N^{-1} is the inverse standard normal *cdf*. We are interested on modelling the PoD as a function of identifiable macroeconomic and financial developments X. We formalize the relationship as

$$Y = XB + e$$

An alternative way to look at this issue is to assume that defaults reflect an underlying, continuous credit change indicator ('normal equivalent deviate' in the language of probit analysis) that has a standard normal distribution. Thus, we can state the relationship as

$$PoD = N(XB + e)$$

where the inverse normal *cdf* transformation converts this equation to a linear problem $Y = XB + e$.

We selected an initial set of explanatory macroeconomic and financial variables that, according to theory and empirical evidence, are likely to affect banks' credit risk. In order to explore the explanatory variables' information content, we computed their fluctuations with respect to a long-term trend, which we denominate 'gaps'. With the obtained gaps, we ran multivariate OLS regressions to identify the specifications that are consistent with economic theory and empirical evidence and that show the best goodness of fit.

Among the theoretical arguments that can be used as a basis to select the initial set of explanatory variables, we find theoretical models with credit constraints and a financial accelerator (Kiyotaki and Moore 1997). The relevant economic theory also includes second-generation models in the currency crisis literature, which stress the role of self-fulfilling expectations and herding behaviour in determining the intensity of the cycles; models which note that under current financially liberalized systems, the scope for risk-taking is increased; and theories that call attention to the creation of perverse mechanisms, such as moral hazard lending and carry trades, that can exacerbate banking and currency crises.[8]

There is a growing empirical literature emphasizing the information content of certain variables. For example, it has been observed that financial liberalization often precedes banking crises. So, variables associated with financial liberalization merit scrutiny. Real aggregate credit in the economy, the ratio of credit to GDP, M2 balances, real interest rates and the ratio of M2 to foreign exchange reserves were considered. Pill and Pradhan (1995), Kaminsky and Reinhart (1999), Eichengreen and Areta (2000) and Borio and Lowe (2002) have reported that real aggregate credit in the economy and the ratio of credit to GDP are important indicators of banking problems. McKinnon and Pill (1996) have reported rapid increases in monetary aggregates linked to banking crises. Galbis (1993) reports that real interest rates have increased after financial liberalization.

The ratio of M2 to foreign exchange reserves may capture the extent to which the liabilities of the banking system are backed by international reserves. In the event of a currency crisis, individuals may rush to convert their domestic currency deposits into foreign currency, so this ratio could capture the ability of the central bank to meet those demands (Calvo and Mendoza 1996). Currency crises may take place after a period of large inflows of foreign short-term capital. Such inflows, usually driven by the combined effect of capital account liberalization and high domestic interest rates, result in an expansion of domestic credit (Khamis 1996). When foreign interest rates rise, domestic ones fall, or when confidence in the economy shifts, foreign investors quickly withdraw their funds and the domestic banking system may become illiquid (Calvo, Leiderman and Reinhart 1993).

We included the current account balance, since this variable indicates the amount of foreign investment needed in the economy and is therefore a variable that could signal the vulnerability of the economy to shifts in investors' confidence. Consumption and investment were also included, since these variables can indicate the uses of funding in the economy and can therefore shape investors' expectations of the capacity of the economy to produce growth

---

[8] See Obstfeld (1995), Calvo (1998) and Flood and Marion (1999) for the first, Allen and Gale (1998) for the second, and Garber and Lall (1996) and Dooley (1997) for the third.

opportunities in the future. Foreign Direct Investment was also included as a measure of the vulnerability of the economy to foreign capital (Sturm, Berger and Haan 2004).[9]

To capture adverse macroeconomic shocks that hurt banks by increasing the share of non-performing loans, we considered changes in real GDP. Equity price, residential property price and aggregate asset price indices were also included,[10] a decision which was motivated by the findings of Borio and Lowe (2002) and Goodhart, Hofmann and Segoviano (2004).[11]

The realized volatility of short-term interest rates was also considered, since this variable can affect banks' balance sheets adversely, if they fail to hedge or to predict the change. Volatile rates and uncertainty affect cash-flow planning and high lending rates result in a larger fraction of non-performing loans (Mishkin 1997).[12] The difference between long and short nominal rates was included as a variable that could indicate market expectations on growth.

Another case of rate-of-return mismatch occurs when banks borrow in a foreign currency and lend in a domestic currency. In this case, an unexpected depreciation of the domestic currency threatens bank profitability and eventually solvency. Banks that raise funds abroad might choose to issue domestic loans denominated in foreign currency, thus eliminating currency mismatches. In this case, foreign exchange risk is shifted onto borrowers, and an unexpected depreciation would still affect bank profitability negatively through an increase in non-performing loans. We have therefore included the nominal foreign exchange rate. Foreign currency loans were a source of banking problems in the Nordic countries in the early 1990s (Drees and Pazarbasioglu 1998) and in Mexico (Mishkin 1997). A real foreign exchange rate index was also included.[13]

Table 8.2 specifies the variables that were analysed, the abbreviation that we used to identify them and their sources.[14]

---

[9] Sturm, Berger and Haan (2004) find that the ratio of investment to GDP is robustly related to the probability that a country receives IMF credit. A low ratio of investment to GDP may indicate limited access to international capital markets. Knight and Santaella (1997) and Vreeland (1999) also provide support for this view.

[10] The aggregate asset price index combines prices of three asset classes: equity, residential property and commercial property. It weights the components by estimates of the shares of the asset classes in private sector wealth. The methodology is described in detail in Borio *et al.* (1994). We thank Claudio Borio for providing us with the aggregate asset price index series.

[11] Note that, as already mentioned, an alternative explanation of the causes and effects of increases in asset prices is provided by the literature on the agency problem of excessive risk-taking associated with limited liability. See Allen and Gale (1999).

[12] See also IMF (2003) for empirical evidence linking financial market volatility and financial system instability.

[13] An increase in the real exchange rate index implies depreciation.

[14] Of course, this is not an exhaustive list of potential variables. In particular, political variables can also be linked to financial stability. Variables capturing the effectiveness of

Table 8.2. Initial set of explanatory variables

Abbreviation	Variable	Source
REPROPRI	Residential property prices	National sources as per detailed documentation and BIS calculations based on national data
SHAPRI	Share price index	IMF International Financial Statistics
AGGASPRI	Aggregate asset price index	National sources as per detailed documentation and BIS calculations based on national data
NEER	Nominal exchange rate	IMF International Financial Statistics
M2	M2 monetary aggregate	IMF International Financial Statistics
REER	Real exchange rate	IMF International Financial Statistics
RESER	International reserves	IMF International Financial Statistics
REINT	Real interest rates	IMF International Financial Statistics
SHINT	Short interest rates	IMF International Financial Statistics
LINT	Long interest rates	IMF International Financial Statistics
MTG	Mortgage bond interest rates	National sources
REGDP	Real GDP	IMF International Financial Statistics and OECD
RECRE	Real aggregate credit	IMF International Financial Statistics and OECD
CON	Consumption aggregate	IMF International Financial Statistics
CA	Current account balance	IMF International Financial Statistics
FDI	Foreign direct investment	IMF International Financial Statistics
REINVE	Investment aggregate	IMF International Financial Statistics
RECON	Real consumption	Authors' calculations based on national data
CREOVGDP	Ratio of aggregate credit in the financial system to GDP	Authors' calculations based on national data
INVOVGDP	Ratio of investment to GDP	Authors' calculations based on national data
CONOVGDP	Ratio of consumption to GDP	Authors' calculations based on national data
RECUAOVREINV	Ratio of real current account to real investment	Authors' calculations based on national data
M2OVRES	Ratio of M2 to international reserves	Authors' calculations based on national data
LOMISH	Difference of long and short interest rates	Authors' calculations based on national data
INREVO	Realized volatility of money market rates	Authors' calculations based on national data

Our aim in this exercise is to analyse combinations of fluctuations in different macroeconomic and financial variables as possible causes of increases in financial risk. We compute fluctuations in these variables using only information that would have been available to the analyst up to the time when the analysis was done. These fluctuations are computed with respect to a long-term trend. When computing movements with respect to a long-term trend, we are interested in

the legal system have also been found to be significant in explaining banking sector problems. Variables reflecting exogenous events can also explain specific crises. None of these are considered here. For the effect of political variables see Mishra (1997). For the effect of legal structures see Akerlof and Romer (1993).

capturing the explanatory power of cumulative processes, rather than growth rates over just one period. The reasoning behind this approach is that vulnerabilities may build up over an extended period, rather than in a single period. We refer to these movements with respect to long-term trends as 'gaps'.

In order to estimate the long-term trend, we employ a 'dynamic' Hodrick–Prescott (HP) filter using information from 1970. This procedure is illustrated in Table 8.3.

For example, let us assume that we were currently at t_3 and we wanted to estimate the gap for a given variable at time t_3 (contemporaneous gap). First, using an HP filter, we would include information from 1970 up until t_3 to compute the trend component (the superscript in the HP trend component, e.g. HTDVariable^3). Second, we would obtain the difference between the value of the variable at t_3 (the subscript in the variable component, e.g. Variable$_3$) and the value of the trend component at t_3 (the subscript in the trend component, e.g. HTDVariable$_3$); therefore

$$\text{GapVariable}_3 = \text{Variable}_3 - \text{HTDVariable}_3^3$$

Note that we only use information up to the period that we analyse, e.g. t_3, because at t_3 an analyst would only have information up to this date.

In order to estimate lags for the gaps we followed a similar procedure. Suppose we were at t_3 and we wanted to estimate the credit gap, lagged one period. First, using an HP filter, we would include information from 1970 up until t_3 to compute the trend component (the superscript in the HP trend component, e.g. HTDVariable^3). However, now in the second step, we would obtain the difference between the value of the variable at t_2 (lagged one period, e.g. the subscript in the variable component, e.g. Variable$_2$) and the value of the trend component at t_2 (lagged one period, e.g. the subscript in the trend component, e.g. HTDVariable$_2$); therefore

$$\text{GapVariable} (-1)_3 = \text{Variable}_2 - \text{HTDVariable}_2^3$$

This procedure was repeated for all the included lags.

Table 8.3. Dynamic HP filtering

Period	Contemporaneous	Lag1 (-1)
t_1	$\text{GapVariable}_1 = \text{Variable}_1 - \text{HTDVariable}_1^1$	$\text{GapVariable}(-1)_1 = \text{Variable}_0 - \text{HTDVariable}_0^1$
t_2	$\text{GapVariable}_2 = \text{Variable}_2 - \text{HTDVariable}_2^2$	$\text{GapVariable}(-1)_2 = \text{Variable}_1 - \text{HTDVariable}_1^2$
t_3	$\text{GapVariable}_3 = \text{Variable}_3 - \text{HTDVariable}_3^3$	$\text{GapVariable}(-1)_3 = \text{Variable}_2 - \text{HTDVariable}_2^3$
t_4	$\text{GapVariable}_4 = \text{Variable}_4 - \text{HTDVariable}_4^4$	$\text{GapVariable}(-1)_4 = \text{Variable}_3 - \text{HTDVariable}_3^4$
t_5	$\text{GapVariable}_5 = \text{Variable}_5 - \text{HTDVariable}_5^5$	$\text{GapVariable}(-1)_5 = \text{Variable}_4 - \text{HTDVariable}_4^3$

Notes: HTD is the HP trend component; subscripts refer to the time of the observation; superscripts refer to the information set included.

Note that we do not consider the long-term trend from which the gaps are defined as 'fundamental values'. This distinction highlights a key issue, especially in the case of price variables, since we do not try to identify asset price bubbles. An asset price bubble can be characterized by a significant overpricing of an asset from its 'fundamental value'. There is no attempt in this paper to assess 'fundamental values' and measure price deviations from them. For the purposes of this exercise, the more relevant issue is to assess the combination of events that has the potential to increase banks' credit risk. Consequently, we do not enter the market efficiency debate.

Using the model defined above, we run multivariate OLS regressions, exploring different combinations of variables' 'gaps' with different lags. For all the countries under analysis, we used up to 28 lags, since the frequency of the data was quarterly.[15]

Since the time series of the dependent variables contain few observations, we tried to be as parsimonious as possible.[16] As a result, we started specifying regression systems with the fewest possible variables and explored how far these could take us. We continued increasing the set of explanatory variables used in the specifications, keeping in mind the trade-off with degrees of freedom when increasing regressors. Therefore, we restricted specifications to contain 2, 3 and 5 explanatory variables for each country under analysis.

Once we defined the number of explanatory variables to be included in each specification, we computed OLS multivariate regressions for all the possible combinations with the defined number of explanatory variables for each specification.

Model specifications were selected on the basis of the consistency of the explanatory variables with theoretical arguments and empirical evidence and on the specifications' goodness of fit, indicated by the adjusted R-squared and Akaike criteria. Under these criteria, Table 8.4 shows the best two specifications with five explanatory variables for Japan, the US, Mexico and Thailand. We chose to show full results for Japan and the US because these are two large economies in different geographical areas. Mexico and Thailand were chosen because these countries represent developing countries that have experienced financial crises in different geographical areas. In order to make our analysis more tractable, we summarize our results in Table 8.5. Full results of any of the analysed countries are available upon request.

From Tables 8.4 and 8.5, we observe that the variables that significantly explained the dependent variable in all the countries under analysis were the gap of credit over GDP (CREDOVGDP) and the gap of aggregate asset prices (AGGASPRI). The gap of real investment and of investment over GDP (REINVE and INVOVGDP) and also seem to be significant in most cases.

---

[15] We assumed that longer lags were not consistent with economic theory.

[16] The number of observations for different countries varied from 40 to 57.

The realized volatility of money market rates (INREVO), the difference of long minus short interest rates (LOMISH), the gap of real GDP (REGDP), the gap of real current account over real investment (RECUAOVREINV), and the gap of nominal exchange rate (NEER) and real exchange rate (REER) showed significant explanatory power in many cases, but not in all the countries.

From the results, we see that the signs of the gap of credit over GDP (CREDOVGDP) and the gap of aggregate asset prices (AGGASPRI) are as expected by economic theory and empirical evidence.

Table 8.4. Significant explanatory variables

(a) **Results for Japan**

Variables	Specification 1		Specification 2	
	Coefficient	p-value	Coefficient	p-value
Constant	0.321869	0.1135	1.867991	0.0000
GapCREDOVGDP(−12)	57.890040	0.0001	36.562740	0.0337
GapAGGPRINDX(−3)	40.137660	0.0000	47.024150	0.0000
GapRECON	−67.0655	0.0023	−47.688830	0.0375
GapREINVE(−19)	−21.0558	0.0001	−8.665556	0.1088
LOMISH(−3)	1.2118	0.0031	—	—
INREVO(−6)	—	—	−7756638	0.0012
R-squared	0.6020		0.4971	
Adjusted R-squared	0.5614		0.4458	
Akaike criterion	3.1351		3.3690	
Schwarz criterion	3.3541		3.5880	
F-statistic	14.8227		9.6876	
Prob (F-statistic)	0.0000		0.0000	

Note: Dependent variable: YJAP. Method: OLS. Sample: 1990:4 –2004:2. Included observations: 55. Newey–West HAC standard errors and covariance (lag truncation = 2).

(b) **Results for US**

Variables	Specification 1		Specification 2	
	Coefficient	p-value	Coefficient	p-value
Constant	−1.617010	0.0000	−1.637664	0.0000
GapCREDOVGDP(−9)	108.017800	0.0000	76.240310	0.0037
GapAGGASPRI(−5)	23.306530	0.0000	21.090670	0.0000
GapM2OVRES(−7)	9.531955	0.0000	9.965453	0.0000
GapRECUAOVREINV(−5)	247.480100	0.0276	—	—
GapLINT(−4)	−1.415808	0.0012	—	—
GapRECUAOVREINV(−7)	—	—	246.080200	0.0023
GapREINVE(−26)	—	—	−24.320960	0.0095
R-squared	0.6886		0.6539	
Adjusted R-squared	0.6581		0.6200	
Akaike criterion	3.5768		3.6824	
Schwarz criterion	3.7919		3.8975	
F-statistic	22.5560		19.2729	
Prob (F-statistic)	0.0000		0.0000	

Note: Dependent variable: YUS. Method: OLS. Sample: 1990:4–2004:4. Included observations: 57. Newey–West HAC standard errors and covariance (lag truncation = 2).

Table 8.4. (*cont.*)

(c) Results for Mexico

Variables	Specification 1		Specification 2	
	Coefficient	p-value	Coefficient	p-value
Constant	2.744820	0.0000	2.762759	0.0000
GapCREDOVGDP(−12)	2.288178	0.0000	2.492706	0.0000
GapAGGASPRI(−20)	8.122759	0.0000	10.634580	0.0000
GapREGDP(−9)	−7.382468	0.0000	−6.049167	0.0000
GapINVEOVGDP(−17)	−2.064286	0.0162	−1.926326	0.0294
GapM2OVRES(−5)	0.487171	0.0038	—	—
INREVO(−3)	—	—	978.410400	0.0591
R-squared		0.8864		0.8635
Adjusted R-squared		0.8530		0.8234
Akaike criterion		0.2020		0.2629
Schwarz criterion		0.4983		1.1753
F-statistic		26.5324		1.5651
Prob (F-statistic)		0.0000		1.7224

Note: Dependent variable: YMEX. Method: OLS. Sample: 1995:2–2004:4. Included observations: 23. Newey–West HAC standard errors and covariance (lag truncation = 2).

(d) Results for Thailand

Variables	Specification 1		Specification 2	
	Coefficient	p-value	Coefficient	p-value
Constant	2.734999	0.0000	2.790529	0.0000
GapCREDOVGDP(−9)	15.77079	0.0000	14.63138	0.0000
GapAGGASPRI(−11)	0.87203	0.0001	0.801764	0.0003
LOMISH(−1)	−0.265676	0.0000	−0.27634	0.0000
GapRECUAOVREINV(−5)	147.5645	0.0005	155.7751	0.0009
INREVO(−5)	—	—	21732.43	0.0334
GapM2OVRES(−11)	4.080393	0.0089	—	—
R-squared		0.8171		0.7984
Adjusted R-squared		0.7855		0.7636
Akaike criterion		2.9318		3.0290
Schwarz criterion		3.1984		3.2956
F-statistic		25.9046		22.9691
Prob (F-statistic)		0.0000		0.0000

Note: Dependent variable: YTHA. Method: OLS. Sample: 1996:2–2004:4. Included observations: 35. Newey–West HAC standard errors and covariance (lag truncation = 2).

Although one might intuitively expect that the higher the amount of investment in the economy, the higher the opportunities for growth and therefore the lower the probabilities of corporate defaults and, as a result, of banking problems, there are, nevertheless, few foundations in economic theory which could support our findings with respect to real investment (REINVE) or investment over GDP (INVOVGDP), e.g. the 'long horizon' variables. Consequently, we would counsel prudence in drawing conclusions about these variables. Although they were highly significant in all the countries under analysis, it could be that the

Table 8.5. Summary results

(a) Common significant variables

Variable	Sign	HOR[a]	ARG	CAN	DNK	FIN	FRA	GER	ITA	JAP	KOR	MEX	NET	NOR	SPA	SWE	THA	UK	US
CREDOVGDP	+	ME	9	6	7	15	7	17	6	12	25	12	5	17	7	8	9	7	9
AGGASPRI	+	ME	12	3	5	19	3	3	6	3	24	20	12	18	7	4	11	9	5
REINVE/ INVEOVGDP	−	LO	17	7	22	16	21	14	21	19	17	17	15	28	21	—	—	24	26
INREVO	+	SH	—	—	—	1	5	3	—	6[b]	1	3	—	1	—	1	5	6	—
LOMISH	−	SH	5	3	4	—	8	—	—	3[b]	—	—	1	—	2	1	1	1	—
REGDP		SH/ME	16	11	3	18	11	3	9	—	7	9	—	1	1	—	—	—	—
RECUAOVREINV	+	ME	21	14	—	—	—	—	—	—	—	—	—	7	—	—	5	8	5
NEER/REER	−	SH	3	14	3	2	5	0	3	—	—	—	3	—	—	3	—	—	—

[a] SH = short; ME = medium; LO = long.
[b] The coefficients of these variables present opposite signs.

(b) Individual-country results

Country	CREDOVGDP p-value	Lag	AGGASPRI p-value	Lag	Other variables[a]	R-squared
Argentina	5.960511 / 0.0883	9	0.941071 / 0.0003	12	LOMISH(−5), M2OVRES(−11), REGDP(−16), NEER(−3), RECUAOVREINVE(−21), REINVE(−17)	0.7266
Canada	26.283130 / 0.0721	6	32.878250 / 0.0000	3	REINVE(−7), LINT(−2), REER(−14), REGDP(−11), RECUAOVREINV(−14), LOMISH(−3)	0.6003
Denmark	23.198240 / 0.0007	7	23.743620 / 0.0000	5	NEER(−3), MTG(−3), LOMISH(−4), REGDP(−3), REINVE(−22)	0.5770
Finland	21.273600 / 0.0015	15	12.276910 / 0.0027	19	INREVO(−1), NEER(−2), REGDP(−18), INVEOVGDP(−16), LINT(−5)	0.5835
France	72.775970 / 0.0000	7	14.298550 / 0.0062	3	INREVO(−5), REGDP(−11), INVEOVGDP(−21), M2OVGDP(−1), NEER(−5), LOMISH(−8)	0.4850
Germany	34.241200 / 0.0002	17	30.433080 / 0.0004	3	NEER, REGDP(−3), INREVO(−3), INVEOVGDP(−14)	0.6456
Itay	24.709120 / 0.0001	6	20.929280 / 0.0000	6	REGDP(−9), NEER(−3), INVEOVGDP(−21), SHINT(−8)	0.6925
Japan	57.890040 / 0.0001	12	40.137660 / 0.0000	3	RECON, REINVE(−19), LOMISH(−3), INREVO(−6)	0.6020
Korea	21.343080 / 0.0005	25	0.849931 / 0.0032	24	REGDP(−7), REINVE(−17), MTG(−1), INREVO(−1), M2OVRES(12)	0.6117
Mexico	2.288178 / 0.0000	12	8.122759 / 0.0000	20	REGDP(−9), INVEOVGDP(−17), M2OVRES(−5), INREVO(−3)	0.8864
Netherlands	79.332200 / 0.0233	5	17.169250 / 0.0273	12	LOMISH(−1), REER(−3), INVOGDP(−15), SINT(−1), INVOVGDP(−15)	0.5864
Norway	17.786020 / 0.0603	17	7.313933 / 0.0331	18	INREVO(−1), RECUAOVREINV(−7), REINVEL(−28), REGDP(−1)	0.6829
Spain	84.548890 / 0.0000	7	27.004740 / 0.0000	7	INVEOVGDP(−21), LOMISH(−2), REGDP(−1), SINT(−6)	0.8309
Sweden	20.420020 / 0.0220	8	3.943797 / 0.0939	4	LOMISH(−1), M2OVRES(−4), LINT(−3), INREVO(−1), NEER(−3)	0.6659
Thailand	15.77079 / 0.0000	9	0.872030 / 0.0001	11	LOMISH(−1), RECUAOVREINV(−5), INREVO(−5), M2OVRES(−11)	0.8171
UK	24.551260 / 0.0065	7	18.178800 / 0.0002	9	LOMISH(−1), LINT(−3), RECUAOVREINV(−8)	0.6962
USA	108.017800 / 0.0000	9	23.306530 / 0.0000	5	M2OVRES(−7), RECUAOVREINV(−5), LINT(−4), REINVE(−26)	0.6886

[a] All of these variables, except LOMISH and INREVO, were transformed to 'gaps', as indicated earlier in this section. Lags are indicated in parentheses.

relationships that we found may be due to a cyclical phenomenon of the data, given that the period under analysis is relatively short (from 1990 onwards).

We would also wish to be cautious in drawing conclusions with respect to the results observed for the realized volatility of money market rates (INREVO) and the gap of real GDP (REGDP), e.g. the 'short horizon' variables. These variables were highly significant for most of the countries under analysis. Note that one would expect that, in environments of high interest-rate volatility, both banks' balance sheets and non-performing loans are affected adversely. Equally, negative GDP performance might increase the share of NPLs. However, the fact that both of these variables appear to be significant at very short lags (although the lags for GDP vary greatly across countries) may be driven by common responses along with the PoDs to a third driving factor (simultaneity in the data). Therefore, although our findings for the 'long horizon' and 'short horizon' variables are superficially quite appealing, we would like to conduct further research before we draw conclusions.

Although the signs of the coefficients of the significant explanatory variables in Table 8.5 are generally consistent with economic theory and empirical evidence,[17] the lag structure of these variables in each of the countries under analysis differs considerably. As policy-makers, we are interested in trying to identify a significant pattern (across countries) in the lag structure of the variables that we have identified as having an effect on banking credit risk. Therefore, we proceeded to perform cross-country panel data analysis.[18]

For this purpose, when we analysed the information summarized in Tables 8.4 and 8.5, we observed that the gap of credit over GDP (CREDOVGDP) was significant at lags varying from 5 to 17 quarters. Equally, the gap of the aggregate asset price index (AGGASPRI) was significant at lags varying between 3 and 24 lags. Finally, the gaps of real investment (REINVE) or investment over GDP (INVOVGDP) were significant at longer horizons, varying between 14 and 28 lags.

From these observations, we decided to analyse the correlation structures of the dependent variable and each of the three most significant variables—i.e. Corr(y,CREOVGDP), Corr(y,AGGASPRI), Corr(y,REINVE/INVOVGDP)—at lags t-4, t-8, t-12, t-16, t-20 and t-24 for the first two variables and t-4, t-8, t-12, t-24 and t-28 for the last variable. The correlation matrices are presented in Table 8.6.

From the correlation matrices, we observe that the highest correlations between the dependent variables and each of the analysed explanatory variables usually coincide with the lags at which the explanatory variables were

---

[17] We mainly focus on the 'medium horizon' variables, since we require further analysis of the 'short horizon' and 'long horizon' variables, as argued above.

[18] Usually, if pooling restrictions are artificially imposed in the presence of different economic structures, there could be cases when the results of panel data regressions do not show significant variables. The methodology proposed below for robust estimators could also be seen as an alternative to panel data estimation that could allow us to deal with small-sample problems without imposing pooling restrictions.

significant in the best (reported) specifications. Furthermore, we see that both Corr(y,CREOVGDP) and Corr(y,AGGASPRI) are usually higher in the medium term (e.g. around t-8), although there are some cases in which the lag structure is much longer. We also observe that Corr(y,REINVE/INVOVGDP) is higher at longer horizons (e.g. most frequently at horizons t-12 or longer). From this prior analysis, we decided to run cross-country panel data regressions, pooling the information for all the countries under analysis, imposing different lag structures (e.g. t-4, t-8, t-12). The results are reported in Table 8.7.

Table 8.6. Dynamic correlations

(a) Corr(y, GapREINVE)

	t-4	t-8	t-12	t-24	t-28
Argentina	0.2938	−0.1720	−0.2362	0.0107	0.2160
Canada	0.0047	−0.4407	−0.3732	−0.3300	−0.2448
Denmark	0.1016	0.0639	0.3008	−0.0617	0.0269
Finland	−0.0045	−0.0322	−0.0493	−0.0843	−0.0319
France	−0.0414	0.1206	0.0339	−0.0646	0.0918
Germany	0.3671	0.1864	−0.0361	0.0961	0.2777
Italy	−0.0910	0.1979	0.3469	−0.2529	−0.1955
Japan	0.3492	0.1044	0.0172	−0.5189	0.0268
Korea	−0.0144	−0.0826	−0.1066	0.0494	0.1198
Mexico	0.0439	−0.6898	−0.1532	0.5141	n/a
Netherlands	0.0321	−0.1119	−0.3317	0.2460	0.2625
Norway	0.1031	−0.0002	−0.1853	−0.1882	−0.2857
Spain	0.1206	0.4360	0.5539	−0.4202	n/a
Sweden	0.0465	0.2962	0.4213	−0.1139	−0.1107
Thailand	0.1262	−0.1026	−0.1264	−0.1814	−0.2961
UK	0.1616	0.5424	0.3985	−0.4340	−0.3505
USA	0.2721	0.2825	0.1994	−0.2369	−0.6638

(b) Corr(y, GapAGGASPRI)

	t-4	t-8	t-12	t-16	t-20	t-24
Argentina	−0.1173	0.1423	0.3196	0.0764	0.2205	0.1447
Canada	0.3561	0.2034	−0.2112	−0.2721	0.2365	−0.2894
Denmark	0.3421	0.3985	0.1231	−0.2244	−0.4301	−0.5868
Finland	−0.0048	−0.1747	−0.1627	−0.1297	0.4133	0.2523
France	0.2188	0.1170	0.0179	−0.0185	0.0770	−0.2690
Germany	0.1580	0.1931	0.1728	0.1355	−0.3037	−0.6535
Italy	0.4348	0.4751	0.2352	0.0052	−0.2544	−0.4447
Japan	0.3974	0.1266	−0.1758	−0.3984	−0.2483	−0.2024
Korea	−0.1224	−0.0985	−0.1394	−0.0065	0.1349	0.1540
Mexico	0.0605	−0.3207	−0.3641	0.1131	0.5302	0.3729
Netherlands	0.1332	0.2585	0.2812	0.1024	−0.3301	−0.6754
Norway	0.3179	0.3197	−0.0347	0.0570	0.4074	−0.3000
Spain	0.3393	0.7753	0.6943	0.2350	−0.4350	−0.8048
Sweden	0.4013	0.2589	0.1655	0.1145	−0.0081	−0.1730
Thailand	−0.2777	0.0038	0.5195	0.0143	−0.0786	0.0995
UK	0.2411	0.5118	0.3713	−0.0729	−0.1264	−0.6082
USA	0.4231	0.4806	0.2309	−0.1399	−0.4365	−0.5337

Table 8.6. (*cont.*)

(c)   Corr(*y*, GapCREOVGDP)

	t-4	*t-8*	*t-12*	*t-16*	*t-20*	*t-24*
Argentina	0.1760	**0.2037**	0.0990	0.0007	−0.0215	−0.3854
Canada	−0.1020	**0.2191**	0.1279	0.0551	−0.2381	−0.1623
Denmark	0.3327	**0.5197**	−0.0091	−0.4758	−0.2916	−0.0147
Finland	−0.1964	0.1937	0.3128	**0.3486**	0.2491	0.1145
France	0.0996	**0.1726**	0.1118	−0.1715	−0.0783	0.1412
Germany	−0.1220	0.0367	0.1335	**0.4153**	0.2706	0.0088
Italy	**0.4318**	0.3523	0.0147	−0.4482	−0.5322	−0.0816
Japan	−0.0181	0.0638	**0.1017**	−0.3682	−0.4526	−0.1924
Korea	−0.0604	−0.0639	−0.2285	−0.1992	−0.2193	**0.1626**
Mexico	−0.6030	−0.3000	**0.5733**	0.1110	0.0063	0.0787
Netherlands	0.2706	**0.4137**	0.1197	−0.2471	−0.3107	−0.0548
Norway	−0.1259	−0.0721	0.2517	**0.6240**	0.1730	−0.0841
Spain	0.2729	**0.6531**	−0.2434	−0.4405	−0.2853	−0.3978
Sweden	0.0315	**0.4094**	0.2381	−0.0433	−0.0829	−0.0654
Thailand	0.0898	**0.5137**	0.1989	−0.3549	−0.4271	−0.1631
UK	0.3946	**0.5688**	0.0425	−0.3692	−0.2023	−0.3571
USA	0.1941	**0.2883**	0.2755	0.1353	−0.3419	−0.4367

Note: The largest correlation for each individual country is in bold.

We turned to this panel exercise to see if we could obtain a better estimate of the relative contribution of these two long-term determinants of financial fragility. When we ran three lags of both the credit and asset gap variables (at *t*-4, *t*-8, *t*-12), either separately or jointly (see Table 8.7), the coefficients of both variables at each of these lags remained significant[19] (apart from that of the asset price gap, at *t*-8, in the joint exercise[20]). We examined various restricted combinations of lags in the two variables, e.g. combining the credit gap variable at *t*-8 with the asset price gap variable at *t*-8, or *t*-12, or *t*-16, but the results remained quite flat, i.e. the adjusted R^2 values remained almost unchanged, and are not shown here.

As already discussed above, these two main explanatory variables interact closely; causality runs in both directions between them, i.e. there is much simultaneity, and it is reinforcing. It is therefore difficult to distinguish their individual effects. This latter exercise—trying to take further account of their individual and interactive effects—is a matter for further research.

The results that have been produced here indicate the need for further research in two specific areas: the interaction between credit and asset prices and the

---

[19] This result differed from that in our earlier exercise using only data from developed countries. In this case the asset price gap variable tended to dominate the credit gap variable in the joint panel exercises where both were included, i.e. only the first set of variables remained significant. This is consistent with a lesser role of capital markets (and of private housing/property) in less developed countries, relative to the role of banks.

[20] When we excluded Thailand from the sample, all the variables seemed to be significant.

Table 8.7. Panel data analysis

	Including credit only		Including asset prices only		Including both credit and asset prices	
	Coefficient	p-value	Coefficient	p-value	Coefficient	p-value
Constant	−0.222234	0.0606	−0.241499	0.0502	−0.233910	0.0462
GapCREDOVGDP(−4)	5.765883	0.0017			6.779743	0.0005
GapCREDOVGDP(−8)	5.614949	0.0045			6.989937	0.0005
GapCREDOVGDP(−12)	2.142127	0.0940			5.594157	0.0000
GapAGGASPRI(−4)			1.321767	0.0148	3.954792	0.0000
GapAGGASPRI(−8)			0.592124	0.0835	0.631641	0.8269
GapAGGASPRI(−12)			1.299631	0.0000	1.232816	0.0000
	Fixed Effects(Cross)					
Argentina	1.544946		1.506961		1.221646	
Canada	−2.389238		−2.350746		−2.376745	
Denmark	−1.332561		−1.364117		−1.313546	
Finland	0.066321		0.027537		0.080117	
France	0.362307		0.377582		0.356009	
Germany	−0.538898		−0.528559		−0.544731	
Italy	0.378045		0.393455		0.352232	
Japan	1.756030		1.784991		1.755848	
Korea	2.304358		2.395774		2.492576	
Mexico	2.801620		2.955473		2.755636	
Netharlands	−1.130550		−1.121113		−1.142975	
Norway	0.346188		0.270682		0.428048	
Spain	−1.586202		−1.569690		−1.535228	
Sweden	0.202090		0.219087		0.184855	
Thailand	2.681911		2.446413		2.540411	
UK	−0.738714		−0.725702		−0.728670	
USA	−1.682592		−1.689582		−1.660340	
R-squared	0.3151		0.3121		0.3467	
Adjusted R-squared	0.2996		0.2965		0.3295	
Akaike criterion	4.5066		4.5110		4.4663	
Schwarz criterion	4.6173		4.6217		4.5936	
F-statistic	20.3170		20.0360		20.1689	
Prob (F-statistic)	0.0000		0.0000		0.0000	

Note: Dependent variable: YPooled. Method: Pooled LS. Sample: 1990:4 –2004:4. Included observations: 57 after adjustments. Cross-sections included: 17. White cross-section standard errors and covariance (d.f. corrected).

estimation of robust estimators. As shown in §8.2, the causality between AGGASPRI and CREDOVGDP goes in both directions and is reinforcing. Although these results show that both variables are significant in explaining banking credit risk, further analysis along the lines of the study presented in §8.3 needs to be done in order to take further account of the interaction between these variables.

Up to now, our attention has focused on selecting the set of explanatory variables to include in the model. For this purpose, we have used multivariate OLS regressions. However, the time series of the probabilities of default (PoDs) are short. The need to analyse short time series is commonly faced by credit risk modellers. Under these circumstances, the OLS estimators have large variances, and OLS estimators can be sensitive to small changes in the data.

So we intend to extend the analysis presented here by recovering the parameters of the selected explanatory variables with a Conditional Probability of Default Methodology (Segoviano 2006). The CoPoD (based on the Jaynes 1957 entropy measure) recovers estimators that, when dealing with short samples, are superior to OLS estimators under the mean-square error (MSE) criterion. Equivalently, the CoPoD greatly reduces the variance of the estimators. This feature should improve the evaluation of the impact of macroeconomic and financial shocks on the credit risk of the financial system.[21]

8.4 Conclusions

This chapter has reconfirmed some empirical relationships that are already well known. First, there is a two-way simultaneous relationship between surges in bank lending and asset prices. This relationship is stronger in the case of real estate, both housing and commercial property, than with equity. The links between bank lending and property are manifold, but differ in strength from country to country.

When such a combined bank lending/property boom occurs, there is an enhanced likelihood of financial fragility occurring, some two to three years after the year of the preceding boom (NB the lags in the process are quite long). Again we would emphasize the relative importance of property, as contrasted with the lesser importance of equity prices. Although there are differences between countries in lag length and the strength of the estimated relationships, the commonality of findings is quite impressive, especially since there are aspects of the empirical tests that still need improvement (notably the excessive reliance of the PoD estimate on the overall variance of (national) equity markets).

What then are the public policy implications of this exercise? As noted earlier, we have not considered the causes of bank lending/asset price surges. Usually these arise in conditions of strong economic growth, allied with structural changes in the banking system, for example liberalization, which encourage the banks to target growth (and to enter new fields of business). Such phenomena were seen in the UK (1972–4), Scandinavia (1988–90) and Japan (1988–90), and are not particularly Asian in character. That said, China and India, and perhaps

---

[21] The CoPoD estimation procedure could be understood as a 'non-parametric' maximum likelihood estimation procedure, in which, rather than finding the estimators by optimizing the parameters of a parametric (given) likelihood function, the likelihood function is inferred from the data observations. Judge and Golan (1992) proved theoretically that this procedure reduces the variance of the estimators in the presence of small samples. Segoviano (2006) presents a Monte Carlo study that shows the reduction of the mean-square error of the CoPoD estimators *vis-à-vis* OLS estimators. For theoretical and implementation details of the CoPoD, we refer interested readers to Segoviano (2006).

Brazil, are countries whose stage of development puts them at risk of repeating this syndrome.

Let us assume that, despite all precautions, a bank lending/property prices surge develops. What then? During such bubbles existing bank regulations, capital adequacy requirements, etc. are not likely to have a restraining effect. During such asset price booms non-performing loans decline and bank profits rise. Capital is not a constraint on bank expansion. This reflects the fact that most financial regulation, notably Basel II, is somewhat procyclical. Consequently such regulatory measures are of little use in counteracting bubble–bust antecedents of financial fragility.

Is it possible to derive contra-cyclical regulatory measures? The Spanish pre-provisioning approach and the Hong Kong time-varying loan-to-value ratios for mortgages are in this genre. Pillar 2 of Basel II enables the supervisory authorities to introduce variations in capital requirements, if they so wish.

One of the problems is that financial intermediation has become a globally competitive industry. Indeed, the need for a 'level playing field' has been one of the primary driving forces behind the Basel regulations. Can any one country introduce counter-cyclical supervisory adjustments, under Pillar 2 or otherwise, without provoking considerable disintermediation either to banks situated abroad or to non-banks? But, if the perceived need is to strengthen domestic banks against boom–bust financial fragility, is such disintermediation necessarily a bad outcome (NB it will be perceived as such by the domestic banks, who will lobby furiously against it)?

Even assuming that policy measures cannot be effectively used to diminish bank lending/property booms to manageable levels, and that this bubble eventually bursts, the lengthy lags in the course of the downwards spiral should give the authorities time to prepare their defences against resulting financial collapse. Stress and scenario tests come into play here. However, the question is not just whether the banks can survive the first-round effect of declines in property prices. They usually can. The deeper question is whether banks' own reactions, for example to limit new bank loans, and that of their (interbank and foreign) depositors, e.g. to withdraw funding, will lead to second-round and subsequent responses that could give a vicious twist to the deflationary spiral. Stress and scenario tests tend to cover only first-round effects. To analyse the resulting possible equilibria, there is a need for general equilibrium models in this area. One of us has been working on this (see Goodhart, Surinand and Tsomocos 2004a, b, 2005, and Goodhart, Tsomocos, Zicchino and Aspachs 2006), but there is a long way yet to go.

Part III

Implications of House Price Fluctuations For Public Policy

9

What Role for House Prices in the Measurement of Inflation?

9.1 Introduction

Our dictionary (Longmans) defines inflation as a fall in the value of money, not as a rise in the consumer price index. If we spend our money now on obtaining a claim on future housing services by buying a house, or on future dividends by buying an equity, and the price of that claim on housing services or on dividends goes up, why is that not just as much inflation as when the price of current goods and services rises? We spend much of our money on such purchases; the value of gross purchases of houses, in those cases where a mortgage was taken out, was 18.5% of post-tax income of the household sector in 1999. In the same year the net value of other financial savings of the household sector was 5.5% of post-tax income.

The argument that an analytically correct measure of inflation should take account of asset price changes was made most forcefully by Alchian and Klein (1973), and has never, in our view, been successfully refuted on a *theoretical* plane, though, as we shall see in §9.2, their *particular* proposals have severe, perhaps incapacitating, *practical* deficiencies. It was therefore a surprise that, at the Conference on The Measurement of Inflation (Silver and Fenwick 2000), at which an earlier version of this chapter (Goodhart 2000) was given, there was no other paper concerning asset prices, and how asset prices—of houses, land, and various other investments, real or financial—might, or might not, fit into a measure of inflation. At the moment most such asset price changes are, in principle, given zero weight, with the index supposedly reflecting only the price of purchases of current consumption of goods and services.

In practice, the distinction between the purchase of a durable asset and current consumption is not easy to make. When we buy an overcoat or a golf club, we expect to benefit from, and consume, their services over many years; yet official data attribute all such consumption, and the pricing thereof, to the year of purchase. This problem is particularly acute with so-called consumer durables (though the average useful life of these may well often be less than that of clothes and shoes), and results in some arcane distinctions in practice: thus the purchase price of new cars has been excluded from the RPI in the UK (because of the difficulty of observing individually bargained discounts), whereas the price of second-hand cars is included, though partly as a proxy for the former (see Office for National Statistics 1998). We shall deal with the even more complex case of how to treat house prices in §9.3. The point here is that the current RPI and CPI statistics are *not* pure measures of the price of current consumption, but a practically convenient mix (though fuzzy at the edges) of prices of short-lived consumer quasi-durable and durable assets alongside the prices of current consumables and services.

Some argue that the question of the appropriate treatment of asset prices in the measurement of inflation has been effectively settled by custom and usage. Thus, an anonymous referee of the previous version of this chapter wrote as follows:

The problem is that the fall in the value of money should be measured by the reciprocal of the increase [*sic*] in the general level of prices, which is a concept impossible to be measured. What we can do is to measure the increases in some basket which can reproduce the general movements of prices. It is commonly agreed that this basket is the consumers' one. As we need to measure the inflation, the best way to do it seems to be using the CPI. Of course, we may question whether to extend the basket in order to take asset price changes into account, but the practical implications appear so severe to advise against any attempt in this direction (as pointed out by Alchian and Klein).

This involves a number of sweeping assertions. As Ralph Turvey, one of our leading experts in this field, has often stated (e.g. Turvey 1989: ch. 2, 2000b, esp. the chapter on 'Purpose Determines Concepts and Coverage'), what kind of index you should want depends on the use that you intend to make of it. Let us rephrase that question. When you want the monetary authorities to control inflation, exactly what do you want to mean by inflation? Current goods and services inflation is far from the same as changes in the value of money, especially when there is a combination of stable consumption prices and wildly fluctuating asset prices, as in Japan over the last two decades. What should we mean by the word 'inflation'?

Of course, there are many uses to which a CPI or an RPI is put for which the focus on the costs of current consumption of goods and services is entirely appropriate. But is that same concentration on the costs of current consumption alone also appropriate when one wishes to concentrate on a general measure of inflation? Put alternatively, what measure of inflation should be, in principle at least, the main focus for monetary policy?

How can one answer that last question? We shall try to divide the question into two parts. First, in §9.2, we shall discuss arguments for including asset prices *in principle* in the measurement of inflation, for the purposes of monetary policy. Here we shall discuss the general theoretical case for so doing (§9.2.1), basing this on the analysis of Alchian and Klein (1973); then we shall turn to practical, empirical policy considerations (§9.2.2), arguing that paying attention to asset prices, in a more formalized manner, could help protect against the worst errors of policy; finally, we shall review why inflation is supposed to harm welfare (§9.2.3), and suggest that welfare losses would be reduced if the inflation measure to be stabilized at a low level also incorporated asset prices.

Even if the arguments *in principle* for including asset prices in measures of inflation, for monetary policy purposes, were to be accepted, the question would still remain as to how to do so in practice. Such practical questions revolve around the issue of what *weightings* to give asset prices in the construction of a price index. This is the topic of §9.3. As is well known, but we shall repeat (§9.3.1), the theoretical arguments of Alchian and Klein (1973) imply such high weights on volatile asset prices that the resulting price indices become unstable, unreliable and unusable. But that does *not* eliminate the case for inclusion of asset prices in price indices. Other, more moderate weighting schemes which are both analytically defensible and practicable can be found. We shall discuss two such approaches. The first involves the weighting of asset prices according to their empirical relationships with goods and services prices (§9.3.2). One such exercise was undertaken in Cecchetti *et al.* (2000); another was carried out by Goodhart and Hofmann (2000a), reproduced as Chapter 2 in this book. The second weighting system is based, even more simply, on the proportion either of total personal incomes, or of total final expenditures, actually spent on assets (§9.3.3).

Arguments such as we make here do not command mainstream support amongst economists (see Gertler *et al.* 1998; Bernanke and Gertler 1999), largely perhaps because they are concerned as to whether excessive weight might be given to volatile financial assets (e.g. equities), thereby making the price index more unstable and less useful. The purpose of §§9.3.2 and 9.3.3 is to demonstrate that such an outcome need not occur. Nevertheless, the result of such disagreements amongst economists has been to halt moves towards any generalized incorporation of asset prices into price indices and associated measures of inflation.

But the one area, in this respect, where the immediate practical policy issues are too intense to be swept under the carpet concerns housing. Housing costs are such a large element in personal spending that the issue cannot be ignored. National statisticians *have* to decide how to deal with housing costs, even if they then—as in some countries—find the problems so severe that they decide to exclude some, or all, aspects of housing altogether from their statistical measures. We touch rather briefly on some of the alternative treatments of housing in consumer price indices in §9.4.

Even if, analytically, the case for some more formalized inclusion of asset prices in the appropriate price index (and measurement of inflation) is strong, we are not starting from a tabula rasa. The United Kingdom, and other countries, have used the RPI (and CPI in some cases) in its existing, or amended, form—as in the case of RPIX as a target for the Monetary Policy Committee—for policy purposes and as a component element in contracts, e.g. indexed contracts, for many years. Continuity, certainty and simplicity all argue against chopping and changing existing procedures. So in §9–5, we do not argue for replacing the present measures, but for paying rather more attention to accompanying, alternative measures which *do* give a more appropriate weighting to asset prices.

9.2 Why asset prices should have a role in the measurement of inflation

9.2.1 The theoretical case

The theoretical case for including asset prices in the measurement of inflation was brilliantly expressed by the economists, Armen Alchian and Benjamin Klein, in their paper 'On the Correct Measure of Inflation' as long ago as 1973. They state that the CPI and the GNP deflator

are frequently considered to be the operational counterparts of what economists call 'the price level'. They, therefore, often are used as measures of inflation and often are targets or indicators of monetary and fiscal policy. Nevertheless, these price indices, which represent measures of current consumption service prices and current output prices, are theoretically inappropriate for the purpose to which they are generally put. The analysis in this paper bases a price index on the Fisherian tradition of a proper definition of intertemporal consumption and leads to the conclusion that a price index used to measure inflation must include asset prices. (173)

Alchian and Klein, following the lead of Irving Fisher (1906) and Paul Samuelson (1961), argue that the utility of any situation is 'a function of a vector of claims to present and future consumption', and hence one should try to assess whether prices have risen, or fallen, by looking at whether the prices of an iso-utility vector of current and future goods and services has risen, or fallen (175). But futures prices for future-consumption goods and services are not generally available, and hence one should proxy these by a full set of asset prices (176–7).

Alchian and Klein are aware of the difficulties of the course they propose. Thus:

[W]ithout future contracts in all commodities, the explicit futures prices and quantities needed for construction of a wealth price index are unavailable. Current prices of assets of different life lengths provide a theoretical substitute since they embody present prices of expected future service flows. But both the asset prices and asset quantities necessary for this index are extremely expensive to determine. We must have prices of a very broad spectrum of assets on which we presently have very little information. Our data must include prices of generally nonmarketable assets, such as human capital, and of assets of varying durability, so that we are able to produce the exact optimum current and future consumption service flows by adjusting the asset mix. We may not be able to determine all these prices with any reasonable expenditure of resources[.] (187)

Moreover,

[E]ven if asset prices and quantities were available, we would have significant problems in the interpretation of asset price changes. A change in the market value of an asset may reflect (i) a change in the price of an unchanged future service flow from the asset, (ii) a shift in preferences for this asset's service relative to other assets, (iii) a shift in preferences for present consumption relative to future consumption, or (iv) a change in the anticipated magnitude of service flow from the asset. Any or all of these changes are likely to be occurring simultaneously and therefore the cause of a change in a particular asset price is difficult to determine. Changes (ii) and (iii) represent a shift in tastes while (iv) represents a change in asset quality; however, they are not conceptually different from the problems encountered in constructing the presently used indices. (188)

They conclude that

[t]he empirical problems involved are enormous. But whatever efforts may be made in this direction and whatever the results, we believe it is an error to assign all of the change in common stock and other asset prices to changes in anticipated future service flows with no change in present prices of such future flows . . . which is what is implicitly done now in commonly used price indices that ignore asset prices. (189)

9.2.2   The practical case

Many of the most serious and least manageable problems of monetary policy relate to the question of whether, and how if at all, the authorities should respond to asset price fluctuations. How we define inflation is quite likely to influence the conduct of monetary policy in practice, whatever should happen in principle.

The most obvious recent case is Japan. If you look at the paths for the level of consumer prices (Figure 9.1), or for the rate of inflation of consumer prices, defined as the percentage increase in the CPI in each quarter over the same quarter in the preceding year (Figure 9.2), then the outcome for Japan appears superior to that of Australia, the USA and the UK. The generally accepted desideratum is for low and stable inflation; some (e.g. Goodfriend and King 2001) even advocate aiming for complete price stability. Figure 9.1 demonstrates that Japan has approximated more closely to this desideratum, with patently lower inflation than its comparators, and Figure 9.2 shows, though less clearly, that it has also had more stable inflation than its comparators.

Yet most of us do not regard Japan's monetary policy as having been exemplary. Why not? The main reason for a more adverse judgement is that the policy-makers in Japan were not able to prevent an asset price bubble and bust over this same period. This bubble and bust occurred in both the equity and real estate markets. As we have argued earlier in this book, the real estate market has the more important linkages with financial intermediation, real output and the CPI/RPI, but movements in equity prices have been more eye-catching, and both are shown below.

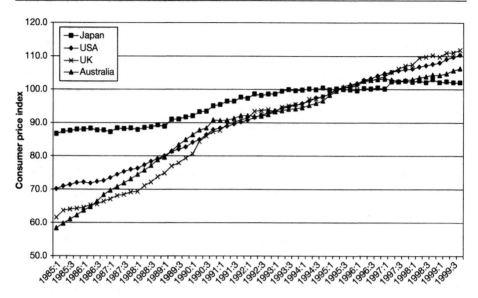

Figure 9.1. Consumer prices, 1985–1999 (1995=100)

Note: Standard deviations: Japan, 5.7; USA, 12.7; UK, 15.8; Australia, 14.1.

Source: OECD, *Main Economic Indicators*, various volumes.

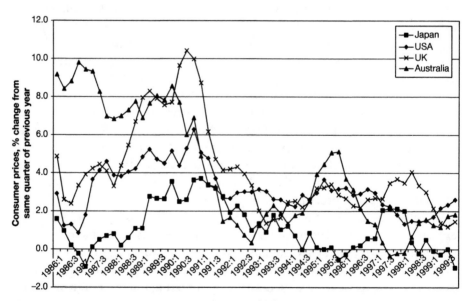

Figure 9.2. Percentage changes in consumer prices, 1986–1999 (year on year)

Note: Standard deviations: Japan, 1.2; USA, 1.2; UK, 2.4; Australia, 3.2.

Source: OECD, *Main Economic Indicators*, various volumes, authors' own calculations.

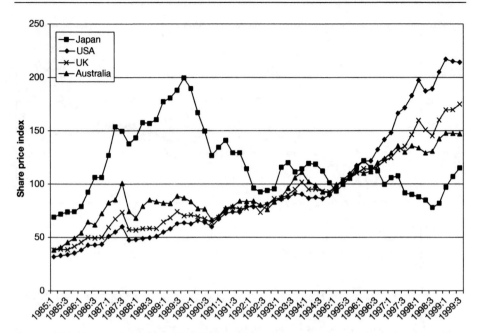

Figure 9.3. Share prices, 1985–1999 (1995 = 100)

Note: Standard deviations: Japan, 32; USA, 53; UK, 36; Australia, 27.

Source: OECD, *Main Economic Indicators,* various volumes.

Figure 9.3 shows the relative movements in equity prices for these same four countries. In the USA, the UK and Australia, there are temporary peaks, in 1987:3 and 1994:1, with subsequent downturns, but otherwise the series trend strongly upwards over the whole period. In Japan, by contrast, a massive rise until 1989:4 is followed by a collapse until 1992 and subsequent stagnation. Moreover the volatility of Japanese share prices, as measured by the standard deviation of year-on-year percentage changes (each quarter relative to the same quarter a year ago), is double that in the USA and the UK (24 compared to 12), while Australia is at 19.

Nevertheless, as reported in Cecchetti *et al.* (2000) and previous chapters of this book, the linkages between housing prices and both output and CPI/RPI inflation measures are much stronger than those between equity prices and output/inflation. In Figure 9.4 we show the time path of housing prices in these same four countries. The same bubble and bust is evident in Japan. In the UK there is a much stronger cyclical pattern, with a very sharp rise until 1989, a sharp decline until 1993, and a fairly steady rise thereafter. In Australia much the same pattern occurs. In contrast, in the USA there has been much less cyclical volatility in housing prices, at least over the whole country. The relationship between local cycles in real estate prices and activity remains to be fully explored.

These discrepant patterns in asset prices, especially in housing prices, appear to have had some influence on the path of real output, the levels of which are shown

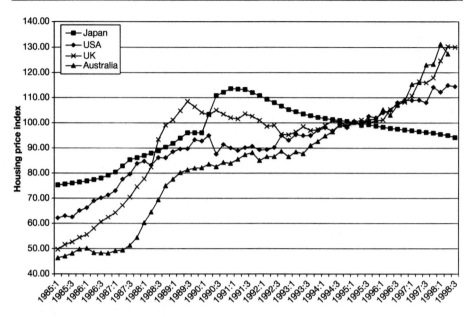

Figure 9.4. Housing prices, 1985–1998 (1995=100)

Note: Standard deviations: Japan, 11.01; USA, 13.92; UK, 20.23; Australia, 23.21.

Source: National central banks; national statistical offices.

in Figure 9.5 and the percentage change over the same quarter in the previous year in Figure 9.6. The rapid rate of growth in real output in Japan until the end of 1991 is then replaced by a period of halting growth. In the UK and Australia, there is a cyclical peak in 1990, following the end of the housing boom, with a subsequent recession until 1992. The US has the steadiest time path for output growth, just as it has also had the steadiest time path for housing price inflation.

The interaction between asset prices, especially real estate, and output has been recently examined in several studies (Cecchetti *et al.* 2000; Goodhart and Hofmann 2000b; Filardo 2000; OECD 2000), and found to be significant.

How, if at all, should the monetary authorities then react to such asset price changes, and how, if at all, should such asset price changes be incorporated into our measures of inflation? These two questions, of action and measurement, are intimately linked. So long as asset price changes are *not* incorporated in the measure of inflation which the authorities are required to stabilize, the authorities are likely to express audible worries about 'exuberance' and 'sustainability', but in practice find themselves paralysed in practice, i.e. largely incapable of any (pre-emptive) action in response to asset price changes

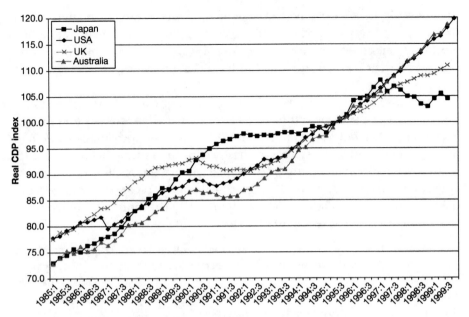

Figure 9.5. Real Gross Domestic Product, 1985–1999 (1995 = 100)

Note: Standard deviations: Japan, 10.5; USA 11.8; UK, 9.0; Australia, 13.0.

Source: OECD, *Main Economic Indicators*, various volumes.

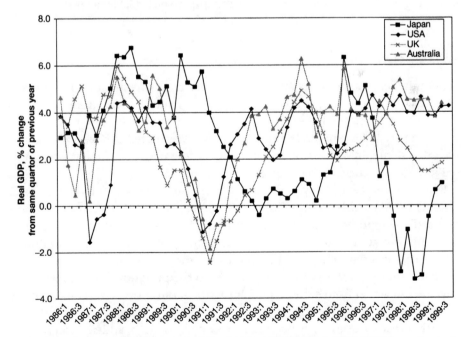

Figure 9.6. Percentage changes in real Gross Domestic Product, 1986–1999 (year on year)

Note: Standard deviations: Japan, 2.5; USA, 1.6; UK, 1.9; Australia, 1.8.

Source: OECD, *Main Economic Indicators*, various volumes, authors' own calculations.

183

themselves in advance of any (consequential) effects coming through onto current goods and services prices—and a good thing that is too, many or perhaps most academic colleagues would reply, stressing, *inter alia*, the volatility of asset prices, and their frequent dysjunction from the fluctuations of the rest of the economy.

There is also, perhaps, a hint of an asymmetric approach to asset price fluctuations, i.e. it is proper to lower interest rates to counter steep asset price declines, as in 1987 and 1998, but not to raise them to counter asset price increases. Perhaps some perception of this asymmetry has been a supporting factor behind the remarkable 'bull run' of equity prices which these diagrams illustrate. This was noted in the *Financial Times* on 30 August 1999 (the day before the Conference on the Measurement of Inflation). When reporting on the monetary conference at Jackson Hole, Gerard Baker reported that

Mr Greenspan devoted his entire contribution to the enlarged role asset prices play in the formulation of policy. But, though he has warned repeatedly in the past that equity prices have become overvalued, he focussed more on trying to understand the forces that have driven prices higher. And, for all the attention he and his colleagues are paying to Wall Street, it is still highly unclear how it will impact policy.

Indeed, the only certainty, he confirmed, was that the Fed would be forced to cut rates if the market fell sharply. This has given rise recently to concerns that the central bank is unwittingly contributing to a form of moral hazard—that it stands by ready to prop up the market if it fails, but will do nothing to stop it going up too high. (Baker 1999)

9.2.3 The welfare case

Economists have historically struggled to understand why inflation is so widely disliked. After all, utility is (one might think) provided by real things, e.g. consumption and leisure; money is mostly just a veil; and a *fully* anticipated rate of inflation should have no costs, unless currency is restricted to have a zero nominal interest rate, in which case second-order costs are involved in replenishing a reduced stock of currency more often from ATMs.

But we owe to Leijonhufvud (1981) the realization that any fully anticipated, and hence *fully* controlled, inflation can be transformed into a zero inflation rate with an appropriate monetary reform (with some consequential benefit in reducing computational costs). So any non-zero inflation rate is by definition at least partially unanticipated, and therefore leads to losses and benefits on contracts and prices/wages based on incorrect expectations. The greater the deviation of actual from expected inflation, the more extreme will be the losses (and gains).

With most ordinary people being risk-averse, such added uncertainty lowers utility. In order to avoid losses when inflation rises to high levels, double-digit and above, much more effort has to be made not only to estimate likely inflationary pressures, but also to withdraw from market positions that might leave one unduly exposed to risk. Some markets cease to function at all, e.g. long-term corporate bond markets, and prices in others become less informative of relative scarcities. Be that as it may, empirical research suggests that when inflation rises to over around 10% it has a significant adverse effect on output. While one can argue that bringing inflation down from, say, 7% to 2% per annum has no clear benefit in terms of raising *trend output*, and a transitional output cost on the way down, there are two counter-arguments. First, there is a continuing loss from the higher inflation itself, to offset against the transitional loss. Second, and perhaps more important, a monetary authority which is not prepared to try to offset stochastic shocks around an *optimal* inflation target is not likely to be able to prevent political, and other, pressures to allow inflation first to creep, and then to gallop, upwards to a point at which trend output growth is worsened. So an inflation target, *au fond*, is there in order to prevent monetary disturbances from affecting output, to provide the basis of financial stability in which growth can prosper.

If one then asks what *measurement* of inflation will do this job best, the answer, we would suggest, depends on the relationship between fluctuations in the inflation series and in the output series. If utility is derived from real variables, then our concern about inflation must relate primarily with respect to its effect in distorting such real variables from their equilibrium path. Hence the definition of inflation that is most relevant would seem to be that most closely related to such deviations. We attempt to measure this by examining the relationship between the variability of output around its trend and the variability of consumer prices and of a set of asset prices (exchange rate, share prices and house prices).

The countries in the sample are: Australia, Belgium, Canada, Denmark, Finland, France, Germany, Ireland, Japan, the Netherlands, Norway, Sweden, the United Kingdom and the United States. The data period is quarterly (annually for Germany) from the early 1970s to 1998.

There were difficulties in selecting an appropriate indicator for the variability of the series, e.g. simple standard deviations led to overlapping observations. After some experimentation, we decided to measure the variability of each variable as the *absolute difference of its growth rate from its trend value*. In particular, for each variable the growth rate at quarter t was calculated as the growth rate of the variable from the corresponding quarter of the previous year. So for each variable we ended up with four series, one for the growth rate of the variable between the first quarters of consecutive years, the second for the growth rate between the second quarters, and so on (for Germany we ended up with one series for each variable because house prices were only available with annual frequency). Both for simplicity and to avoid overfitting we used a linear trend for all the series.

Having calculated this indicator for all the variables, we specified two alternative models, therefore running eight regressions for each country (two for Germany):

$$|DevGDP|_t = C + |DevGDP|_{t-1} + |DevCPI|_t + |DevEXCH|_t + |DevSP|_t + |DevHP|_t$$

$$|DevGDP|_t = C + |DevGDP|_{t-1} + |DevCPI|_{t-1} + |DevEXCH|_t + |DevSP|_{t-1} + |DevHP|_{t-1}$$

where $DevX = \Delta \ln X - TREND\Delta \ln X$. The two models differ only in their lag structure. In the first model fluctuations of asset and consumer prices are expected to affect the volatility of GDP (as measured by our proxy) instantaneously, while in the second model they are expected to affect the volatility of output with a lag of one year. Both models included an autoregressive term because of the strong autocorrelation in the growth rate of output.

In Table 9.1 we summarize the results of our exercise, recording the number and name of the countries for which the specified explanatory variable was significant and with the expected sign in i regressions.

All the series were extremely noisy, and the included explanatory variables appear to have power in explaining the volatility of GDP only in *some* of the regressions (concentrated in *a few* countries). However, despite the necessary caution, this simple exercise suggests that the variable that appears to explain best the volatility of GDP is the volatility of consumer prices, as might have been expected. Perhaps more interesting is that the volatility of house prices appears the second most important explanatory variable for at least three countries

Table 9.1. Summary of results for individual country output growth volatility regressions

Number of equations	Share prices	House prices	Exchange rate	CPI	GDP
4	1 (Japan)	1 (Germany: 1 out of 2)[a]	0	1 (Netherlands)	0
3	0	2 (Netherlands, UK)	0	2 (Belgium, Japan)	0
2	3 (Finland, UK, USA)	1 (Finland)	1 (Denmark)	3 (Denmark, France, USA)	3 (Australia, Belgium, Japan)
1	3 (Australia, Canada, Netherlands)	2 (Canada, US)	2 (France, UK)	4 (Canada, Finland, Ireland, Sweden)	3 (Denmark, Netherlands, USA)

Note: The table reports the number and the name of the countries for which the respective variable was significant (at least at the 10% level) and with the expected (positive) sign.
[a] For Germany, since house prices were available only with annual frequency, we ran one regression for each model.

(Germany, the Netherlands, and the UK) for which we found reasonable evidence of its importance. By comparison we only found reasonable evidence (i.e. significance in at least three equations) for share prices in one country (Japan). The least important regressors appeared to be the autoregressive term (GDP(-1)) and the exchange rate. Therefore, and with due caution, if we were to infer policy implications from this simple exercise, we would be tempted to propose a role for house prices in the measurement of inflation (besides consumer prices), but no role for share prices or for the exchange rate.

In so far as the welfare effect of inflation relates ultimately to its impact on output and on consumption per head, the implication of this preliminary study is that the most relevant measure of inflation *should* give considerable weight to housing prices, though less, perhaps none, to equity prices. The econometric instability of the relationship between exchange rates and output implies that no weight should be given to them beyond their indirect effect already picked up in the CPI. This provides yet another reason for doubting the use of Monetary Conditions Indices (MCI) combining interest and exchange rates via some weighting function as a measure of the (overall?) stance of monetary policy (e.g. Batini and Turnbull 2000). Clearly, however, the relative weights to be given to the various assets (in some cases, perhaps, zero) is the crucial issue, and it is to this issue that we turn in §9.3.

9.3 What weights should be given to asset prices in the construction of a price/inflation index?

9.3.1 The Alchian–Klein theoretical position

As one might have expected, greater efforts have been made to follow up Alchian and Klein's conceptual proposals with concrete empirical and numerical estimates in Japan than anywhere else. Shiratsuka (1996, 1998, 1999) and Shibuya (1992) have taken the lead on this, though see also Shimizu (1992) and Goodhart (1995). The conclusions, however, are largely negative about the value and usefulness of such a constructed index. Asset price changes are caused by too many factors, and many such assets, such as land prices and human capital, are too badly measured. Moreover, unless the rate of subjective time discount, or time preference, is taken to be very high, an empirical application of the Alchian–Klein approach will give a huge weighting to asset prices relative to current goods prices (in Shibuya's exercise 0.97 and 0.03 respectively). And this relatively large weight on asset prices, of course, then exaggerates all the idiosyncratic causes of variance in asset prices as a measure of, or guide to, inflation more generally. Shiratsuka concludes that

Although the concept of a dynamic equilibrium price index is highly evaluated from the viewpoints of theoretical consistency, it is difficult for monetary policy makers to expect the DEPI to be more than supplementary indicators for inflation pressures. This is because such modification of the conventional price indices is hardly operational. (Shiratsuka 1999: 19)

9.3.2   An empirically based measure

The main recent work on this issue is by Cecchetti *et al.* (2000), particularly §3, and also §4. Thus they write:

There is a notion pervading much of the discussion of the inclusion of asset prices in measure of inflation, and it concerns that idea that asset-price movements somehow give information about *future* inflation . . . .

However, note that if the underlying justification for inclusion of asset prices in the measure of inflation is that they help to predict future inflation, then it is far from obvious that they should attract a weight based on the discount rate. Instead, the weight should be more closely related to their relative contribution to an inflation forecast.

But once we formulate the problem in this way, we can see that the issue of including or excluding any given nominal price is an empirical one, having to do with their informativeness about the common trend. If, for example, we knew that the price of a particular variety of shoes never experienced any relative price changes, then we could save government statistical agencies quite a bit of money. Alternatively, if there were only two goods in the economy, and they experienced substantial relative price shocks, then focussing attention on one price alone, rather than a properly constructed average, would be very misleading.

The computation of a DFI [Dynamic Factor Index] involves the calculation of the relative weights to put on the different prices that we observe. Starting with a set that includes asset prices, we can ask whether their inclusion adds any information to our estimate of the common trend.

We study the properties of two sets of price data. First, we examine the same set of quarterly data for 12 countries used by Goodhart and Hofmann [Chapter 2 of this book]. The data are described in the appendix to their paper . . . . The results are what we would expect. Since stock prices are so much more volatile than consumer prices, their implied weight is very low, never exceeding 2.5%, and usually below 2%. Housing is quite a different story, however, because in this case prices can have a substantial effect.

To examine this a bit further, we have collected a more comprehensive monthly data set for the United States, with a sample from the beginning of 1967 through 1999. Here we are able to assemble data for energy prices, food prices, housing purchase prices, housing rental and operating costs (labelled 'CPI Shelter'), stock prices, and a residual category of the consumer price index that excludes food, energy and shelter. Here we look at the inflation rate over a 12-month period, and examine the consequences of computing variances of rolling ten-year periods. The results . . . suggest that stock prices are much too volatile to be useful in computing a price index, but that the treatment of housing is crucial . . . .

The conclusion from this expository exercise is that straightforward attempts to include asset prices in measures of inflation need to proceed with care. While there may be justification for including equity prices, their inclusion is likely to create more problems than they solve. Specifically, the extremely high variance of stock returns (hundred of times that of conventional inflation measures) will simply add noise. Housing, though, needs to be considered very carefully. Here, we believe that there is clear room for improvement of price indices. (Cecchetti *et al.* 2000: 81–85)

In a similar vein, Goodhart and Hofmann (2000a), reproduced in Chapter 2 of this book, examined the relationship between CPI inflation and previous values of sets of explanatory variables, examining whether the inclusion of certain asset prices, notably housing, equity and the yield spread, improves the fit. Our conclusion was that

[i]f there is a message in these results, it is that monetary variables in general, and house price movements in particular, need to be given more weight in the assessment of inflation, particularly at a two-year horizon, than is done in some current models, which primarily incorporate the monetary transmission mechanism via the effects of real interest rates on real expenditures (and of nominal interest rates on exchange rates) . . . .

At the beginning of this paper we noted that most economists would agree that movements in asset prices *should* be taken into account by the monetary authorities in so far as they signal changes in expected inflation. What we have done here is to run a horse-race between a benchmark forecasting equation with and without a set of non-standard asset prices. We claim that such asset prices, especially house prices, do help in the majority of cases in the context of our data set to assess (predict) future CPI inflation. (Goodhart and Hofmann 2000a: 134)

Thus one method of weighting asset prices in a reformed price index is to use weights derived from empirical studies of the econometric relationships between the various series.

9.3.3 A statistically based measure

Another alternative is to relate the weights to the share of expenditures on each item. The CPI and RPI concentrate on personal expenditures, but omit almost entirely expenditures on real and financial assets. Thus direct (net) expenditures on buying houses (from other sectors, i.e. houses built by the company sector or sold to it from the government sector, when public sector dwellings are sold to their occupants) amounted to slightly over $3\frac{1}{2}\%$ of the usage of personal incomes in the UK in 1999. So the weight on the price of new housing could be that same percentage.

Besides being (net) purchasers of houses, households save by buying (mostly financial) assets. Changes in such asset prices affect the value of money as much as do changes in current goods and services prices. A net acquisitions approach is therefore, perhaps, the best.

What one is buying with a financial asset is a claim to a flow of interest or dividend payments. Dividend payments change over time, and there will be expectations of these which may turn out to be correct, or incorrect. But the present level of dividends is measurable, and a rise in the price of a claim on such a dividend, or more simply in the case of a rise in the price of a claim on an interest payment (though there is default risk here), seems (to us) a perfectly reasonable measure of inflation.

The argument may be made that the household sector, even after taking into account indirect purchases via financial intermediaries such as pension funds, may be net sellers of financial assets, as for example currently in the USA. In that case, the higher the price–dividend ratio the lower would be measured inflation. But that also seems reasonable. The more that we are a net seller of something highly valued, the higher is our utility, and the better off we are for a given cash income.

Why should one be concerned only with the level of inflation affecting individuals (persons), taking no notice of the inflationary pressures on other domestic sectors, companies and government? Perhaps, particularly if one is concerned about the conceptual and practical difficulties of taking account of (volatile) financial assets in a measure of inflation, a much broader index, covering all domestic sectors (so that financial assets net out, ignoring net claims on the rest of the world for this purpose), would seem suitable.

The GDP deflator at least has a broader coverage than the RPI or CPI, and includes estimates of prices of newly produced investment goods and houses. In that sense it partly avoids one of the main deficiencies of the narrow focus of the RPI/CPI measure of inflation.

However, it has other drawbacks. It does not, for example, resolve the theoretical problems identified by Alchian and Klein. Thus they state that the GNP deflator

includes the prices of newly produced assets but does not include the prices of previously existing items of wealth and therefore is conceptually distinct from our iso-utility wealth price index. Therefore, although it is useful for other purposes, a current output price index also provides a biased estimate of changes in the money cost of consumer utility . . . . Prices of already produced assets will, we conjecture, generally be more flexible than prices of currently produced goods, which are based on current costs that are often made less flexible by long-term contracts. (Alchian and Klein 1973: 181)

Moreover, this deflator is a somewhat arbitrary and abstract concept partly obtained as a derived residual which coordinates estimates of nominal and real output, themselves measured with considerable error. As a consequence it is only available quarterly, and is subject to large revisions as often as the output measures are changed. It is a somewhat noisy series. Few understand its conceptual basis, and even fewer pay it much attention as a preferred measure of inflation.

A better index that has been developed in response to user requests for such a broader measure of inflation is the Final Expenditure Price Index, or FEPI (see Wall 2000; Wall and O'Donoghue 2000; also note a similar exercise being undertaken in Australia, by Woolford 2000). While these indices have been constructed to overcome several of the deficiencies of the GDP deflator as a broader measure of inflation, they are still somewhat experimental and, in some fields, problematical. Wall (2000) is concerned with one such difficult area, concerning the public sector, and Woolford's paper touches on others. A few years' experience will be required before it will be possible to discern exactly how valuable these additional and broader measures of inflation will be to our assessments of such trends. In these, as in other, measures of inflation the treatment of owner-occupied housing tends to remain a stumbling block, though FEPI does contain an index for new dwellings as a component of its investment index.

9.4 Housing

These arguments on the appropriate treatment of asset prices in an inflation index perhaps reach their most practical and operational nub in the treatment of housing. For a large proportion of the population, our house is our most important and valuable asset. Personal expenditures on housing services, in one form or another—down-payments, mortgage payments, rent and repairs—represent a considerable chunk of personal expenditures. So statisticians, and others, can hardly avoid trying to decide how to deal with this major question for the construction of price indices.

The International Labour Organization (ILO) manual (Turvey 1989; see also Turvey 2000a and Office for National Statistics 1998), lists three general approaches to the treatment of housing. The first is the net acquisition approach, which is the change in the price of newly purchased owner-occupied dwellings, weighted by the net purchases of the reference population. This is an asset-based measure, and therefore comes close to our preferred measure of inflation as a change in the value of money, though the change in the price of the stock of existing houses rather than just of net purchases would in some respects be even better. It is, moreover, consistent with the treatment of other durables. A few countries, e.g. Australia and New Zealand, have used it, and it is, we understand, the main contender for use in the euro area Harmonised Index of Consumer Prices (HICP), which currently excludes any measure of the purchase price of (new) housing, though it does include minor repairs and maintenance by home-owners, as well as all expenditures by tenants.

The second main approach is the payments approach, measuring actual cash outflows, on down-payments, mortgage repayments and mortgage interest, or some subset of the above. This approach always, however, includes mortgage interest payments. This, though common, is analytically unsound. First, the procedure is not carried out consistently across purchases. Other goods bought on the basis of credit, e.g. credit-card credit, are usually not treated as more expensive on that account (though they have been in New Zealand). Second, the treatment of interest flows is not consistent across persons. If a borrower is worse off in some sense when interest rates rise, then equivalently a lender owning an interest-bearing asset is better off; why measure one and not the other? If we sell an interest-earning asset, say a money-market mutual fund holding, to buy a house, why are we treated differently to someone who borrows on a (variable-rate) mortgage? Third, should not the question of the price of any purchase be assessed separately from the issue of how that might be financed? Imports, inventories and all business purchases tend to be purchased in part on credit. Should we regard imports as more expensive when the cost of trade credit rises? Money, moreover, is fungible. As we know from calculations of mortgage equity withdrawal, the loan may be secured on the house but used to pay for furniture. When interest rates rise, is the furniture thereby more expensive? Moreover, the actual cash out-payments totally ignore changes in the ongoing value of the house whether by depreciation or capital loss/gain, which will often dwarf the cash flow. Despite its problems, such a cash-payment approach was used in the UK until 1994 and is still used in Ireland.

As the Reserve Bank of New Zealand (1997) puts it:

The rate of interest paid in order to advance consumption in time is not a 'price' any more than the rate of interest on saving is a 'negative price'. Consumers do not 'consume' debt. They consume the goods and services purchased with borrowed funds in the same way as they consume out of current income or past savings. The CPI should measure current consumption prices, not the way in which that consumption is financed. It is for these reasons that interest rates are excluded from the national accounts and GST frameworks and from the CPIs of most OECD countries.

The third approach is some variation of a user-cost approach. The most straight-forward, and perhaps the best of these, is to pretend that all housing is rented, and ask what is the change in the cost of renting current housing services. There is a practical difficulty with this in many countries, in that the rented sector in reality is too dissimilar and often too small to provide a good basis for calculation, though the US, Germany, Denmark and the Netherlands try to use this approach. Meanwhile, of course, we have a difficulty in principle, which is that people buy houses; they mostly do not rent them. This means that this kind of rental approach consciously aims to ignore the cost of buying access now to such future rental services.

In the absence of a sufficiently large rental market, there is a plethora of approx-imations to a user-cost approach. The method used now in the UK, following the advice of the RPI Advisory Committee (1994), and also in Canada, Sweden and Finland, is a combination of mortgage payments plus depreciation at replace-ment cost. Analytically this really is a dog's breakfast. We have already stated why we believe that the use of mortgage payments is wrong. As for depreciation, it is neither a cash payment, nor the true change in the price of an asset over any period, since depreciation over any period is likely to be dwarfed by shifts in the current value of the asset.

An even more theoretical user-cost approach is to measure the cost forgone by living in an owner-occupied property as compared with selling it at the beginning of the period and repurchasing it at the end (see Blinder 1980). But this gives the absurd result that as house prices rise, so the opportunity cost falls; indeed the more virulent the inflation of housing asset prices, the more negative would this measure become. Although it has some academic aficionados, this flies in the face of common sense; we are glad to say that no country has adopted this method.

In view of all these difficulties it is, perhaps, not surprising that another popular option is to exclude owner-occupied housing from the index altogether: none of France, Belgium, Italy, Spain, Greece, Austria, Luxembourg or Portugal included it in their index, at least when a survey of such practices was taken in 1998. And currently, neither does the HICP. A working party at Eurostat is considering owner-occupied housing costs in the HICP. At present it is prohibited by law from including prices that are non-observable or that do not involve an actual monetary transaction. Partly for this reason, the approach, we understand, that is most likely to be implemented, if one is at all, is to use the purchase price of new houses bought by the household sector from another sector (e.g. the corporate or government sectors).

9.5 Conclusions

In the earlier sections of this chapter we have set out some general arguments for incorporating asset prices into measures of price indices and inflation. Yet there is also a very strong case for leaving our present measures unchanged. The status quo has the inestimable advantage that it has the power of inertia on its side. Change is disruptive, perhaps even more so in the statistical world than elsewhere, and the case for change has to be demonstrable to have a chance. It is of crucial importance in the first place to have a nominal inflation target which is understood and reliable. Monkeying about with it on minor points of academic nicety could provoke confusion and cynicism. So long as all such measures are cointegrated the choice between measures is less important than having and sticking with the measure with which we have already become accustomed.

Moreover, there are strong arguments for keeping the status quo. On the negative side it can be correctly claimed that the valuation of asset prices depends on expectations about the future. Such expectations are hard to measure, ephemeral, not factual as price tags are factual, and often falsified; ex ante is not the same as ex post. If we should expect the price of London housing services to rise in future at a steady 10% per annum, a two-room flat in, shall we say, Notting Hill priced at £500,000 is not expensive, but cheap!

The more positive argument is that there is no *necessity* for the authorities to remain paralysed into inaction in the face of asset price changes, even with the present definition of inflation. In so far as those, like us, concerned about asset price changes can demonstrate econometrically that asset price changes *now* feed through significantly into *future* goods and services inflation, then the authorities should react *now*. And if they cannot find such a robust link, then it is right to ignore such asset price movements.

What does emerge from the empirical studies which have been done, we believe, is that the links between equity prices (and exchange rates) and subsequent movements in output and (goods and services) inflation is weak. In contrast, the relationship between housing price movements and subsequent output and inflation is much stronger. So the appropriate methodology for incorporating measures of housing price inflation into our overall statistics for inflation remains an urgent and important issue. It cannot be dismissed or ignored. It has to be addressed.

10

A Second Central Bank Instrument?

10.1 Why central banks need a second instrument

There has been a welcome and continuing trend of improvement in economic outcomes over recent decades, from the turbulent years of the 1970s, through the cycles of the 1980s (and in the early 1990s), to the recent decade of stable, low inflation and much milder cycles of real output. Some (large?) part of this improvement has been due to beneficial structural changes in the monetary policy framework, with the successful achievement of EMU, and the practical adoption of inflation targeting (IT) as a means of achieving price stability, being key milestones in this successful process.

But the decline in volatility in goods and services prices, as measured for example by the HICP, has not been matched by any equivalent decline in the volatility of asset prices. Moreover, the globalization and liberalization of banking and financial systems, though highly desirable for long-run trend growth, may nevertheless exacerbate shorter-run asset price booms and busts worldwide. An occasion of real fundamental improvement in the economy may generate rising profits and asset prices, which encourages greater bank lending, which raises asset prices yet further, and so on. Meanwhile improving productivity, appreciating exchange rates and strong tax revenues may help to keep consumer goods prices quiescent, so monetary policy does not automatically offset such an asset price cycle.

However desirable on other grounds, the recent changes to the accounting and regulatory regimes, with the shift to fair (market) values under the International Accounting Standards (IAS) and the adoption of Basel II, will do nothing to check such bank lending/asset price cyclical volatility. Indeed, if some of the more pessimistic prognostications about procyclicality turn out to be justified, such volatility may be exacerbated.

In the meantime the sole instrument that central banks currently wield, their command over short-term interest rates, is predicated on the maintenance of stability in the consumer price index, and rightly so. Despite proposals to shade interest rate decisions to offset asset price volatility (e.g. Cecchetti *et al.* 2000), the difficulties of doing so are considerable (see Greenspan 2002; Bernanke and Gertler 1999). Rather than distort the use of the interest rate instrument to try to achieve a second objective, what is needed is a second instrument. The purpose of this second instrument would be to maintain systemic financial stability. This latter objective remains a core purpose of central banks, whether or not they also supervise the individual banks, and is complementary to their primary role in achieving price stability, but—at least at present—is a field where central banks have few, if any, stabilizing instruments at hand, apart from emergency liquidity assistance to help mop up after something goes wrong in the financial system.

10.2   The form of a second instrument

So the main problem that we diagnose is a dynamic interaction between bank lending and asset prices, particularly property prices (see Chapters 6 and 8), leading to asset bubbles and busts. We fear that such (systematic) volatility may be unwittingly exacerbated by the new accounting (IAS) and regulatory measures (see Chapter 7). The need is to introduce an instrument that will have counter-cyclical characteristics, which could serve to check bank lending during asset price hikes, and vice versa.

The BIS have been advocating such general measures for some time (Borio, Furfine and Lowe 2001; Borio and Lowe 2002; Borio and White 2003). In the Conclusions to their 74th Annual Report, they wrote,

Fortunately, the global economy now appears to be on an upward path, and there is less call for macroeconomic stimulus. We should use this opportunity to reflect on the processes that allowed our armoury of macroeconomic instruments to become so depleted. An obvious point, but not without objections, is that this situation should be addressed directly through more aggressive tightening in good times. In addition, policies to strengthen the financial system, and to encourage more prudent lending behaviour in upturns, might help to mitigate the damage in downturns and reduce the need to resort to aggressive policy easing in the future. (BIS 2004: 143)

The next question is, how do you do this? In Chapter 3 we suggested that, analogously to the method of measuring output gap, we could use deviations of asset prices from a smoothed (Hodrick–Prescott filter) trend to assess the gap between the current asset price and its 'fundamental' value. But that was roundly criticized on the grounds of inconsistency with efficient market hypotheses. Borio and Lowe (2002) suggest that the rate of growth of bank lending itself is the key determinant of future asset price movements, but the lags are long and the relationship subject to structural changes in financial intermediation, etc.

Our view now is that a better (perhaps best) approach would be to relate the capital requirement on bank lending to the rate of change of asset prices in the relevant sector. Thus the capital adequacy requirement (CAR) on mortgage lending could be related to the rise in housing prices (relative to HICP inflation), and lending to construction and property companies to the rise in property prices. For manufacturing and services more broadly, the CAR could be related to the rise in equity prices: up when equity prices are appreciating, down when prices are falling. Similarly, required solvency ratios for life insurance companies would be adjusted counter-cyclically in response to shifts in equities, bond and property prices.

The purpose of the exercise would be both to build up reserves and to restrain bank lending during asset price booms, so as to release these during asset price depressions. In this respect it has much in common with the current Spanish pre-provisioning policy proposals. The flip side, however, is that it appears to relax prudential requirements most during bad recessions, just when individual banks and other financial intermediaries are individually at their most fragile. But when the concern of the central bank is for the aggregate, systemic state of the system, surely this is the right course.

10.3   Disintermediation

This proposal that CARs should be raised in line with the increase in the relevant asset price (relative to the general increase in the CPI) has quite a lot in common with earlier proposals to vary margin requirements for the purpose of limiting fluctuations in equity prices on the NYSE. Hardouvelis, both when at the Federal Reserve Bank of New York and subsequently, has advocated this (e.g. Hardouvelis 1990, 1992, 1995, 2002). This has been heavily criticized, partly with the argument of inappropriate intervention into private sector markets, but more so on the grounds that there are so many other ways of speculating on a stock exchange that a margin call would distort the pattern of flows without having much, or any, effect on overall trading, or prices.

Similarly it might be argued that state- (time-)varying CARs would lead to pure disintermediation without much net effect. The extent of disintermediation to other domestic lenders would, we would expect, be quite limited. In Europe at least, the CARs are imposed on all credit-extending intermediaries, and thus the state (time) variation in CARs would affect them all equally, so there would be no distortion between different forms of mortgage institution.[1] Moreover, small and medium-sized enterprises have no real alternative to banks. Large companies do, and this exercise, which would have the (desired, but probably slight) effect of

---

[1] Branches, but not subsidiaries, of foreign banks would not be subject to such time-varying CARs. If, and when, the business of such branches becomes large, the host country often requires that it become a subsidiary. Moreover the friction involved in switching between banks will usually outweigh any small pricing differentials that might arise.

widening bank spreads in (asset price) booms and lowering them in asset price busts, might induce the bigger companies to raise slightly more of their funds in the capital market during booms and slightly less during recessions. But that too might be considered on balance a desirable outcome, with the effect of further dampening asset price fluctuations.

On this view the more serious concern about disintermediation, in respect to this proposal, relates to disintermediation abroad, not domestically. Absent exchange controls, which we are not advocating, the most obvious loophole is for a bank simply to book domestic currency loans to residents through a foreign subsidiary, financing that through an internal transfer of funds. It would probably be necessary to subject all domestic currency lending to national residents to be subject to the time-varying CARs, wherever booked. That would, of course, leave the possibility of lending in foreign currency in foreign subsidiaries with the borrower swapping back into domestic currency. Again the frictions involved would probably outweigh the comparative benefit from avoiding such differentials in CARs as might arise between national jurisdictions. Moreover asset price booms and busts, even in spatially fixed and segmented assets such as housing and property, tend to be quite closely correlated internationally, so that differentials between nations in their time-varying CARs would tend to be small.

Overall we doubt that the effects of time-varying (state-varying) CARs would, like margin requirements on stock purchases, be much reduced by systemic disintermediation.

10.4   Empirical details

Even if the principle of state- (time-)varying CARs were to be accepted, there would be a mass of detail to work through carefully first. If the variation in CARs were to be based on the rate of change of some benchmark index, what would be the period(s) over which that change would be estimated, what would be the coefficient(s), and how often would the calculation be revised—(e.g. would the massive collapse in equities in October 1987 be reflected in revised (lowered) capital requirements the next day, or on December 31, or when? Some categories of bank lending relate fairly obviously to certain asset price indices, e.g. mortgages to housing prices, or property and construction companies to property prices. What do you do with other private sector loans—do you not apply time-varying CARs to them, or do you relate the time-varying CARs to some index of cycles in real output or of equity prices? If the latter, how far do you seek to disaggregate by sector, if at all?

Next, what might be the effect of time-varying CARs on bank behaviour, loan pricing and margins, and hence on borrower responses and bank profitability? There are large unknowns, especially as time- (state-)varying CARs have never, to our knowledge, been previously introduced. Under these circumstances it would seem sensible to proceed quite cautiously, initially introducing relatively mild cyclical adjustments in required CARs, with, say, a maximum variation of plus or minus 200 basis points (i.e. a trough-to-peak change of at most 400 basis points).

We could do some partial equilibrium counterfactual simulations showing how, for a given, historical pattern of bank credit extension, different methods of varying CARs would have led to a different time path of CARs for each country. Depending on the enthusiasm for this basic idea, we could quite easily do this in subsequent research. A much more difficult exercise would be to embed this into a dynamic general equilibrium model whereby commercial bank and borrower responses would affect total lending, asset price and real output, though in principle this could be done in models of the kind developed by Goodhart, Sunirand and Tsomocos (2004a,b, 2005).

For the purpose of this exercise, however, we have sought to illustrate how our approach might work by examining a mechanism quite closely akin to a time-varying CAR, in the shape of time-varying loan-to-value ratios (LTVs) in mortgage lending. Mortgage institutions have introduced, for their own prudential purposes, time-varying LTVs, and in a few cases, and a few countries (notably in Hong Kong, e.g. in 1991), these were varied as a result of pressure from the authorities for public policy purposes. So in the next section we assemble the evidence from prior research studies on the effects of changing LTVs on financial markets, and consider how the use of this instrument could be an addition to the authorities' armoury.

10.5 The effects of time-varying LTVs

Only a few studies have assessed the effect of varying LTVs on credit creation and property prices. Gerlach and Peng (2005) analyse the interaction between bank lending and property prices in Hong Kong. They show that the effect of property prices on bank lending in Hong Kong was significantly reduced after banks started to apply the maximum LTV guideline of the HKMA in 1991. Almeida *et al.* (2002) assess the effect of cross-country variation in the maximum loan-to-value ratio on the sensitivity of house prices to changes in real income and find that the reaction of house prices to such changes is larger the higher the LTV.

Data on maximum or average LTVs are not readily available. Almeida *et al.* (2002) report maximum LTVs compiled from various sources for a large panel of countries, but the data are only rough estimates and are available only as decennial averages. Thus, as there is not much variation in the data at the individual-country level, we have to assess the effect of LTVs on bank lending and property prices from an international perspective, on the basis of data for a panel of 16 countries. Following the analysis in Hofmann (2003), we model both aggregate bank lending to the private non-bank sector (bank credit) as a function of GDP, property prices and the short-term real interest rate, and also property prices as a function of GDP, bank credit and interest rates.[2] The sample period is the first quarter of 1985 till the fourth quarter of 2001.

First, we investigated the long-run link between bank credit, GDP and property prices. Prior unit-root tests suggested that real bank lending, real GDP and real property prices are I(1), while the real interest rate appears to be a borderline case between I(1) and I(0). We therefore decided to allow only bank credit, GDP and property prices to enter the long-run relationship. We first tested for the presence of panel cointegration based on the panel cointegration trace test proposed by Larsson *et al.* (2001). The test statistic is the standardized average of the N individual Johansen trace test statistics:

$$\psi_{LR} = \frac{\sqrt{N}(\overline{LR} - \mu)}{\sqrt{\delta}} \tag{1}$$

where $\overline{LR}$ is the average of the individual trace test statistics and μ and δ are respectively the mean and the variance of the asymptotic distribution of the trace test statistic, which are tabulated in Osterwald-Lenum (1992). Larsson *et al.* (2001) show that the test statistic has a standard normal distribution. The test is one-sided, with large positive values of the test statistics suggesting a rejection of the null hypothesis of no cointegration. The 1%, 5% and 10% critical values are 1.96, 1.64 and 1.28 respectively. The test results, which are reported in Table 10.1, suggest the presence of a single cointegrating relationship.

As the next step, we estimate the long-run coefficients linking real bank lending, real GDP and real property prices based on a fixed-effects panel dynamic OLS (DOLS) estimator proposed by Kao and Chiang (2000). The results are also reported in Table 10.1 and suggest that there is a significant positive link between real bank lending and both real GDP and real property prices in the long run.

In order to assess the effect of LTV on bank credit and property prices we estimate error-correction models (ECMs) for the change in bank credit and the change in property prices. The regressors are the lagged error-correction term, i.e. the deviation of the log of bank credit from the long-run relationship estimated above, four own lags, the current change in real GDP, the lagged change in the short-term real interest rate and the current change in real property prices for the bank credit ECM; and the current change in real bank credit for the property price ECM. In order to prevent simultaneity bias from affecting the estimation, the contemporaneous variables included in each equation were instrumented for, using four own lags as instruments. The systems were estimated by pooled fixed-effects three-stage least squares in order to account for potential contemporaneous correlation in the errors across equations.

---

[2] For a detailed description of the data and their sources see Hofmann (2003).

Table 10.1. Panel cointegration analysis of the credit-property price nexus

Panel cointegration test			Cointegrating relationship
$r = 0$	$r \leqslant 1$	$r \leqslant 2$	
9.69	1.14	0.44	$C = 1.22Y + 0.26P$
			(0.11) (0.05)

Note: The panel cointegration test is that proposed by Larsson *et al.* (2001). The 1%, 5% and 10% critical values for the panel cointegration test are respectively 1.96, 1.64 and 1.28. The cointegrating relationship was estimated on the basis of a fixed-effects panel dynamic OLS (DOLS) estimator proposed by Kao and Chiang (2000). Standard errors are in parentheses.

Table 10.2. Error-correction models for bank credit and property prices

$\Delta C_t = -0.027ECT_{t-1} + 0.176\Delta C_{t-1} + 0.204\Delta C_{t-2} + 0.143\Delta C_{t-3} + 0.055\Delta C_{t-4} + 0.092\Delta Y_t + 0.0001\Delta r_{t-1}$
$\quad\;\;(-7.48)\qquad\quad(6.3)\qquad\quad\;(7.65)\qquad\quad(5.28)\qquad\quad(2.08)\qquad\quad(0.39)\qquad\quad(0.21)$
$\quad + 0.154\Delta P_t + 0.12LTV_t$
$\quad\;\;\;(3.04)\qquad\;(4.44)$

$\Delta P_t = -0.003ECT_{t-1} + 0.372\Delta P_{t-1} + 0.072\Delta P_{t-2} + 0.131\Delta P_{t-3} - 0.101\Delta P_{t-4} + 0.83\Delta Y_t - 0.002\Delta r_{t-1}$
$\quad\;\;(-0.65)\qquad\quad(9.72)\qquad\quad\;(2.15)\qquad\quad(4.07)\qquad\quad(-3.60)\qquad\quad(1.97)\qquad\;(-4.75)$
$\quad + 0.189\Delta C_t$
$\quad\;\;\;(2.559)$

Note: T-statistics are in parentheses.

We allowed LTVs to enter both EMCs. We did not find evidence that LTVs had a significant influence on the effect of property prices on credit, as suggested by Gerlach and Peng (2005), or that LTVs influenced the effect of real GDP on property prices, as suggested by Almeida *et al.* (2002). What we did find is a strong and highly significant direct effect of LTVs on credit growth. So we included the current level of the LTV, instrumented by its own four lags, in bank credit ECM. The results are reported in Table 10.2.

The results suggest that long-run causality goes from property prices to bank lending, rather than conversely. The error-correction term in the ECM for bank lending is significantly negative, but insignificant in the property price ECM. Short-run causality appears to go in both directions: the change in real property prices has a significantly positive effect on bank lending and vice versa. GDP growth and real interest rates appear to matter more for property prices than for bank lending.

The LTV, on the other hand, has a significantly positive effect on bank lending. This finding suggests that countries with higher maximum LTVs also have experienced faster credit expansion. This result implies, in turn, that variations in the maximum LTV may be used to stabilize bank credit. The average standard deviation of the change in real house prices in our sample of 16 countries is about 5.

Since the effect of a change in house prices and of a change in the LTV on credit are not significantly different (see Table 10.2), appropriate adjustments of the LTV within a band of plus or minus 10 percentage points around its mean would already suffice to offset the effect of 95% of the fluctuations of house prices on credit growth. Given an average LTV of 80% in our sample of countries, this would imply a 70–90% band for the variation in the LTV in response to changes in property prices.

10.6   Conclusions

Central banks have two, core purposes, to wit the maintenance of price and financial stability. They have one main instrument, the setting of short-term interest rates, which is correctly predicated on the achievement of price stability, or inflation targets. Another instrument, emergency lending to banks under pressure, is normally only used after financial stability has already come under threat, and, owing to concerns about moral hazard, can only be used sparingly.

So, there is a currently unfulfilled need for a second instrument, which could be varied by a central bank to help maintain financial stability. We suggest that time- and state-varying capital adequacy requirements (CARs) could play this role. We have examined a closely related issue, whether time- and state-varying loan-to-value ratios (LTVs) for mortgage lending could be used to stabilize either the housing market or bank lending to it. Our preliminary results suggest that changes in LTVs do not affect property prices directly, but do have a significant effect on bank lending.

11

House Price Fluctuations and Public Policy

Persistent inflation is a monetary phenomenon. When monetary policy is subject to proper discipline and becomes well anchored, there should be no persistence in inflation. In the last 15 or so years, that has been the experience of most developed countries. During these years the target for inflation has not been zero, but a low rate of about 2 to $2\frac{1}{2}$%. The preference for a low, but positive, inflation rate (over a target for zero inflation) is due partly to concerns over whether the statistical indices may exaggerate inflation slightly (see the Boskin Report 1996), partly to a belief that workers would be unwilling to negotiate, or to accept, nominal wage cuts, so that grinding inflation down from 2% to zero might be very costly in forgone output (Akerlof and Yellen 1985, 1990), and, even more, to a fear that, given the zero nominal floor to short-term interest rates, it could be hard for (conventional) monetary policy measures to counteract a deflationary shock when the economy already has price stability. The poor economic experience of Japan over these same last 15 years has strongly reinforced these latter concerns. This makes it unlikely that the policy target for inflation will be revised down to zero (or below: see the arguments of Selgin 1996 in favour of a target of zero labour costs) in the foreseeable future.

Be that as it may, the persistence, or first-order autocorrelation, of inflation around the mean target has collapsed, even becoming negative since the start of inflation targeting in the UK in 1992 (see Benati 2005: table C). In this respect the recent period of inflation targetry has been as well 'anchored' as the gold standard. During the intervening periods—interwar, Bretton Woods, and from Bretton Woods to the start of inflation targetry—the persistence of inflation (relative to its mean) increased from period to period.

This will have been due to a variety of causes, but the mismanagement of monetary policy will rank high, notably the inability of the monetary authorities to prevent deflation in the early 1930s, and to stop worsening inflationary trends in the early 1960s and 1970s. This latter was partly out of a belief that monetary policy should be targeted at outcomes other than domestic price inflation, for example at unemployment or the maintenance of an exchange rate peg, and partly out of a view that such monetary policy was both relatively unimportant and impotent, a view represented by the Radcliffe Report (1959) and now recorded in historical studies by Nelson (2004) and Batini and Nelson (2005).

In any case, the experience of the years from about 1955 to about 1975 was of regular cycles of inflation and output around an increasing trend in inflation. Each time that there was a surge in inflation, restrictive policies, both fiscal and monetary, would be introduced, either directly to counter the inflation or indirectly to offset its effects on the balance of payments and hence on the exchange rate. While the inflationary booms were countered by restrictive policies, the subsequent recessions led to policies being eased again in pursuit of higher employment, growth and political popularity.

It was not until 1979 that Arthur Volcker in the USA, and Margaret Thatcher in the UK, made control of inflation the prime objective of monetary policy, though that had been the main objective of the Bundesbank since its foundation in 1957 (Marsh 1992). Not only, however, did it take quite a long time to eliminate excess inflation from the system, but also several strategies for monetary policy management, notably various forms of monetary targetry and, in the case of the UK, entry into the Exchange Rate Mechanism of the European Union, were tried first and found wanting.

During this whole long period, from 1945 until the early 1990s, the determining forces that drove monetary policy decisions were clear. Inflationary pressures, which in an open economy in a pegged exchange rate regime would also emerge in the guise of balance of payments difficulties, would put upwards pressure on interest rates (or induce a tightening of credit and exchange controls). By contrast, increases in unemployment and/or comparatively sluggish growth rates would put downwards pressure on interest rates (and lead to a relaxation of direct controls).

From the early 1990s onwards, the conjuncture changed in certain respects. The success of inflation targetry, whether overt as in the inflation targeting countries or covert, as in the USA, led to that target becoming credible. Inflation expectations became 'anchored' by the target. Consequently fluctuations in both demand and monetary impulses had less effect on wage/price negotiations. The Phillips curve, relating the cyclical component of unemployment to the cyclical component of inflation, became much flatter; in other words unemployment could vary more without affecting goods and services price inflation (see Benati 2005: chart 2, p. 164 and Morris, Shin and Tong 2006). With both inflation, and inflation expectations, held stable by the monetary anchor, fluctuations in those series no longer provided such a clear mirror wherein the monetary authorities could see the reflections of their own actions (Morris, Shin and Tong 2006).

The same condition had existed under the gold standard in the nineteenth and early twentieth centuries. The achievement of overall medium- and longer-term price stability (weather-related agricultural supply fluctuations led to much short-term price volatility) did not, however, lead to output or financial stability more widely. Often such output (and financial) fluctuations had their foundation in technological advances, e.g. canals, railways, steel, chemicals, electricity. That would lead to a related financial market expansion, with a combination and interaction of bank lending expansion and asset price surge. When the profitability arising from the investment boom peaked, there was often an accompanying sharp asset price downturn and financial crisis, as in 1873, 1893 and 1907 (see Delargy and Goodhart 1999).

By the same token, once the monetary anchor had been restored in the early 1990s, and inflationary expectations anchored, monetary developments, as under the gold standard, became more closely reflected in asset price fluctuations than in goods and services price inflation. In one respect this was a natural outcome. Bank lending is much more closely related to transactions in assets, especially in property, than to consumption expenditures. One example of this is that mortgage lending to persons in most countries far outstrips credit card and other consumer loans. This is reflected in a rather close correlation between property prices and credit creation (see Chapters 6–8 above).

Indeed in numerous cases and countries, monetary and asset price expansion during the last 15 years has been accompanied by below-target goods and service price inflation. This is because such expansion may be related to an initial favourable shock, raising productivity (and thus reducing unit labour costs), as in the USA, and/or raising investment opportunities (and hence, via capital inflows, leading to an appreciation of the currency), as in Asia. Moreover, the strong economy raises tax revenue and reduces the fiscal deficit. So, just before a potential crash, an economy can look remarkably sound, with high growth, high investment, stable prices and a low fiscal deficit (as in East Asia in 1997/8).

This leads to a new conundrum for monetary policy. During the period 1950–90 monetary tightening in the shape of higher interest rates would largely have its effect on domestic price inflation through the external channel. An increase in interest rates would lead to higher capital inflows and cause an appreciation of the exchange rate. But in the last few decades a larger proportion of capital flows, both direct and portfolio, have been profit- (equity-)related. So a rise in interest rates can lead, via its effect in reducing expected domestic profitability, to a diminution in capital inflows and hence a depreciation (not an appreciation) of the exchange rate. Particularly in emerging economies, a financial crisis can lead to a combination of depreciation, higher interest rates, falling output and rising inflation. This conjuncture has caused particular difficulties for the IMF, whose standard remedies for financial crises in the shape of tighter monetary and fiscal policies, if pressed too far, can arguably worsen the situation; and Stiglitz (2002), indeed, has argued just that.

Be that as it may—and certainly such policy issues remain contentious—the external channel has become both less reliable and in most cases, perhaps, less potent as an element in the transmission mechanism of monetary policy. At the same time the personal sector has been accumulating much more wealth, both non-financial in the form of property, and financial. In most countries the gross value of persons' direct property holdings is of similar magnitude and sometimes even larger than their gross financial asset holdings (see Table 1.1 above), though such property has usually been initially purchased by borrowing through mortgages, so gross personal financial indebtedness has also been climbing rapidly, not only absolutely, but as the ratio to disposable income (see Figure 1.2 above).

Interest rate changes have an effect on debtors' cash flow, depending on the form of their mortgage, whether variable or fixed-rate, and such rate changes affect the present value of assets, both financial and non-financial. There is a growing literature, both theoretical and empirical, on the likely effect of such factors on personal consumption and on the housing market (see e.g. Maclennan *et al.* 2000; ECB 2003; OECD 2004; Tsatsaronis and Zhu 2004; Aoki *et al.* 2004). The empirical evidence also suggests that in the wake of the liberalization and deregulation of financial and credit markets since the late 1970s, the effect of interest rate changes on property prices as well as the effect of property prices on bank lending and economic activity appear to have become stronger over time (Iacoviello and Minetti 2003).

So there is a developing two-way interaction between asset price fluctuations and monetary policy. With goods and services price inflation (expectations) largely anchored by monetary policy, demand shocks (and perhaps supply shocks too) are likely to be reflected to a greater extent in asset price adjustments. Such asset price fluctuations will not only have implications for future movements in real output and consumer price indices, but they may also have potential implications for systemic financial stability. In the middle of an asset price boom, when expectations of future returns are high and probabilities of default are low, the bubble can be hard to restrain by minor shifts in interest rates. On the other hand, when asset prices are trending down and defaults high, reductions in interest rates may do little to encourage bank lending, as in Japan.

Despite the fact that the impact of interest rate changes on asset prices (notably on exchange rates, property prices and equities) can be uncertain and variable, it is largely via such reactions that monetary policy bites. So monetary policy measures, primarily interest rate changes, affect asset prices, and asset price changes induce monetary policy responses, primarily through their effect on real output and future expected inflation. One of the main objectives of this book has been to illustrate and, where possible, to quantify this two-way interaction, as has been done in Chapters 6, 8 and 10.

The particular purpose of this chapter, however, is to assess how the authorities might react to this new conjuncture, whereby economic shocks have become reflected more in asset price fluctuations, and less so in consumer price fluctuations. There are two main camps of thought. The first, represented by Bernanke and Gertler (1999), argues that monetary policy, in the form of interest rate changes, ought to react to the extent that such asset price fluctuations lead to predictable changes in future output and inflation, but no more than that. A major problem with such a prescription is that it is very hard to predict how an asset price bubble, or bust, may affect future output and inflation. There is always a danger that a burst bubble, interacting with a weakened banking system, could lead to a debt/deflation crisis. In some sense similarly, the Bank of Japan has worried that sufficient monetary expansion to offset fully the depressive effect of an asset price collapse could potentially lead to hyperinflation.

Given the considerable uncertainty, but potential strength, of the effects of any major asset price bubble, or bust, there are therefore strong arguments for trying to lean against such developing asset price fluctuations, to head them off at the pass. That said, in so far as variations in housing prices already enter the target price index, that will occur quasi-automatically. This takes us back to the discussion in Chapter 9, about how far asset prices in general, and housing prices in particular, should enter into the target price index.

If such asset prices do not enter into the price index, or insufficiently so, there remains a question of how to respond to the separate movement of such asset prices. There are numerous problems. First, asset prices move in differing ways; how, if at all, should one aggregate over such classes of asset prices, e.g. exchange rates, property and equities? Our Chapter 3, describing the construction of a Financial Conditions Index (FCI), points in one such direction.

Second, the simplicity, transparency and theoretical support resulting from defining the role of monetary policy as maintaining medium-term price stability, with the latter defined in terms of a consumer price index, are of great value; this definition provides a heuristic, and easily understandable, rule for the authorities' behaviour, with one instrument to hit one target. Trying to balance an objective function containing (some index of) asset prices separately from consumer prices would lead to greater complexity, discretion and noise, and would be less likely to provide an anchor for expectations.

Third, the argument for responding to asset prices, over and above their (predictable) effect on future output (and inflation), usually involves some belief that such asset prices have moved away from their 'fundamental equilibrium', and may harm the economy when they snap back to their 'proper' level, or perhaps overshoot. The concept that asset prices may be in disequilibrium is, however, contentious. Clearly asset prices are what they are at any time because there is as much buying as selling, as many bulls as bears, at that price. So for a central bank to raise (lower) interest rates without being able to point to a forecast of future inflation exceeding (falling below) target, just because it viewed an asset price as being intrinsically too high (low), would be difficult to justify publicly and politically. Central bank officials are not universally known for their prescience in calling the turn of asset markets. It is, perhaps, worth recalling that Alan Greenspan termed the US equity market as exhibiting 'irrational exuberance' in 1996, when the Dow stood at about 6500, not only far below its subsequent January 2000 peak of 11,580, but even well below its subsequent trough in October 2002 of 7535.

For such reasons we share the conventional, and consensus, view that the straightforward allocation of monetary policy, in the form of interest rate adjustments, to the maintenance of consumer price stability is appropriate, though we believe that house price inflation should be represented in that index. This does not mean, however, that we would not respond at all to perceived asset price fluctuations. What we would try to do is to find another instrument.

Note that a main concern—perhaps the main concern—about asset price bubbles is that their collapse will weaken the banking system, causing systemic financial instability, and thereby leading to a debt/deflation spiral (Fisher 1932). This was a large part of the story in many nineteenth-century cases, in 1929–33 in the USA and much of continental Europe, in Scandinavia in the early 1990s, in East Asia in 1997/8 and in Japan more recently. In so far, therefore, as the central bank has a prime concern for systemic financial stability, it should want to promote a program of counter-cyclical prudential regulations which become restrictive during asset price bubbles and relax during asset price downturns.

Unfortunately the system of financial regulation is developing in a manner which will have exactly the reverse proclivity. Under the Basel II accord for financial regulation, this will become more procyclical, as shown in Chapter 7 above and also in Danielsson *et al.* (2001), Goodhart and Segoviano (2004), and Goodhart and Taylor (forthcoming). The main aim of Basel II is to make capital adequacy requirements (CARs) more risk-sensitive. But the probability of default (PoD) of a borrower increases in downturns, even though the risky venture itself is usually initiated, and financed, in the preceding upturn. So measured risk rises in slumps, and falls in booms, as do non-performing loans. The Basel Committee of Banking Supervision was not only aware of the likely procyclicality of (Pillar 1) Basel II, but also took steps to try to ameliorate that problem, for example by requesting banks to 'look through the cycle' in assessing PoDs. Even so, the implementation of Basel II is likely to cause CARs to vary in a significantly more procyclical fashion than did Basel I, with the consequence that the dynamic interaction of bank lending and asset price cycles could become even more pronounced.

There is, however, an opportunity, under Pillar 2 of Basel II, for the regulatory/supervisory authorities in any country to superimpose additional capital requirements on their own banks. So if the authorities wanted to do so, they could require the banks under their control to build up capital, even more than required under Pillar 1, during periods of asset price appreciation.

The main problem facing any one country trying to introduce counter-cyclical financial regulation is that in a global financial system, such banking business might just be transferred abroad; geographical disintermediation would take place. The main danger would arise from domestic banks booking business through subsidiaries abroad (the business of foreign branches being treated as part of the domestic bank). Supplementary measures would have to be taken to deal with this, for example by imposing some direct controls on certain transactions between domestic banks and their subsidiaries.

If that loophole were closed, informational frictions, both of banks with respect to new borrowers and of borrowers with respect to alternative (foreign) loan opportunities, could limit the extent of disintermediation. In any case, if the concern is that a domestic asset price downturn could lead to financial fragility emerging in domestic banks, would it not be beneficial to divert some of the lending which is supporting that asset price bubble to foreign banks? In earlier years when the development of the London Docklands financial centre at Canary Wharf appeared risky, considerable comfort was afforded by the fact that a large part of its bank finance came from foreign banks.

There is, nonetheless, a political-economy concern about the contra-cyclical use of Pillar 2. This is that one of the main objectives of the Basel Accords, both Basel I and II, has been to bring about an international level playing field, so that there can be fair competition between banks headquartered in different countries whenever they compete. The application of Pillar 2 by an individual country would, and indeed would be intended to, handicap banks subject to such extra CAR *vis-à-vis* other banks. Depending on circumstances this could cause resentment among, and strong lobbying by, those banks that were affected.

Be that as it may, one of the best leading indicators of financial fragility in an individual bank or for an aggregate banking system is a rapid expansion of lending, taking such lending well above trend levels. This was documented for national banking systems in Chapter 8. So the need is to have some mechanism for restraining such growth, whether in aggregate or by sector, when it interacts with an asset bubble. One could try to design Pillar 2 in a quasi-automatic fashion, so that the greater the rate of expansion of such lending, the higher the CAR.

There are, perhaps, other ways of achieving the same objective. In Hong Kong and in South Korea the monetary authorities sought to require the banks to apply more conservative loan-to-value ratios (LTVs) as housing prices rose (see for example Gerlach and Peng 2005) and Wong, Fung, Fong and Sze 2004). Relating LTV requirements to the ratio of housing prices to incomes could be done more commonly. The Spanish pre-provisioning initiative (see Saurina 2004 and Fernandez de Lis *et al.* 2001) was also a way of trying to get banks to build up additional reserves in good times, to provide greater strength during adverse periods. Whether this scheme will continue to be acceptable under the new fair-value accounting procedures of the International Accounting Standards (IAS) remains to be seen.

The objective is fairly obvious and straightforward—to find a contra-cyclical instrument, or set of instruments, that will directly dampen the asset price/bank lending cycle. It has to be said, however, that there seems relatively little enthusiasm or will among regulators, banks, politicians or public for driving this agenda forward at this juncture. At the present time (2006), the initial, transitional effort of implementing Basel II and IAS almost simultaneously has led to considerable regulatory exhaustion. The current wish is to allow the new regulatory systems time to settle before considering further reforms and alternatives.

It would probably not be until the application of Basel II may be seen as having exacerbated the asset price/bank lending cycle, if indeed it does so, that serious attention will be given to the policy proposals set out here. But if that time should come, we will be ready to put forward these suggestions.

References

Abiad, A., and A. Mody (2003), 'Financial Reform: What Shapes it? What Shakes it?', IMF Working Paper no. 03/70.

Acharya, V., S. Bharath and A. Srinivasan (2003), 'Understanding the Recovery Rates on Defaulted Securities', CEPR Discussion Paper no. 4098.

Akerlof, G., and P. Romer (1993), 'Looting: The Economic Underworld of Bankruptcy for Profit', *Brookings Papers on Economic Activity*, 2: 1–73.

Akerlof, G., and J. Yellen (1985), 'A Near Rational Model of the Business Cycle with Wage and Price Inertia', *Quarterly Journal of Economics*, 100: 823–38.

—— —— (1990), 'The Fair Wage-Effort Hypothesis and Unemployment', *Quarterly Journal of Economics*, 105: 255–83.

Alchian, A., and B. Klein (1973), 'On a Correct Measure of Inflation', *Journal of Money, Credit and Banking*, 5: 173–91.

Allen, F., and D. Gale (1998), 'Bubbles and Crises', *The Economic Journal*, 110: 236–55.

—— —— (1999), 'Bubbles, Crises, and Policy', *Oxford Review of Economic Policy*, 15: 9–18.

Almeida, H., M. Campello and C. Liu (2002), 'The Financial Accelerator in Household Spending: Evidence from International Housing Markets', mimeo New York University.

Altissimo, F., E. Georgiou, T. Sastve, M. Valderrama, G. Strene, M. Stocker, M. Weth, K. Whelan, and A. Willman (2005), 'Wealth and Asset Price Effects on Economic Activity', ECB Occasional Paper no. 29.

Altman, E. (2002), *Altman Report on Defaulted Bonds and Bank Loans*, Salomon Smith Barney, United States Corporate Bond Research.

—— B. Brady, A. Resti, and A. Sironi (2002), 'The Link between Default and Recovery Rates: Implications for Credit Risk Models and Procyclicality', working paper, New York University.

—— A. Elizondo, and M. Segoviano (2002), *Medicion integral del riesgo de credito*, ed Limusa, Mexico.

Ando, A., and F. Modigliani (1963), 'The "Life Cycle" Hypothesis of Saving: Aggregate Implications and Tests', *American Economic Review*, 53: 55–84.

Andrews, D. (1993), 'Tests for Parameter Instability and Structural Change with Unknown Change Point, *Econometrica*, 61: 821–56.

Aoki, K., J. Proudman, and G. Vlieghe (2004), 'House Prices, Consumption, and Monetary Policy: A Financial Accelerator Approach', *Journal of Financial Intermediation*, 13: 414–35.

Arthur, S. (2003), 'Obtaining Real Estate Data: Criteria, Difficulties and Limitations', BIS Papers no. 21, 63–69.

Bagliano, F., C. Favero, and F. Franco (1999), 'Measuring Monetary Policy in Open Economies', CEPR Discussion Paper no. 2079.

Baker, G. (1999), 'Wall St Asks Fed Questions—and May Hold the Answers', *Financial Times*, 30 Aug.

References

Bank of England (1971), *Competition and Credit Control* (London: Bank of England).

Basel Committee on Banking Supervision (1999), 'Capital Requirements and Bank Behaviour: The Impact of the Basel Accord', Basel Committee on Banking Supervision Working Paper no. 1.

Batini, N., and E. Nelson (2005), 'The UK's Rocky Road to Stability', Federal Reserve Bank of St. Louis Working Paper no. 2005–020A.

—— and K. Turnbull (2000), 'Monetary Conditions Indices for the UK: A Survey', Bank of England External MPC Unit Discussion Paper no. 1.

Benati, L. (2003), 'Evolving Post-World War II U.K. Economic Performance', paper presented at the James Tobin symposium organized by the Chicago Federal Reserve Bank.

—— (2005), 'The Inflation-Targeting Framework from an Historical Perspective', *Bank of England Quarterly Bulletin*, 45: 160–8.

Berger, A., and G. Udell (1994), 'Did Risk-Based Capital Allocate Bank Credit and Cause a "Credit Crunch" in the United States?', *Journal of Money, Credit and Banking*, 26: 585–628.

Bernanke, B. (1983), 'Nonmonetary Effects of the Financial Crisis in the Propagation of the Great Depression', *American Economic Review*, 73: 257–76.

—— (2003), 'An Unwelcome Fall in Inflation?', paper presented to the Economics Roundtable, University of California, San Diego; available <www.federalreserve.gov/boarddocs/speeches/2003/20030723/default.htm>.

—— and A. Blinder (1988), 'Credit, Money and Aggregate Demand', *American Economic Review: Papers and Proceedings*, 78: 435–9.

—— and M. Gertler (1989), 'Agency Costs, Collateral and Business Fluctuations', *American Economic Review*, 79: 14–31.

—— —— (1995), 'Inside the Black Box: The Credit Channel of Monetary Policy Transmission', *Journal of Economic Perspectives*, 9: 27–48.

—— —— (1999), 'Monetary Policy and Asset Price Volatility', in Federal Reserve Bank of Kansas City, *New Challenges for Monetary Policy*, proceedings of the Jackson Hole Conference, 17–51.

—— —— and S. Gilchrist (1999), 'The Financial Accelerator in a Quantitative Business Cycle Framework', in J. Taylor and M. Woodford (eds), *Handbook of Macroeconomics*, vol. 1C, Amsterdam and Oxford: Elsevier Science, 1341–93.

Bernholz, P. (2003), *Monetary Regimes and Inflation: History, Economic and Political Relationships*, Cheltenham: Edward Elgar.

BIS (1999), 'The Monetary and Regulatory Implications of Changes in the Banking Industry', BIS Conference Papers no. 7.

—— (2001a), Annual Report 71st, Basel: Bank for International Settlements.

—— (2001b), 'The Financial Crisis in Japan During the 1990s: How the Bank of Japan Responded and the Lessons Learnt', BIS Papers no. 6.

—— (2004), Annual Report 74th, Basel: Bank for International Settlements.

Black, F., and M. Scholes (1973), 'The Pricing of Options and Corporate Liabilities', *Journal of Political Economy*, 81: 637–59.

Blanchard, O., and J. Galí (2005), 'Real Wage Rigidities and the New Keynesian Model', paper presented to the FRB/JMCB conference on Quantitative Evidence on Price Determination.

Blinder, A. (1980), 'The Consumer Price Index and the Measurement of Recent Inflation', *Brookings Papers on Economic Activity*, 2: 539–73.

Boone, L., C. Giorno, and P. Richardson (1998), 'Stock Market Fluctuations and Consumption Behaviour: Some Recent Evidence', OECD Economics Department Working Paper no. 208.

212

Bordo, M., B. Eichengreen, D. Klingebiel, and M. Martinez-Peria (2001), 'Is the Crisis Problem Growing More Severe?', *Economic Policy*, 32: 51–82.

—— and O. Jeanne (2002), 'Monetary Policy and Asset Prices: Does "Benign Neglect" Make Sense?', *International Finance*, 5: 139–64.

Borio, C. (1996), 'Credit Characteristics and the Monetary Policy Transmission Mechanism in Fourteen Industrial Countries: Facts, Conjectures and some Econometric Evidence', in K. Alders, K. Koedjik, and C. Kool (eds), *Monetary Policy in a Converging Europe*, Amsterdam: Kluwer Academic Publishers, 77–116.

—— and W. Fritz (1995), 'The Response of Short-Term Bank Lending Rates to Policy Rates: A Cross-Country Perspective', BIS Working Paper no. 27.

—— C. Furfine, and P. Lowe (2001), 'Procyclicality of the Financial System and Financial Stability: Issues and Policy Options', in *Marrying the Macro and Micro-Prudential Dimensions of Financial Stability*, BIS Papers no. 1, 1–57.

—— N. Kennedy, and S. Prowse (1994), 'Exploring Aggregate Asset Price Fluctuations across Countries: Measurement, Determinants and Monetary Policy Implications', BIS Economic Papers no. 40.

—— and P. Lowe (2002), 'Asset Prices, Financial and Monetary Stability: Exploring the Nexus', BIS Working Paper no. 114.

—— —— (2004), 'Securing Sustainable Price Stability: Should Credit Come Back from the Wilderness?', BIS Working Paper no. 157.

—— and W. White (2003), 'Whither Monetary and Financial Stability? The Implications of Evolving Policy Regimes', in Federal Reserve Bank of Kansas City, *Monetary Policy and Uncertainty: Adapting to a Changing Economy*, proceedings of the Jackson Hole Symposium.

Boskin, M., E. Dulberger, R. Gordon, Z. Griliches, and D. Jorgensen (1996), *Towards a More Accurate Measure of the Cost of Living*, Final Report to the Senate Finance Committee (the Boskin Report).

Bover, O., J. Muellbauer, and A. Murphy (1989), 'Housing, Wages and UK Labour Markets', *Oxford Bulletin of Economics and Statistics*, 51: 97–136.

Brennan, M. (2004), 'How Did It Happen?', *Economic Notes*, 33: 3–22.

Brunner, K., and A. Meltzer (1972), 'Money, Debt and Economic Activity', *Journal of Political Economy*, 80: 951–77.

Buiter, W., and N. Panigirtzoglou (1999), 'Liquidity Traps: How to Avoid Them and How to Escape Them', NBER Working Paper no. 7245.

—— —— (2003), 'Overcoming the Zero Bound on Nominal Interest Rates with Negative Interest on Currency: Gesell's Solution', *Economic Journal*, 113: 723–46.

Calvo, G. (1983), 'Staggered Prices in a Utility-Maximizing Framework', *Journal of Monetary Economics*, 12: 383–398.

—— (1998), 'Varieties of Capital-Market Crises', in G. Calvo and M. King (eds), *The Debt Burden and its Consequences for Monetary Policy*, New York: Macmillan Press.

—— L. Leiderman, and C. Reinhart (1993), 'Capital Inflows and Real Exchange Rate Appreciation: The Role of External Factors', *IMF Staff Papers*, 40: 108–51.

—— and E. Mendoza (1996), 'Petty Crime and Cruel Punishment: Lessons from the Mexican Debacle', *American Economic Review*, 86: 170–5.

Calza, A., C. Gartner, and J. Sousa (2001), 'Modelling the Demand for Loans to the Private Sector in the Euro Area', ECB Working Paper no. 55.

Caprio, G. and D. Klingebiel (2003), 'Episodes of Systemic and Borderline Financial Crises', World Bank, mimeo.

Case, K., J. Quigley, and R. Shiller (2001), 'Comparing Wealth Effects: The Stock Market versus the Housing Market', Cowles Foundation Discussion Paper no. 1335.

Cecchetti, S. (1995), 'Inflation Indicators and Inflation Policy', *NBER Macroeconomics Annual 1995*, 81–85.

—— (1999), 'Legal Structure, Financial Structure and the Monetary Policy Transmission Mechanism', NBER Working Paper no. 7151.

—— H. Genberg, J. Lipsky, and S. Wadhwani (2000), *Asset Prices and Central Bank Policy*, Geneva Reports on the World Economy, 2, London: Centre for Economic Policy Research.

Chen, N.-K. (2001), 'Bank Net Worth, Asset Prices and Economic Activity', *Journal of Monetary Economics*, 48: 415–36.

Chiuri, M., and T. Japelli (2003), 'Financial Market Imperfections and Home Ownership: A Comparative Study', *European Economic Review*, 47: 857–75.

Christiano, L., M. Eichenbaum, and C. Evans (2005), 'Nominal Rigidities and the Dynamic Effects of a Shock to Monetary Policy', *Journal of Political Economy*, 113: 1–45.

Christofides, L., and M. Leung (2003), 'Nominal Wage Rigidity in Contract Data: A Parametric Approach', *Economica*, 70: 619–38.

Clarida, R., J. Galí, and M. Gertler (1999), 'The Science of Monetary Policy: A New Keynesian Perspective', *Journal of Economic Literature*, 37: 1661–1707.

Coenen, G. (2003), 'Zero Lower Bound: Is it a Problem in the Euro Area?', in O. Issing (ed.), *Background Studies for the ECB's Evaluation of its Monetary Policy Strategy*, Frankfurt: European Central Bank, 139–56.

Collyns, C., and A. Senhadji (2002), 'Lending Booms, Real Estate Bubbles and the Asian Crisis', IMF Working Paper no. 02/20.

Danielsson, J., P. Embrechts, C. Goodhart, C. Keating, F. Muennich, and H. Shin (2001), 'An Academic Response to Basel II', LSE Financial Markets Group Special Paper no. 130.

Davey, M. (2001), 'Mortgage Equity Withdrawal and Consumption', *Bank of England Quarterly Bulletin*, Spring: 100–4.

Davis, E., and H. Zhu (2004), 'Bank Lending and Commercial Property Prices: Some Cross-Country Evidence', BIS Working Paper no. 150.

Deaton, A. (1992), *Understanding Consumption*, Oxford: Oxford University Press.

Debelle, G. (2004), 'Household Debt and the Macroeconomy', *BIS Quarterly Review*, March: 51–64.

Delargy, P., and C. Goodhart (1999), 'Financial crisis: Plus ça change, plus c'est la même chose', *International Finance*, 1: 261–88.

Demirgüc-Kunt, A., and E. Detriagiache (1998), 'The Determinants of Banking Crises: Evidence from Developing and Developed Countries', *IMF Staff Papers*, 45: 81–109.

—— —— (1999), 'Financial Liberalization and Financial Fragility', World Bank Policy Research Working Paper no. 1917.

—— —— (2005), 'Cross-Country Empirical Evidence of Systemic Banking Distress: A Survey', IMF Working Paper no. 05/96.

Dickey, D., and W. Fuller (1981), 'Likelihood Ratio Statistics for Autoregressive Time Series with a Unit Root', *Econometrica*, 60: 423–33.

Dooley, M. (1997), 'A Model of Crises in Emerging Markets', NBER Working Paper no. 6300.

Dornbusch, R., C. Favero, and F. Giavazzi (1998), 'A Red-Letter Day?', CEPR Discussion Paper no. 1804.

Drees, B., and C. Pazarbasioglu (1998), 'The Nordic Banking Crises: Pitfalls in Financial Liberalization?', IMF Occasional Paper no. 161.

ECB (2003), *Structural Factors in the EU Housing Market*, Frankfurt am Main: European Central Bank.

The Economist (2002), 'Going Through the roof', 28 Mar. 2002.

Eichengreen, B. (1992), *Golden Fetters: The Gold Standard and the Great Depression 1919–1939*, Oxford: Oxford University Press.

—— and C. Areta (2000), 'Banking Crises in Emerging Markets: Presumptions and Evidence', Center for International and Development Economics Research Paper no. C00–115.

—— and M. Bordo (2003), 'Crises Now and Then: What Lessons from the Last Era of Financial Globalisation?', in P. Mizen (ed.), *Monetary History, Exchange Rates and Financial Markets: Essays in Honour of Charles Goodhart*, vol. 2, London: Edward Elgar, 52–91.

Eika, K., N. Ericsson, and R. Nymoen (1996), 'Hazards in Implementing a Monetary Conditions Index', *Oxford Bulletin of Economics and Statistics*, 58: 765–90.

Elsinger, H., A. Lehar, and M. Summer (2002), 'Risk Assessment of Banking Systems', Oesterreichische Nationalbank Working Paper no. 79.

Ericsson, N., E. Jansen, N. Kerbeshian and R. Nymoen (1998), 'Interpreting a Monetary Conditions Index in Economic Policy', in Bank for International Settlements, *Topics in Monetary Policy Modelling*, BIS Conference Papers, vol. 6, Basel: Bank for International Settlements, 237–56.

Fama, E. (1975), 'Short-Term Interest Rates as Predictors of Inflation', *American Economic Review*, 65: 269–82.

Fase, M. (1995), 'The Demand for Commercial Bank Loans and Lending Rates', *European Economic Review*, 39: 99–111.

Fernández de Lis, S., J. Martinez, and J. Saurina (2001), 'Credit Growth, Problem Loans and Credit Risk Provisioning in Spain', in *Marrying the Macro- and Micro Aspects of Financial Stability*, BIS Papers, no. 1, Basel: Bank For International Settlements, 331–53.

Filardo, A. (2000), 'Monetary Policy and Asset Prices', *Federal Reserve Bank of Kansas City Economic Review*, Third Quarter: 11–37.

Fisher, I. (1906), *Nature of Capital and Income*, New York: Macmillan.

—— (1932), *Booms and Depressions*, New York: Adelphi.

—— (1933), 'The Debt-Deflation Theory of Great Depressions', *Econometrica*, 1: 337–57.

Flood, R., and N. Marion (1999), 'Perspectives on the Recent Currency Crisis Literature', *International Journal of Finance and Economics*, 4: 1–26.

Friedman, B., and K. Kuttner (1993), 'Economic Activity and the Short-Term Credit Markets: An Analysis of Prices and Quantities', *Brookings Papers on Economic Activity*, 2: 193–283.

Friedman, M., and A. Schwartz (1963), *A Monetary History of the United States 1867–1960*, Princeton: Princeton University Press.

Fuhrer, J. (1997), 'The (Un)importance of Forward-Looking Behavior in Price Specifications', *Journal of Money, Credit and Banking*, 29: 338–50.

—— (2000), 'Habit Formation in Consumption and its Implications for Monetary Policy Models', *American Economic Review*, 90: 367–90.

—— and G. Rudebusch (2004), 'Estimating the Euler Equation for Output', *Journal of Monetary Economics*, 51: 1133–53.

Furfine, C. (2003), 'Interbank Exposures: Quantifying the Risk of Contagion', *Journal of Money, Credit and Banking*, 35: 111–28.

Galbis, V. (1993), 'High Real Interest Rates under Financial Liberalization: Is There a Problem?', IMF Working Paper no. 93/7.

References

Galí, J., and M. Gertler (1999), 'Inflation Dynamics: A Structural Econometric Analysis', *Journal of Monetary Economics*, 44: 195–222.

—— —— and D. López-Salido (2001), 'European Inflation Dynamics', *European Economic Review*, 45: 1237–70.

Garber, P., and S. Lall (1996), 'Derivative Products in Exchange Rate Crises', *Federal Reserve Bank of San Francisco, Proceedings*, 206–31.

Gerlach, S., and W. Peng (2005), 'Bank Lending and Property Prices in Hong Kong', *Journal of Banking and Finance*, 29: 461–81.

Gertler, M. (1988), 'Financial Structure and Aggregate Economic Activity: An Overview', *Journal of Money, Credit and Banking*, 20: 559–88.

—— M. Goodfriend, O. Issing, and L. Spaventa (1998), *Asset Prices and Monetary Policy: Four Views*, London: CEPR.

Girouard, N., and S. Blöndahl (2001), 'House Prices and Economic Activity', OECD Working Paper no. 279.

Glick, R., and M. Hutchison (1999), 'Banking and Currency Crises: How Common are the Twins?', Federal Reserve Bank of San Francisco Pacific Basin Working Paper no. PB 99–07.

Goodfriend, M., and R. King (1997), 'The New Neoclassical Synthesis and the Role of Monetary Policy', *NBER Macroeconomics Annual 1997*, 231–83.

—— (2001), 'The Case for Price Stability', NBER Working Paper no. 8423.

Goodhart, C. (1995), 'Price Stability and Financial Fragility', in K. Sawamoto, Z. Nakajima, and H. Taguchi (eds), *Financial Stability in a Changing Environment*, London: Macmillan, 439–510.

—— (2000), 'Time, Inflation and Asset Prices', in M. Silver and D. Fenwick (eds), *Proceedings of the Conference on 'The Measurement of Inflation'*, Cardiff: Cardiff Business School, 518–34.

—— (2001), 'What Weight Should Be Given to Asset Prices in the Measurement of Inflation?', *The Economic Journal*, 111: 335–56.

—— (2003), 'Intervention in Asset Markets', in R. Pringle and N. Carver (eds), *How Countries Manage Reserve Assets*, London: Central Banking Publications, 55–69.

—— (2004), 'The Bank of England, 1970–2000', in R. Michie (ed.), *The British Government and the City of London in the Twentieth Century*, Cambridge: Cambridge University Press, 340–71.

—— and B. Hofmann (2000a), 'Do Asset Prices Help to Predict Consumer Price Inflation?', *The Manchester School*, suppl., 68: 122–40.

—— —— (2000b), 'Financial Variables and the Conduct of Monetary Policy', Sveriges Riksbank Working Paper no. 112.

—— —— (2001), 'Asset Prices, Financial Conditions and the Transmission of Monetary Policy', paper presented to the Federal Reserve Bank of San Francisco and Stanford Institute for Economic Policy Research conference on 'Asset Prices, Exchange Rates, and Monetary Policy'.

—— —— (2003), 'Deflation', paper presented to the ECB Workshop on Asset Prices and Monetary Policy.

—— —— (2004a), 'Deflation, Credit and Asset Prices', in R. Burdekin and P. Siklos (eds), *Deflation: Current and Historical Perspectives*, Cambridge: Cambridge University Press, 166–88.

—— —— (2004b), 'A Second Central Bank Instrument?', in P.B. Sørensen (ed.), *Monetary Union in Europe: Historical Perspectives and Prospects for the Future. Essays in Honour of Niels Thygesen*, Copenhagen: DJØF Publishing, 261–72.

————— (2005a), 'The IS Curve and the Transmission of Monetary Policy: Is There a Puzzle?', *Applied Economics*, 37: 29–36.

————— (2005b), 'The Phillips Curve, the IS Curve and Monetary Transmission: Evidence for the US and the Euro Area', *CESifo Economic Studies*, 51: 757–76.

————— and M. Segoviano (2004), 'Bank Regulation and Macroeconomic Fluctuations', *Oxford Review of Economic Policy*, 20: 591–615.

————— ————— (2005), 'Default, Credit Growth and Asset Prices', paper presented to the IMF conference on 'Financial Stability—Central Banking and Supervisory Challenges'.

————— and M. Segoviano (2004), 'Basel and Procyclicality: A Comparison of the Standardised and IRB Approaches to an Improved Credit Risk Method', London School of Economics Financial Markets Group, Discussion Paper no. 524.

————— P. Sunirand, and D. Tsomocos (2004a), 'A Model to Analyse Financial Fragility: Applications', *Journal of Financial Stability*, 1: 1–30.

————— ————— (2004b), 'A Time Series Analysis of Financial Fragility in the UK Banking System', Oxford Financial Research Centre Working Paper no. 2004-FE-18.

————— ————— (2005), 'A Risk Assessment Model for Banks', *Annals of Finance*, 1: 197–224.

————— and A. Taylor (Forthcoming), 'Procyclicality and Volatility in the Financial System: The Implementation of Basel II and IAS 39', Forthcoming in S. Gerlach and P. Gruenwald (eds), *Procyclicality of Financial Systems in Asia*, London: Palgrave Macmillan.

————— D. Tsomocos, L. Zicchino and O. Aspachs (2006), 'Towards a Measure Of Financial Fragility', Financial Markets Group Discussion Paper no. 554.

Gordon, R. (1998), 'Foundations of the Goldilocks Economy: Supply Shocks and the Time-Varying NAIRU', *Brookings Papers on Economic Activity*, 2: 297–333.

Gordy, M., and B. Howells (2004), 'Procyclicality in Basel II: Can We Treat the Disease without Killing the Patient?', Board of Governors of the Federal Reserve System mimeo.

Granger, C., and P. Newbold (1974), 'Spurious Regressions in Econometrics', *Journal of Econometrics*, 35: 143–59.

Greenspan, A. (2002), 'Economic Volatility', remarks at the Symposium of the Federal Reserve Bank of Kansas City at Jackson Hole.

Hamilton, J. (1994), *Time Series Analysis*, Princeton: Princeton University Press.

Hansson, B., and H. Lindberg (1994), 'Monetary Conditions Index—A Monetary Policy Indicator', *Sveriges Riksbank Quarterly Review*, 3: 12–17.

Hardouvelis, G. (1990), 'Margin Requirements, Volatility, and the Transitory Component of Stock Prices', *American Economic Review*, 80: 736–62.

————— and D. Kim (1995), 'Margin Requirements, Price Fluctuations and Market Participation in Metal Futures', *Journal of Money, Credit and Banking*, 27: 659–71.

————— and S. Peristiani (1992), 'Margin Requirements, Speculative Trading and Stock Price Fluctuations: The Case of Japan', *Quarterly Journal of Economics*, 107: 1333–70.

————— and P. Theodossiou (2002), 'The Asymmetric Relation between Initial Margin Requirements and Stock Market Volatility across Bull and Bear Markets', *Review of Financial Studies*, 15: 1525–60.

Hayami, M. (2001), 'Recent Economic Developments and Monetary Policy', speech at the Research Institute of Japan, available at <www.boj.or.jp/en/press/press_f.htm>.

Hilbers, P., Q. Lei and L. Zacho (2001), 'Real Estate Market Development and Financial Sector Soundness', IMF Working Paper No. 129.

HM Treasury (2003), *Housing, Consumption and EMU*, London: Stationery Office.

References

Hofmann, B. (2001), 'The Determinants of Private Sector Credit in Industrialised Countries: Do Property Prices Matter?', BIS Working Paper No. 108.

—— (2003), 'Bank Lending and Property Prices: Some International Evidence', HKIMR Working Paper no. 22/2.

—— (2004), 'The Determinants of Private Sector Credit in Industrialised Countries: Do Property Prices Matter?', *International Finance*, 7: 203–34.

—— (Forthcoming), 'EMU and the Transmission of Monetary Policy: Evidence from Business Lending Rates', Forthcoming in *Empirica*.

—— and P. Mizen (2004), 'Interest Rate Pass-Through and Monetary Transmission: Evidence from Individual Financial Institutions' Retail Rates', *Economica*, 71: 99–124.

Hoshi, T., and A. Kashyap (1999), 'The Japanese Banking Crisis: Where Did It Come From and How Will It End?', NBER Working Paper no. 7250.

Iacoviello, M. (2004), 'Consumption, House Prices and Collateral Constraints: A Structural Econometric Analysis', *Journal of Housing Economics*, 13: 304–20.

—— and R. Minetti (2003), 'The Credit Channel of Monetary Policy: Evidence from the Housing Market', Boston College Working Paper no. 541.

IMF (2000), *World Economic Outlook, May 2000*, Washington, DC: IMF.

—— (2003), *Global Financial Stability Report, September 2003*, Washington, DC: IMF.

Jaynes, E. (1957), 'Information Theory and Statistical Mechanics', *Physics Review*, 106: 620–30.

Johansen, S. (1988), 'Statistical Analysis of Cointegration Vectors', *Journal of Economic Dynamics and Control*, 12: 231–54.

—— (1991), 'Estimation and Hypothesis Testing of Cointegration Vectors in Gaussian Vector Autoregressive Models', *Econometrica*, 59: 1551–81.

—— (1995), *Likelihood-Based Inference in Cointegrated Vector Autoregressive Models*, Oxford: Oxford University Press.

Judge, G., and A. Golan (1992), 'Recovering Information in the Case of Ill-Posed Inverse Problems with Noise', University of California, Berkeley mimeo.

Kaminsky, G., and C. Reinhart (1999), 'The Twin Crisis: The Causes of Banking and Balance-of-Payments Problems', *American Economic Review*, 89: 473–500.

—— and S. Schmukler (2003), 'Short-Run Pain, Long-Run Gain: The Effects of Financial Liberalization', NBER Working Paper no. 9787.

Kao, C. and M. Chiang (2000), 'On the Estimation and Inference of a Cointegrated Regression in Panel Data', *Advances in Econometrics*, 15: 179–222.

Kashyap, A., and C. Stein (2004), 'Cyclical Implications of the Basel-II Capital Standard', *Federal Reserve Bank of Chicago Economic Perspectives*, First Quarter: 18–31.

—— and J. Stein (1997), 'The Role of Banks in Monetary Policy: A Survey with Implications for the European Monetary Union', *Federal Reserve Bank of Chicago Economic Perspectives*, Sept./Oct.: 2–18.

—— —— and D. Wilcox (1993), 'Monetary Policy and Credit Conditions: Evidence from the Composition of External Finance', *American Economic Review*, 83: 8–98.

Kennedy, N., and P. Andersen (1994), 'Household Saving and Real House Prices: An International Perspective', BIS Working Paper no. 20.

Keynes, J. (1972), 'The Consequences for the Banks of the Collapse in Money Values', *The Collected Writings of John Maynard Keynes*, vol. 9, *Essays in Persuasion* (1931), London: Macmillan, 150–8.

Khamis, M. (1996), 'Credit and Exchange Rate-Based Stabilization', IMF Working Paper no. 96/51.

Kindleberger, C. (1973), *The World in Depression, 1929–1939*, Berkeley, Calif.: University of California Press.

—— (1978), *Manias, Panics and Crashes: A History of Financial Crises*, New York: Basic Books.

Kiyotaki, N., and J. Moore (1997), 'Credit Cycles', *Journal of Political Economy*, 105: 211–48.

Kiyotaki, N., and J. Moore (2001), 'Liquidity, Business Cycles and Monetary Policy', Clarendon Lecture, London School of Economics.

Klaeffling, M., and V. Lopez Perez (2003), 'Inflation Targets and the Liquidity Trap', in O. Issing (ed.), *Background Studies for the ECB's Evaluation of its Monetary Policy Strategy*, Frankfurt: European Central Bank, 139–56.

Knight, M., and J. Santaella (1997), 'Economic Determinants of IMF Financial Arrangements', *Journal of Development Economics*, 54: 405–36.

Kuroda, S., and I. Yamamoto (2003), 'Are Japanese Nominal Wages Downwardly Rigid?', *Bank of Japan Monetary and Economic Studies*, 21: 1–68.

Kyodo News (2000), 'Hayami Says Economy Strong Enough to Endure Further Reform', 29 May.

La Porta, R., F. Lopez-de-Silanes, A. Shleifer, and R. Vishny (1997), 'Legal Determinants of External Finance', *Journal of Finance*, 52: 1131–50.

—— —— —— —— (1998), 'Law and Finance', *Journal of Political Economy*, 106: 113–55.

Larsson, R., J. Lyhagen, and M. Lothgren (2001), 'Likelihood-Based Cointegration Tests in Heterogeneous Panels', *Econometrics Journal*, 4: 41–56.

Leahy, M., S. Schich, G. Wehinger, F. Pelgrin, and T. Thorgeirsson (2001), 'Contributions of Financial Systems to Growth in OECD Countries', OECD Economics Department Working Paper no. 280.

Leijonhufvud, A. (1981), *Inflation and Economic Performance*, Kiel: Institut für Weltwirtschaft.

Levine, R. (1997), 'Financial Development and Economic Growth: Views and Agendas', *Journal of Economic Literature*, 35: 688–726.

Lindé, J. (2005), 'Estimating New-Keynesian Phillips Curves: A Full-Information Maximum Likelihood Approach', *Journal of Monetary Economics*, 52: 1135–49.

Ludwig, A., and T. Sløk (2004), 'The Relationship between Stock Prices, House Prices and Consumption in OECD Countries', *Topics in Macroeconomics*, 4, article 4, Berkeley Electronic Press.

Lütkepohl, H. (1993), *Introduction to Multiple Time Series Analysis*, Berlin: Springer Verlag.

MacDonald, R. (2000), 'Concepts to Calculate Equilibrium Exchange Rates: An Overview', Economic Research Group of the Deutsche Bundesbank Discussion Paper no. 3/00.

MacKinnon, J. (1991), 'Critical Values for Cointegration Tests', in R. Engle and C. Granger (eds), *Long-Run Economic Relationships: Readings in Cointegration*, Oxford: Oxford University Press, 267–76.

Maclennan, D., J. Muellbauer, and M. Stephens (2000), 'Asymmetries in Housing and Financial Market Institutions and EMU', in T. Jenkinson (ed.), *Readings in Macroeconomics*, Oxford: Oxford University Press, 34–63.

Marsh, D. (1992), *The Bundesbank: The Bank that Rules Europe*, London: Heinemann.

McCallum, B. (2000), 'Theoretical Analysis Regarding a Zero Lower Bound on Nominal Interest Rates', *Journal of Money, Credit and Banking*, 32: 870–904.

McCallum, B., and E. Nelson (1999a), 'Performance of Operational Policy Rules in an Estimated Semi-Classical Structural Model', in J. Taylor (ed.), *Monetary Policy Rules*, Chicago: University of Chicago Press, 5–54.

—— —— (1999b), 'Nominal Income Targeting in an Open-Economy Optimizing Model', *Journal of Monetary Economics*, 43: 553–78.

McKinnon, R., and H. Pill (1996), 'Credible Liberalizations and International Capital Flows: The Over Borrowing Syndrome', in T. Ito and A. Krueger (eds), *Financial Deregulation and Integration in East Asia*, Chicago: University of Chicago Press, 7–45.

Mehra, Y. (2004), 'The Output Gap, Expected Future Inflation and Inflation Dynamics: Another Look', *Topics in Macroeconomics*, 4, article 17, Berkeley Electronic Press.

Meltzer, A. (1999a), 'The Transmission Process', Carnegie Mellon University mimeo.

—— (1999b), 'A Policy for Japanese Recovery', Carnegie Mellon University mimeo.

—— (1999c), 'Commentary: What More Can the Bank of Japan Do?', *Bank of Japan Monetary and Economic Studies*, 17: 189–91.

—— (2003), *A History of the Federal Reserve. Volume 1: 1913–1951*, Chicago: University of Chicago Press.

Merton, R. (1974), 'On the Pricing of Corporate Debt: The Risk Structure of Interest Rates', *Journal of Finance*, 29: 449–70.

Minsky, H. (1964), 'Financial Crisis, Financial Systems, and the Performance of the Economy', in I. Friend, H. Minsky and V. Andrews, *Private Capital Markets*, Englewoods Cliffs, NJ: Prentice-Hall.

—— (1982), *Can "It" Happen Again? Essays on Instability and Finance*, Armonk, NY: M. E. Sharpe.

—— (1986), *Stabilizing an Unstable Economy*, New Haven, Conn.: Yale University Press.

Mishkin, F. (1990), 'What Does the Term Structure Tell Us about Future Inflation?', *Journal of Monetary Economics*, 25: 77–96.

—— 'Understanding Financial Crises: A Developing Country Perspective', in M. Bruno and B. Pleskovic (eds), *Annual World Bank Conference on Development Economics 1996*, Washington, DC: International Bank for Reconstruction and Development, 29–61.

Mishra, D. (1997), 'Political Determinants of Currency Crises: Theory and Evidence', University of Maryland mimeo.

Mitchell, B. (1962), *Abstract of British Historical Statistics*. Cambridge: Cambridge University Press.

Morgenstern, O. (1959), *International Financial Transactions and Business Cycles*, Princeton: Princeton University Press.

Morris, S., H. Shin, and H. Tong (2006), 'Social Value of Public Information: Morris and Shin (2002) is Actually Pro Transparency, Not Con: Reply', *American Economic Review*, 96: 453–5.

Muellbauer, J. (1994), 'The Assessment: Consumer Expenditure', *Oxford Review of Economic Policy*, 10: 1–41.

Nelson, E. (2001), 'What Does the UK's Monetary Policy and Inflation Experience Tell Us about the Transmission Mechanism?', CEPR Working Paper no. 3047.

—— (2002), 'Direct Effects of Base Money on Aggregate Demand: Theory and Evidence', *Journal of Monetary Economics*, 49: 687–708.

—— (2004), 'The Great Inflation of the Seventies: What Really Happened?', Federal Reserve Bank of St. Louis Working Paper no. 2004–001A.

Nickell, S., and G. Quintini (2003), 'Nominal Wage Rigidity and the Rate of Inflation', *The Economic Journal*, 113: 762–81.

Obstfeld, M. (1995), 'Models of Currency Crises with Self-Fulfilling Features', NBER Working Paper no. 5285.

OECD (2000), *Economic Outlook 68*, Paris: OECD.

—— (2004), 'Housing Markets, Wealth and the Business Cycle', *OECD Economic Outlook*, 75: 127–47.

Office for National Statistics (1998), *The Retail Prices Index: Technical Manual*, London: HM Stationery Office.

Osterwald-Lenum, M. (1992), 'A Note with Quantiles of the Asymptotic Distribution of the Maximum Likelihood Cointegration Rank Test Statistics', *Oxford Bulletin of Economics and Statistics*, 54: 461–72.

Peersman, G., and F. Smets (1999), 'The Taylor Rule: A Useful Monetary Policy Benchmark for the Euro Area?', *International Finance*, 1: 85–116.

Peeters, M. (1999), 'Measuring Monetary Conditions in Europe: Use and Limitations of the MCI', *De Economist*, 147: 183–203.

Perron, P. (1989), 'The Great Crash, the Oil Price Shock and the Unit Root Hypothesis', *Econometrica*, 57: 1361–1401.

—— (1990), 'Testing for a Unit Root in a Time Series Regression with a Changing Mean', *Journal of Business and Economic Statistics*, 8: 153–62.

—— (1997), 'Further Evidence from Breaking Trend Functions in Macroeconomic Variables', *Journal of Econometrics*, 80: 355–85.

Pill, H., and M. Pradhan (1995), 'Financial Indicators and Financial Change in Africa and Asia', IMF Working Paper no. 95/123.

Posen, A. (2000), 'The Political Economy of Deflationary Monetary Policy', in R. Mikitani and A. Posen (eds), *Japan's Financial Crisis and its Parallels to U.S. Experience*, Institute for International Economics Special Report 13, Washington, D.C.: Institute for International Economics.

Radcliffe Report (1959), *Radcliffe Report: Committee on the Working of the Monetary System*, Cmnd 827, London: HMSO.

Reid, M. (1982), *The Secondary Banking Crisis, 1973–75: Its Causes and Course*, London: Macmillan.

Reinhart, C., and I. Tokatlidis (2001), 'Before and After Financial Liberalization', University of Maryland mimeo.

Reserve Bank of New Zealand (1997), 'Recommendation to the 1997 CPI Revision Advisory Committee', available at <www.rbnz.govt.nz/cpi.htm>.

Reuters News Services (1996), 'JGBs end Tokyo Lower after BOJ Governor Comments', 16 Apr.

Roberts, J. (1995), 'New Keynesian Economics and the Phillips Curve', *Journal of Money, Credit and Banking*, 27: 975–84.

Rotemberg, J. (1982), 'Sticky Prices in the United States', *Journal of Political Economy*, 60: 1187–1211.

—— and M. Woodford (1999), 'Interest Rate Rules in an Estimated Sticky Price Model', in J. Taylor (ed.), *Monetary Policy Rules*, Chicago: University of Chicago Press, 57–119.

RPI Advisory Committee (1994), *Treatment of Owner Occupiers Housing Costs in the Retail Prices Index*, Cmnd 2717 (London: HMSO).

References

Rudebusch, G., and L. Svensson (1999), 'Policy Rules for Inflation Targeting', in J. B. Taylor (ed.), *Monetary Policy Rules*, Chicago: University of Chicago Press for NBER, 203–46.

Samuelson, P. (1961), 'The Evaluation of Social Income: Capital Formation and Wealth', in F. Lutz and D. Hague (eds), *The Theory of Capital*, London: Macmillan, 32–57.

Saurina, J. (2004), 'Principles versus rules and the Definition of Regulatory Bank Capital: Evidence from a Unique Environment', paper presented to the Conference on Prudential Regulation and Banking Supervision, Banco de España.

Secretariat of the Basel Committee on Banking Supervision (2001), *The New Basel Capital Accord: An Explanatory Note*, Basel: BIS.

Segoviano M. (2006), 'The Conditional Probability of Default Methodology', Financial Markets Group Discussion Paper no. 558.

—— and P. Lowe (2002), 'Internal Ratings, the Business Cycle and Capital Requirements: Some Evidence from an Emerging Market Economy', BIS Working Paper no. 117.

Selgin, G. (1996), 'Less than Zero: The Case for a Falling Price Level in a Growing Economy', Institute of Economic Affairs Occasional Paper.

Shapley, L., and M. Shubik (1977), 'Trading Using One Commodity as a Means of Payment', *Journal of Political Economy*, 85: 937–68.

Shibuya, H. (1992), 'Dynamic Equilibrium Price Index: Asset Price and Inflation', *Bank of Japan Monetary and Economic Studies*, 10: 95–109.

Shimizu, Y. (1992), 'Problems in the Japanese Financial System in the Early 1990s', *Hitotsubashi Journal of Commerce and Management*, 27: 29–49.

Shiratsuka, S. (1996), 'Shisan kakaku hendo to bukka shisu' (Asset price fluctuations and price index), *Kinyu Kenkyu*, 14: 45–72.

—— (1998), *Bukka no keizai bunseki* (Economic analysis of inflation measures), Tokyo: University of Tokyo Press.

—— (1999), 'Asset Price Fluctuation and Price Indices', Institute for Monetary and Economics Studies, Bank of Japan Discussion Paper no. 99-E-21.

Shubik, M. (1973), 'Commodity Money, Oligopoly, Credit and Bankruptcy in a General Equilibrium Model', *Western Economic Journal*, 11: 24–38.

—— (1999), *The Theory of Money and Financial Institutions*, Cambridge, Mass.: MIT Press.

—— and D. Tsomocos (1992), 'A Strategic Market Game with a Mutual Bank with Fractional Reserves and Redemption in Gold', *Journal of Economics*, 55: 123–50.

—— and C. Wilson (1997), 'The Optimal Bankruptcy Rule in a Trading Economy Using Fiat Money', *Journal of Economics*, 37: 337–54.

Silver, M., and D. Fenwick (2000), Proceedings of the Conference on 'The Measurement of Inflation', Cardiff: Cardiff Business School.

Sims, C. (1980), 'Macroeconomics and Reality', *Econometrica*, 48: 1–48.

Smets, F., and R. Wouters (2003), 'An Estimated Dynamic Stochastic General Equilibrium Model for the Euro Area', *Journal of the European Economic Association*, 1: 1123–75.

Stiglitz, J. (2002), *Globalization and its Discontents*, New York: W. W. Norton.

Stock, J., and M. Watson (1999), 'Forecasting Inflation', *Journal of Monetary Economics*, 44: 293–335.

—— —— (2003), 'Forecasting Output and Inflation: The Role of Asset Prices', *Journal of Economic Literature*, 41: 788–829.

Sturm, J., H. Berger, and J. Haan (2004), 'Which Variables Explain Decisions on IMF Credit? An Extreme Bounds Analysis', University of Groningen, Faculty of Economics mimeo.

Svensson, L. (2001), 'The Zero Bound in an Open Economy: A Foolproof Way of Escaping from a Liquidity Trap', *Bank of Japan Monetary and Economic Studies*, 19(S-1): 277–312.

Tsatsaronis, K., and H. Zhu (2004), 'What Drives Housing Price Dynamics: Cross-Country Evidence', BIS Quarterly Review, Mar., 65–78.

Taylor, J. (1980), 'Aggregate Dynamics and Staggered Contracts', *Journal of Political Economy*, 88: 1–23.

Tett, G. (2001), 'A Hard Choice for Japan', *Financial Times*, 2 Dec.

Tobin, J. (1969), 'A General Equilibrium Approach to Monetary Theory', *Journal of Money, Credit and Banking*, 1: 15–29.

Tornell, A., F. Westermann, and L. Martinez (2004), 'The Positive Link between Financial Liberalization, Growth and Crises', NBER Working Paper no. 10293.

Turvey, R. (1989), *Consumer Price Indices: An ILO Manual*, Geneva: International Labour Organisation.

—— (2000a), 'Owner-Occupiers and the Price Index', *World Economics*, 1: 153–9.

—— (2000b), 'Consumer Price Index Methodology: A Manual', available at <www.turvey.demon.co.uk>.

Upper, C., and A. Worms (2004), 'Estimating Bilateral Exposures in the German Interbank Market: Is There a Danger of Contagion?', *European Economic Review*, 48: 827–49.

Vassalou, M., and Y. Xing (2002), 'Default Risk in Equity Returns', Columbia University Working Paper.

Vickers, J. (1999), 'Monetary Policy and Asset Prices', Bank of England Quarterly Bulletin, 39: 428–35.

von Hagen, J., and B. Hofmann (2003), 'Monetary Policy Orientation in Times of Low Inflation', EMU Monitor Background Paper.

Vreeland, J. (1999), 'The IMF: Lender of Last Resort or Scapegoat?', Yale University Department of Political Science, Leitner Working Paper no. 1999–03.

Wall, D. (2000), 'The Final Expenditure Prices Index (FEPI): Improving the Index of Government Prices and Other Issues', in M. Silver and D. Fenwick (eds), *Proceedings of the Conference on 'The Measurement of Inflation'*, Cardiff: Cardiff Business School, 511–16.

—— and J. O'Donoghue (2000), 'Development Plans for the Final Expenditure Price Index', *Economic Trends*, 555: 51–4.

Walsh, C. (2003), Monetary Theory and Policy, MIT Press, Cambridge (MA).

Walsh, C., and J. Wilcox (1995), 'Bank Credit and Eonomic Activity', in J. Peek and E. Rosengreen (eds), *Is Bank Lending Important for the Transmission of Monetary Policy?*, Federal Reserve Bank of Boston Conference Series no. 39 (Boston: Federal Reserve Bank of Boston).

Wells, S. (2002), 'UK Interbank Exposures: Systemic Risk Implications', *Financial Stability Review, Bank of England*, Dec. 175–82.

Werner, R. (1996), 'The BoJ Prolonged Japan's Recession', *Asian Wall Street Journal*, 13 June.

—— (2002), 'The "Enigma" of Japanese Policy Ineffectiveness', *The Japanese Economy*, 30: 25–95.

—— (2003), *Princes of the Yen: Japan's Central Bankers and the Transformation of the Economy*, Armonk, NY: M. E. Sharpe.

White, H. (1980), 'A Hetroskedasticity-Consistent Covariance Matrix and a Direct Test for Heteroskedasticity', *Econometrica*, 48: 817–38.

Wong, J., L. Fung, T. Fong, and A. Sze (2004), 'Residential Mortgage Default Risk and the Loan-to-Value Ratio', *Hong Kong Monetary Authority Quarterly Bulletin*, Dec.: 35–45.

References

Woodford, M. (1994), 'Non-Standard Indicators for Monetary Policy: Can Their Usefulness be Judged from Forecasting Regressions?', in N. G. Mankiw (ed.), *Monetary Policy*, Chicago: University of Chicago Press, 95–115.

Woodford, M. (2003), *Interest and Prices*, Princeton University Press.

Woolford, K. (2000), 'Measuring Inflation: A Framework based on Domestic Final Purchases', in M. Silver and D. Fenwick (eds), *Proceedings of the Measurement of Inflation*, Cardiff: Cardiff Business School, 518–34.

Yamaguchi, Y. (1999), 'Monetary Policy and Structural Policy: A Japanese Perspective', speech given at the Colloque Monetaire Internationale, Banque de France, October 8–9, available at <www.boj.or.jp/en/press/press/_f.htm>.

Yates, A. (1998), 'Downward Nominal Rigidity and Monetary Policy', Bank of England Working Paper no. 82.

Zhu, H. (2003), 'The Importance of Property Markets for Monetary Policy and Financial Stability', in *Real Estate Indicators and Financial Stability*, BIS Papers no. 21, Basel: Bank for International Settlements, 9–29.

Index